Psychology, Ethics and Change

Susan Fairbairn and Gavin Fairbairn

Routledge & Kegan Paul
London and New York

First published in 1987 by
Routledge & Kegan Paul Ltd
11 New Fetter Lane, London EC4P 4EE

Published in the USA by
Routledge & Kegan Paul Inc.
in association with Methuen Inc.
29 West 35th Street, New York, NY 10001

Set in 10 on 12 point Sabon
by Pentacor Ltd., High Wycombe, Bucks
and printed in Great Britain
by T.J. Press Ltd, Padstow, Cornwall

Library of Congress Cataloguing in Publication Data
Psychology, ethics, and change.
Includes bibliographies and index.
1. Psychotherapists—Professional ethics.
2. Clinical psychologists—Professional ethics.
I. Fairbairn, Susan. II. Fairbairn, Gavin.
[DNLM: 1. Ethics. 2.Psychology, Clinical.
3. Psychotherapy. WM 62 P9745]
RC455.2.E8P84 1987 174'.2 87–12772

British Library CIP Data also available
ISBN 0–7102–0558–9 (C)
0–7102–1268–2 (P)

To our parents and children

Contents

Notes on Contributors

Annabel Broome qualified at Durham and Newcastle-upon-Tyne Universities, and has been District Psychologist at Dudley Health Authority since 1979. She has worked and published extensively in Health Psychology, including gynaecology, pain and health promotion.

Rudi Dallos is staff tutor in psychology at the Open University, South West Region and is a member of the course team for the course D307 Social Psychology: Development, Experience and Behaviour in a Social World. He has been teaching and carrying out research into family therapy for the past six years and has published work in both social psychology and family therapy.

Gavin Fairbairn was born in Edinburgh and educated at the Universities of Edinburgh and Manchester and at the Open University. From 1971 until 1985 he worked in special education and child, adolescent and adult psychiatry. He has a particular interest in the moral dilemmas that arise from our needs to care and to be cared for. He has published in medical and social work ethics, and in nursing. With Susan Fairbairn he is joint editor of *Ethical Issues in Caring* (Gower, 1987) and is joint organiser of the annual Ethical Issues in Caring conferences. He is currently Senior Lecturer in Primary Education at the North East Wales Institute, Cartrefle, where he teaches psychology, philosophy and special education.

Susan Fairbairn was born in Cambridge and educated at the Universities of Edinburgh, Strathclyde and Stirling. She is currently Research Associate in the Department of Nursing at Manchester

University where she is undertaking research on nurses' communication skills with cancer patients. She has published in environmental psychology and medical and nursing education and is a Tutor in Social Psychology for the Open University. With Gavin Fairbairn she is joint editor of *Ethical Issues in Caring* (Gower, 1987) and is joint organiser of the annual EIC conferences.

Rom Harré was born in New Zealand where he studied engineering and mathematics. He read philosophy at Oxford and subsequently held posts at Birmingham and Leicester Universities. His current post is Fellow of Linacre College, Oxford. Since 1974 he has been Adjunct Professor of the History and Philosophy of the Social and Behavioural Sciences at the State University of New York at Binghampton. His books include *Social Being*, *Personal Being*, *The Explanation of Social Behaviour* (with P.F.Secord) and *The Rules of Disorder* (with P.Marsh and E.Rossern). He is co-editor of the *Blackwell Encyclopedic Dictionary of Psychology* and is currently working on the theory of a psychology of the body.

Richard Lindley is a lecturer in philosophy at Bradford University, and a founder member of the Society for Applied Philosophy. His book *Autonomy* was published in 1986 by Macmillan. He is currently co-authoring (with a consultant psychiatrist) a book on ethical and political issues in psychotherapy.

Sue Llewelyn is currently employed as a Lecturer in Psychology at the University of Nottingham. She trained as a clinical psychologist in Nottingham, Leeds and Sheffield, where she has worked therapeutically with individuals and groups since 1975. Her particular interests include helpful factors in therapy, and the psychology of women.

Ron McKechnie was born in Glasgow in 1943 and educated at the Scottish Congregational College, Edinburgh, Strathclyde University and Leeds University. After working as a shipping clerk, divinity student and school teacher he came into clinical psychology in 1971. His special interests are in drinking problems, sexual problems and in overcoming the limitations of traditional scientific methodology in psychology. He is currently Top Grade Clinical Psychologist at the Crichton Royal Hospital, Dumfries.

Don Mixon was born in Detroit in 1930 and educated at De Pauw, Hedgerow Theatre, Black Mountain, San Francisco State, University of Nevada/Reno, and in various fields, factories and workshops. He has taught at Humboldt State, University of Massachussetts/Boston, San Francisco State and at Wollongong since 1981.

Glynn Owens is lecturer in clinical psychology at Liverpool University, Honorary Principal Clinical Psychologist at Moss Side Hospital, and the author of a number of articles, chapters and books on various aspects of psychology. His current research includes studies of the relationship between psychology and general health.

Dorothy Rowe has recently retired from being the Head of the Clinical Psychology Department for North Lincolnshire. As a psychotherapist and researcher she has been studying the experience of depression for almost twenty years. She has written a number of books including *The Experience of Depression* (Wiley, 1978), *Depression: The Way Out of Your Prison* (RKP, 1983) and most recently *Living with the Bomb* (RKP, 1985).

Rob Sanson-Fisher is currently Professor and Head of Behavioural Science in Relation to Medicine at the University of Newcastle, NSW, Australia. His specific areas of interest include modification of health risk behaviours, aspects of the doctor-patient interaction and assessment of quality of medical care.

David Smail was educated at University College, London and is District Psychologist for Nottingham Health Authority. He is author of *Psychotherapy: A Personal Approach* and *Illusion and Reality: The Meaning of Anxiety*.

Peter Trower graduated from Bristol University in 1969 with a joint honours in psychology and philosophy and from Leeds University in 1971 with an MSc in clinical psychology. He then joined the social skills research team in Oxford until 1977, returning to full-time clinical work in Birmingham for the next five years. In 1982 he became lecturer in clinical psychology at Leicester University, a post he currently holds.

ACKNOWLEDGMENTS

We wish to thank all the contributors for their perseverance and good humour during the time we have been working on the book. In particular we wish to thank David Smail for his support in the early stages and Sue Llewelyn for helping us to continue.

David and Sandra Canter, Ann Faulkner, John Harris, Peter Maguire and Miller Mair have provided us with an example of academic endeavour and creativity. We wish to acknowledge our debt to them.

We are very grateful to Morris Cunningham formerly Principal Clinical Psychologist, Crichton Royal Hospital, Dumfries, for creating the little figures on the cover.

Introduction: Psychology, Ethics and Change

Gavin and Susan Fairbairn

INTRODUCTION

Practitioners in the caring professions face moral decisions every day. They must decide how to allocate their time and the other resources at their disposal, who to help and who not to help. They must decide how they will interact with those who seek their help: for example, whether in general they will regard them as autonomous beings with rights and responsibilities, or rather as helpless individuals, incapable of rational choice. They must decide what their position is in relation to the political and social pressures that impinge upon them in their caring task. For example, in a world where resources in the welfare services are limited because of competing interests, they are faced daily with the dilemma of whether to continue to 'make do' with the resources provided, or rather to take political action to ensure that their clients are better provided for. All caring practitioners face the problems of confidentiality that being in possession of privileged information causes. And all face the problem of deciding how much of themselves to give to their professional work and how much to keep for themselves, their families and friends. These are general moral issues which face practitioners throughout the whole spectrum of caring professions. In addition there are other, more particular problems which arise in relation to the special tasks of each context of human caring.

Our concern as editors has been to bring together contributions which draw attention to the ethical dimension of the psychological processes used in attempting to bring about change in human well being, both mental and physical. Although the book focuses mainly on the practice of clinical psychology and behavioural medicine, many of the issues raised, or other very similar issues, will also arise for psychiatrists, social workers and nurses working in psychiatric settings and for others whose work is concerned with psychological change including educational psychologists, counsellors and teachers of children with special needs. In order to avoid clumsiness of style, we have used the terms 'psychologists' and 'psychology' in an all encompassing way rather than referring for example to 'the clinical psychologist' or 'the psychologist working in behavioural medicine'. We hope context will make clear the group to whom we are referring. It is also worth noting that at times some of what we say about 'psychologists' could be taken as referring to any individual who is engaged in bringing about psychological change.

Both clinical psychology and behavioural medicine are involved in the business of change and both take place primarily within medical settings. Each is concerned with change relating to the well being of individuals; they differ both in the kinds of changes they aim to achieve and in the emphasis they lay on ways of achieving change. Both are concerned to some extent with both physical and mental well being but the emphasis within each discipline is different. Whereas most clinical psychologists, even the most behavioural of behaviourists, would acknowledge that their primary aim was to enhance the psychological well being of their clients, much of behavioural medicine relates to physical well being. However, psychologists working within behavioural medicine or health psychology will often be aiming to promote psychological well being within the context of physical illness, for instance working to improve coping strategies for cancer patients or investigating the use of techniques of relaxation in the control of physical pain. Conversely the work of clinical psychologists may affect physical health, eg where clients are drug or alcohol dependent or are prone to self harm. In some instances the physical benefits to a client may even be a primary aim of clinical psychology. Glynn Owens, in his chapter in this book, discusses the use of punishment in the treatment of severely self-mutilating clients: clearly in such cases the psychologist is more concerned with physical well being.

Clinical psychologists mostly work in face-to-face contact with clients, either one to one, or with groups or families. The approaches and techniques they use are designed to promote change in the client, and sometimes in his family or social system. In instances where they have a consultancy role, clinical psychologists work indirectly for change by providing guidance and supervision of treatments carried out by other health care professionals, for example in token economy regimes or rehabilitation programmes. In their day to day work they are likely to face ethical issues relating to the nature of their relationship with clients, concerned for example with autonomy and paternalism, confidentiality, honesty, authority and power. On the other hand psychologists, who work in behavioural medicine or health psychology, are likely to be engaged in larger scale change for example in health promotion or in health-related research aimed at indirect improvements in patients' or clients' physical or mental welfare. In addition to sharing many of the ethical problems already mentioned, such psychologists are likely to face other more large scale and perhaps more overtly political problems, relating, for example, to resource allocation and questions of autonomy and choice within whole communities. Bob Sanson-Fisher raises many such issues in his chapter. Community psychologists whose work is concerned with changing views of mental problems are also likely to face larger scale ethical and political issues as well as interpersonal ones.

In approaching the ethical dimension of psychological change the contributors to the book focus attention both on some of the conceptual frameworks and ideologies that underlie psychology as a clinical discipline and on practical issues. The contributors come from different theoretical backgrounds and do not necessarily share beliefs about the nature of folk, of psychological change, or of the aims of psychological interventions. Contributors such as Susan Llewelyn, Glynn Owens, Peter Trower, Ron McKechnie and Rudi Dallos, whose chapters are concerned with clinical psychology, elaborate moral problems faced by practitioners adopting a range of approaches from individual psychotherapy to radical behavioural approaches, family and group therapy. Those considering behavioural medicine elaborate issues arising from the application of psychology in changing health behaviours and beliefs (Becker *et al.*, 1977) and in medical education.

Contributors were asked to address ethical issues which particularly concerned or interested them, and therefore the chapters do not provide a comprehensive coverage of all key issues in this field; nor do they cover the entire range of contexts in which psychologists play a clinical role. The book is not intended to represent the whole range of ethical issues that may arise in clinically applied psychology. Rather it should be seen as an hors-d'œuvre to whet the appetite for more ethical discussion. Nor do the contributors to the book represent any kind of fair sampling of the range of ethical concerns and opinions among clinical psychologists. Our hope for the volume is that it should encourage and contribute to thinking and discussion about an important, and perhaps rather neglected, dimension in psychological practice. We are pleased that contributors came up with unsettling and thought-provoking pieces, questioning assumptions at a profound level. For example, Don Mixon examines the basis for the scientific claims of much psychology, David Smail questions the reasons for changes in attitudes towards therapy and therapists from suspicion to eager acceptance when proof of their efficacy is lacking and Rom Harré brings into question the crucial neglect of the context in which diagnostic procedures or clinical interviews take place. These and other contributors are seeking to find out what is happening at a non-superficial level. They are disclosing meta-rules in much the same way as the small boy, by pointing out the non-existence of the Emperor's 'new clothes', drew attention, albeit unwittingly, to the implicit rule about not noticing the Emperor's nakedness.

ETHICS AND PSYCHOLOGY

Ethics has received relatively little attention in psychology in comparison with other disciplines. Many other professions engaged in caring for people, such as medicine, nursing and social work have a developed literature dealing with the ethics of their practice. For example, in Britain the *Journal of Medical Ethics* is issued quarterly and a new journal, *Bioethics*, is being launched in 1987. The medical and nursing journals frequently publish articles dealing with ethical issues and there are many books dealing with ethics in these disciplines (see, for example, Harris, 1985; Thompson, Melia and Boyd, 1983; Campbell and Higgs, 1982; Bloch and Chodoff, 1981). The British Association of Social Workers (BASW) recently sponsored a volume of papers addressing issues arising from their Code of Ethics (Watson, 1985) and there are many books addressing philosophical and ethical issues in social work (see, for example, Timms, 1984; Watson, Leighton and Stalley, 1983). In psychology outside the USA the situation is different. There is a considerable literature on the ethics of psychological research (eg Heinz, 1982) and on specific treatment modes and specialised contexts in clinical psychology, eg on the use of behaviour modification with the mentally handicapped (Williams *et al.*, 1984) and on clinical psychology within child-development centres (Middleton, 1985). And from time to time the British Psychological Society (BPS) issues statements or guidelines about ethical matters. However, little work exists in Britain addressing the practical ethical issues faced by psychologists.

ETHICS AND MORALS

In philosophy a distinction is often made between 'ethics' and 'morals' or 'morality'. 'Ethics' is used to refer to the systematic study of morality in terms, for example, of the principles that are used in making decisions about courses of action, for example about whether their consequences are good or bad, and about whether the motives behind them are good or bad. 'Morals' or 'morality', on the other hand, is used to refer to the situations, actions, beliefs, attitudes, intentions etc., to which ethical theories are a systematic response. Used in accordance with this strict definition, ethics is more abstract than morality; it is that branch of philosophy which is sometimes, perhaps confusingly, referred to as moral philosophy.

In terms of this distinction between ethics and morals, what we want to encourage is a consideration of the moral problems that arise in clinical practice in ethical terms. However, these terms are often used interchangeably by non-philosophers and indeed by some philosophers (see, for example, Singer, 1979), and we are not committed to distinguishing them in this introduction. The way in which a person uses the terms morals, ethics and all their variations seems to depend upon the way in which she thinks about questions of value. For example, someone who believes that morality is primarily about being prissy about sex, about restricting people's opportunities for enjoyment or about the imposition of archaic values drawn from out-of-date religions, is likely to think that anything discussed in terms of 'morality' is beyond the pale and hence to prefer the term 'ethics' to refer to the questions of value that arise in her life. The use that we make of these terms and their variations is simply intended to focus attention on questions of value.

We want to draw attention to the kinds of problems in clinical practice which readers might find themselves discussing, using evaluating words like 'right', 'wrong', 'should', 'ought', 'good' and 'bad'. One way in which moral philosophers attempt to provide a way of thinking about moral problems is by attempting to 'unpack' the meaning of such words to make clear what is meant when they are used. Different ethical theories offer different ways of thinking about these terms.

For example, 'utilitarianism' would generally suggest that the meaning of such terms should be understood in terms of the amount of benefit or harm that will come about as a result of a particular action or decision. Utilitarians emphasise the consequences of actions. Good consequences are balanced against bad consequences and decisions about what to do are made on the basis of which action will produce the most benefit and the least harm. Utilitarianism is difficult to apply in a thorough-going way, because it requires that one should consider the benefits and harms to all who will be affected by an action, even those affected indirectly and at some spatio-temporal distance from the action in question. Stated crudely, its aim is to produce the greatest happiness, or whatever the chief good for people is, for the greatest number.

An 'absolutist' stance, on the other hand, would suggest that the meaning of evaluative words should be understood in terms of the extent to which the actions or decisions, to which the words are applied, agree with the dictates of a system of rules. The absolutist position in ethics is opposed to utilitarianism. The major thesis of absolutist ethical positions is that certain actions are intrinsically wrong, whatever the consequences, and can never be justified, and that moral judgments are universally applicable. Acts like murder, for example, are considered in an absolutist sense always to be wrong. Religious morality is often, but need not be, of an absolutist kind.

The ethical issues that arise in the caring professions are part of the network of ethical problems that arise for all people. Of course, many situations faced by psychologists involved in clinical practice will not arise for lay people or for other caring professionals because they will arise for the psychologist in virtue of her special role. However, the ethical thinking required to deal with such problems will be no different than that required to deal with ethical issues in other areas of life; it is just that the circumstances in which it will have to be applied will be different. One way in which a psychologist might prepare for the ethical problems that she will meet in her work would therefore be to study ethical theory in order that she can reason about such problems from a more educated, if not necessarily a more ethical, position. But we are not concerned in this introduction to argue for a particular ethical theory, rather to stimulate readers to a consideration of the moral questions that they face and the conceptual and ethical equipment with which they deal with such questions. The problem with ethical theories is that although one may work them out in great detail they are difficult to apply in specific situations. How can it be possible to apply general ethical principles to situations in clinical practice, each of which is unique? Perhaps it is a weakness of the book that it does not include chapters offering arguments concerning the applicability of various ethical theories to psychological practice. None of the chapters attempts a detailed overview of ethical theories and we do not propose to do so here. Readers who wish to familiarise themselves with such theories in discussions of practical issues may wish to read *Moral Dilemmas in Medicine* (Campbell, 1975), *Causing Death and Saving Lives* (Glover, 1977), *Practical Ethics* (Singer, 1979) or the introductory chapter of *Ethical Issues in Modern Medicine* (Arras and Hunt, 1983) all of which offer interesting overviews.

THE NEGLECT OF ETHICS

Some people might think that a consideration of ethics is a luxury with no relationship to practice; they might fail to see how considering ethics could possibly change the way in which the needs of clients are met. Some might argue that there is no need for a book addressing ethical issues in psychology, because psychologists involved in clinical work are concerned to promote the welfare of their clients, that they naturally have their clients' best interests at heart as if this somehow guarantees that they will act ethically. They might cite the British Psychological Society's Code of Conduct for Psychologists, which states that psychologists will 'hold the interests and welfare of those in receipt of their services as paramount' (*BPS*, 1985). But Codes of Conduct cannot guarantee ethical behaviour. It is one thing for a professional body to proclaim that members of that profession should always treat their clients' interests as of the greatest importance and quite another to expect that they will, or even can, actually do this. Very few psychologists are so committed that they do what they do solely in the interests of their clients. Conflicts of interests are bound to arise and these indeed will be the source of ethical problems.

Against those who see ethics as a frill – interesting but inessential (or uninteresting and inessential), we would argue that a consideration of the ethical dimension of psychological change is fundamental to the development of practice. Moral difficulties may be small-scale interpersonal issues, wider interdisciplinary conflicts or global and political in nature. They include the kinds of problems and issues which readers might 'go home and cry about': sensed failures, injustices or impossible working situations. Such difficulties may form the basis of moans or gossiping to family or colleagues or may be shared with no one. Many of the most burning issues that affect people in their tasks in the caring professions are at root moral issues. Ask yourself what it is that you get most upset/alarmed/despondent about in your work. We guess that if you apply a 'laddering' technique to this question you will end up finally with an ethical issue. A rather more informal technique might involve simply elaborating the nature of the issue by repeatedly asking yourself questions of this kind 'Why does that upset you?', 'What is it that you find upsetting here?' in relation to situations you identify as being upsetting. Perhaps an example might help. When asked the question 'What is it that you get most upset/alarmed/despondent about in your work?' Lesley, who did not believe that a consideration of ethics had a place in her work in a child psychiatric unit, said that the thing that upset her most was the way in which situations of conflict with children were handled by the nursing staff. After a few more questions she was talking about how the nursing staff failed to respect the children as people. 'Every one of them is a person like you and me and should be treated with the same respect as everyone else.' As Kelly (1955) says, superordinate constructs are evaluative, ie ethical. It seems clear to us that unresolved conflicts and dilemmas in one's practice can be personally damaging and debilitating. This can in turn make therapeutic change for clients less likely as psychologists become less effective and more likely to attend to self-preservation than to treat the interests of clients as paramount. Of course problems of this kind are not peculiar to psychology. It is perhaps because the moral problems that caring practitioners face can be so personally damaging that they manage to devise so many different strategies for avoiding moral decisions.

Another reason for the neglect of ethics in the psychological literature is that any discussion of 'ethics' may become confused with *moralising*. Independent minded psychologists are likely to have little truck with undefended imperative statements telling them what they 'should', 'ought' or 'must' do or not do. A psychologist who misguidedly associates ethics with moralising may reject any examination of the ethics of her profession.

Apart from a general distaste for some of the language of ethical debate, two other not uncommon beliefs seem likely to lead away from the explicit consideration of professional ethics and values in psychological practice. The first is the belief in the notion of psychology as a value-free science, the second the belief in the idea that therapists should be value neutral and 'nondirective'. The second of these may gain strength from the first.

Psychology as value-free science

Sutton (1981) states, 'in one respect psychological practice faces unique problems, because psychology stands at the intersection of the helping professions with "science".' Psychological science has traditionally been thought of as developing through careful, value-free investigations. The notion of an objective (and hence, so it is thought, value free) clinical psychology, favoured by many psychologists, rests on the possibility of a foundation in positivist science. Critical discussion of the nature of psychology as positivist science is now common, eg Mixon's chapter in this volume, Pilgrim (1984), Kelly (1955). Shotter (1974, 1975) has proposed that psychology as a discipline is better considered a 'moral science of action' than as a 'natural science of behaviour'.

One question for discussion is the extent to which ideas and techniques used by clinical psychologists are actually founded upon systematic scientific research. Sutton (1981) views this question as ethically important, arguing that psychologists are obliged to do research. 'If the practising psychologist is to retain his status as a scientist rather than to be simply a purveyor of ideas and techniques developed by other psychologists, then (s)he has an obligation to undertake scientific work.' Sutton seems here to be arguing for clinical research to become one of the principal means by which clinical psychology is practised.

In a scientifically based clinical psychology the ethics of scientific research may be examined and discussed. However, it seems probable that the greater the emphasis on the scientific credibility of research the less likely interpersonal and professional values and ethics are to be widely and seriously debated. If its practitioners view clinical psychology as having a firm foundation in positivist science, they may disregard questions of professional values and ethics because these are not amenable to objective consideration. Discussion of ethical issues in the context of journals and conferences may sit rather badly alongside reports of research and interventions couched in objective language. This might lead to reticence in putting forward ethical observations and discussion.

However, clinical psychology viewed as closely linked to science cannot indefinitely avoid ethical debate. Even if the psychological knowledge utilised in clinical practice was always the result of the application of an objective scientific method, at the point at which it is applied, moral questions of an interpersonal kind are bound to arise. Something similar is true of all applications of scientific knowledge. Consider, for example, scientific research in genetic engineering and nuclear power; there is no doubt that the applications of these scientific discoveries including human cloning and the atom bomb are of ultimate moral importance. Similarly applications of findings in sensory deprivation, behaviour modification and intelligence testing bring along with them questions of ethics.

The scientific nature of clinical psychology is called into question by Smail in this book and at more length in *Illusion and Reality* (1984). Smail portrays the therapeutic enterprise as being more akin to magic than to science; he also places the therapeutic relationship on a continuum with prostitution, thus noting its nature as charitable love for which the therapist is paid. Neither of these metaphors seem to demand the exclusion of interpersonal values in the same way that construing psychological practice as part of the prevailing positivist scientific orthodoxy does.

The value-free therapist

The Division of Clinical Psychology *Guidelines for the Professional Practice of Clinical Psychology* (BPS, 1983), state 'In considering therapeutic goals, psychologists seek to ensure that neither their own values nor those of the institution or organisation in which care is provided, are unreasonably imposed upon the client' (16.2). Providing help and support in what they construe as a nondirective and value-free manner is something of a tradition for psychotherapists and counsellors. Smail (1987) characterises the apparently value-free stance of the therapist thus 'the therapist. . . .apparently steps out of the moral arena and offers his or her services on the basis of a kind of ethically neutral technological efficacy, in principle no different from that which might be claimed by motor mechanics . . .'

It is worth noting the possibility of confusion between the idea of conducting therapy in a way that does not impose values on the client and recognising the importance of the values that the therapist brings to the therapeutic encounter. Acting in what is thought to be a value-free way may lead therapists towards the adoption of an assumed persona which is non-judgmental, calm, rather removed and neutral with respect to values. The adoption of such a therapeutic self is likely to involve the submersion of the therapist's real self with real interests and concerns outside the therapeutic context. To the client she may appear rather distant and rather unlike other people he knows and seem to have rather bland views about the world; or she may seem warm, friendly and enthusiastic without actually sharing anything of her true self.

Refraining from self-disclosure is common among caring practitioners of all kinds. Therapists may feel constrained to limit self disclosure because of their role. Hiding everyday remarks and comments from clients, when with acquaintances they would not hesitate to say those parts of themselves, may seem useful; or they may consider it part of their clinical responsibility not to become too friendly with clients. A therapist may not disclose her personal values for reasons which relate to issues of power in the therapist/client relationship. The distant, uninvolved therapist, disclosing little of herself, is more likely to be able to maintain her role as an unchallenged expert; recognising important personal values in the professional relationship, on the other hand, may make this position more difficult to maintain. The psychologist may limit self-disclosure because she wishes to maintain her values, perhaps without having to defend or even examine them in her professional work or because, for reasons of self protection, she wishes to control the quality of the relationship and the quantity of time in her life that it takes up. The degree of role distance and accessibility of the psychologist is crucially important for professional and personal survival. The gnawing burden of being excessively available to clients is vividly conveyed by Konrad (1975) in his description of the nightmare effect of an overly dependent client on a caseworker.

A relationship with a client in which the therapist is not personally present, is probably of a fundamentally different kind to the therapist's other relationships with people. It could be argued that the therapist who is not personally present in the encounter and who does not stand alongside the client, is not treating him with respect as a person and that this can never be in the client's best interests. Of course, being present with a client need not imply that the psychologist should disclose herself to him, only that the whole of her self should be available in the interaction with him. It is for each individual to decide how much of their available self, how much of their experience, of their value and belief systems, they manifest in their relationship with others. But it could be seen as disrespectful of a client as a person if the psychologist enters a therapeutic relationship with the intention of remaining distant and of avoiding becoming known as the person she really is. Mishler (1984) argues for professional-client relationships to be based on statements by the professional which affirm the common humanity of professional and client, their similarity as persons, rather than on discourse emphasising their differences and separation due to their special roles in this situation. Clearly there are differences between the client and the therapist, for example in terms of their expertise in dealing with the kinds of problems they have come together to consider and of their knowledge about the particular problems with which they are presently concerned. But if the therapeutic relationship is to be based on respect for clients as people, as it must be if the client is to be treated as a person, then it also has to be acknowledged that it takes place between two people. We cannot respect another as a person unless we recognise that he is a person like us; and we cannot do this in a therapeutic situation unless we are present, as a person, with the other.

Of course given the special nature of a therapeutic relationship and the responsibilities it places upon the psychologist, it is necessary for her to be selective as to the parts of herself that she utilises with clients. For example, since the relationship is, by definition, one in which she is engaged to offer help to the client and not to gain help for herself (though, of course, she may gain help for herself by the way), any disclosure of her self that goes on should ideally be in the client's best interests. The BPS Guidelines make the point that interaction on a personal or social level or self-disclosure should take place 'only in the best interests of the client' (19.1).

Adopting what is thought to be a value-free position in therapy may lead the therapist to deny the importance or influence of her own moral values. Therapists' values are frequently hidden in therapy and so their importance may be ignored or overlooked. But the purpose of the psychologist is commonly to promote change which frequently involves movement towards the therapists's perceived best, ie valued, solution: that is, in some sense, by some means, the therapist's values are imposed upon the client, albeit implicitly rather than explicity. It is important therefore to consider the extent to which therapists' values are or should be, explicitly present and available within the therapeutic relationship as foundations for therapeutic change. Smail (1987) recognises the importance of the therapist's personal value system in therapy 'Much of the time it is the therapist's *personal* qualities – personal experience and personal judgement, and indeed personally constructed ethical stance – which determine his or her view both of the patient's situation and of what course he or she feels the patient should take in dealing with it.' And in a paper on ethical confrontation in counselling, Brian Thorne (1987) discusses what he considers is the necessity for therapists, however non-directive they might wish to be, to bring their own moral position into play in the therapeutic situation at times. Moral qualms probably arise for most therapists only at the point at which the power and influence held by the therapist as a consequence of her relationship with the client begins to be wielded heavy-handedly in persuading the client to adopt the therapist's moral values. Apart from anything else, such persuasion might be considered to remove autonomy from the client if he merely conforms to the views of the therapist. The consequences might be that therapists who wish to avoid such a possibility will adopt an extreme value-free position.

But even for the most ardent adherent to the importance of a value-free stance in therapy, there may be limitations to the extent to which they can, in conscience, remain morally neutral. For example, even such therapists may feel direct influence is necessary where moral positions involving violence or serious crime are concerned.

CODES OF ETHICS

There is another use of the term 'ethics', as well as the sense in which it is used by philosophers to refer to the systematic study of human conduct with respect to its rightness and wrongness. This is the sense in which 'ethics' is used to refer to a body of more or less explicit guidelines or rules for conduct by the members of a profession; it is in this sense that we have codes of ethics for doctors, nurses, psychologists, the advertising industry etc. Such codes are sometimes refered to as codes of practice or codes of conduct. We have already mentioned the relative lack of discussion of ethics in British psychology and here it is worth noting that only 12 per cent of members of the BPS voted in the ballot on the resolution adopting the Code of Conduct for psychologists. By contrast 37 per cent voted on a resolution to transfer the society's funds from a bank involved with the apartheid system in South Africa (BPS, 1985). Given the low percentage of members of the BPS voting on the Code of Conduct resolution one might question the extent to which it represents the views of the majority of BPS members. And it is interesting to speculate on the reason for members being sufficiently morally concerned to be motivated to demonstrate outrage at the apartheid system in this way while being somewhat reticent about voting on the adoption of an ethical code concerning their own conduct as psychologists. Perhaps we are right in thinking that there is some confusion between ethics and 'moralising'.

THE NATURE OF ETHICAL CODES

When people talk about 'ethics' sometimes what they mean is something akin to '*etiquette*', and at their least helpful codes of professional ethics are little more than statements of rules for conduct. Statements of rules are likely to be unhelpful because in practice situations are likely to be more complex than rules suggest. Although rules of conduct might seem to give clear indications for action in given circumstances, they are likely at times to conflict with one another and so ultimately rules of conduct can serve to muddle rather than clarify issues. If one's basis for moral action is a primitive adherence to rules, what can one do when the rules suggest conflicting courses of action?

Codes of ethics in the caring professions are often expressed in very general terms. Even where they are more specific and closely linked to disciplinary procedures, they are ultimately unenforceable and depend upon the integrity of the individual. The individual is finally responsible for the ways in which she conducts herself professionally as well as personally. Ethical codes are often criticised because the generality of the language in which they are stated makes them open to different interpretations. Often they lack any attempt at an analysis of the apparently simple words in which they are stated, words which would-be upholders may think that they understand but about which they may disagree with others; words such as responsibility, duty, obligation, accountability, value, dignity, respect and confidentiality. Even if it is possible for practitioners to agree about what they mean by such words it is worth remembering that the clients towards whom they intend to act ethically may understand something very different by them. Weiss (1982) points this out in an interesting account of a comparison of the understandings held by clients, doctors, and medical students of confidentiality, arguably the most advocated ethical principle throughout the caring professions. Weiss found that the expectations of clients about the way in which privileged information will be treated are very different from those of doctors and medical students; it seems a fairly safe bet to guess that something similar would be true if such a comparison were made between the views of clinical psychologists and their clients. If codes of ethics are created at least in part to ensure that clients are protected, perhaps clients should be consulted about their expectations of the ethical standards of practitioners. Perhaps the best of such codes are those in which an attempt is made to overcome difficulties of interpretation or at least to point out that they exist, where the intention of the code is clearly to encourage ethical reasoning and to provide some guidelines for such reasoning.

BPS STATEMENTS ON MATTERS OF ETHICS RELATING TO THE CLINICAL PRACTICE OF PSYCHOLOGY

The BPS has issued a number of documents that address issues of ethics that impinge upon the practice of clinical psychologists including the 'Report of the Working Party on Behaviour Modification' (1978), the 'Principles Governing the Employment of Psychological Tests' (1981) and the 'Ethical Principles for Research on Human Subjects' (1978). The 'A Code of Conduct for Psychologists' (1985) and the *Guidelines for the Professional Practice of Clinical Psychology* (1983) have a particular bearing on clinical practice. This is not the place to enter into a detailed analysis of these; however it is worthwhile making a few observations in relation to each.

The BPS Code of Conduct for Psychologists

In many ways the Code of Conduct serves as a kind of primitive rule book for professional conduct of the kind that the *Guidelines* (BPS, 1983) rejects. It contains some interesting ambiguities and internal conflicts. For example, it maintains that psychologists 'shall normally carry out investigations or interventions only with the valid consent of participants . .' (paragraph 3). Now it seems right and proper for psychologists to seek the valid consent of those who will be most directly affected by their actions. However, this statement allows that valid consent need not always be sought. The Code is prescriptive about what should happen in circumstances where it is thought necessary to withhold full information from participants in an investigation. It states that psychologists shall 'always consult experienced professional colleagues when considering withholding information about an investigatory procedure, and withhold information only when it is necessary in the interests of the objectivity of the investigatory procedure or of future professional practices' (3.1). However, it fails to outline the kinds of occasions on which it might be considered appropriate, even right, not to seek consent. And even its prescription that participants who have not been fully informed prior to the investigation should be retrospectively provided with such full information, contains the proviso that this should only happen 'in so far as it is consistent with a concern for the welfare of the participants'. No indication is given about the kinds of circumstances that might warrant the failure retrospectively to 'come clean'; this is worrying in view of the lack of prescription that investigations should in themselves be consistent with a concern for the welfare of the participant. These statements about research seem to conflict somewhat with paragraph 1 which maintains that psychologists 'shall hold the interests and welfare of those in receipt of their services to be paramount at all times and ensure that the interests of participants in research are safeguarded' (paragraph 1). Presumably it is most often in an individual's interests to be aware of what is happening to him in order that he can decide if this is what he really wants to be happening. Another ambiguity arises concerning the question of who is to count as the recipient of services. In clinical practice the patient or client is the recipient but conflict may arise for a psychologist who is working as part of an interdisciplinary team where her role is that of an agent of, say, a consultant psychiatrist. In such a case the psychologist may perceive herself as offering a service to the patient/client while the consultant sees her as offering a service to him. In the terms of the Code the psychologist has a difficulty: if she is to safeguard the interests of those in receipt of her services she will have to do what she considers best for the client and this might conflict with the expectations of the consultant.

The Guidelines

The *Guidelines for the Professional Practice of Clinical Psychology* (BPS, 1983) represent the attempt to spell out in detail what the exemplary practice of clinical psychology would consist in. The authors recognise that the *Guidelines* do 'not represent' "the final word" on the professional practice of clinical psychology' and intend that 'to remain effective the *Guidelines* will be revised and improved on a regular basis'. The *Guidelines* adopt a positive approach to the development of good practice in 'giving guidance as to the nature of *good* practice rather than taking the negative approach of trying to identify and thereafter outlaw all forms of bad practice'. Much of what they spell out in considerable detail seems to constitute sound practical as well as ethical advice. Much is said about the need to maintain professional competence, about not allowing false impressions of competence to be entertained by others and about safeguards regarding the work of trainee psychologists. The necessity to obtain valid consent to treatment and the problems of privacy and confidentiality are addressed in a thorough and thought-provoking manner.

Several areas of possible conflict are addressed. For example, the possibility of conflict between the psychologist's responsibilities to her client and to the medical practitioner who has primary responsibility for the client is discussed. Here the *Guidelines* are unequivocal and recognise that the responsibility to ensure that 'the client receives the care that he or she is considered to require' is superordinate over loyalty to colleagues.

However, despite having much to commend them, the *Guidelines* have many weaknesses. One major weakness is that possible ambiguities of meaning are not teased out and points where ambivalence or doubt about an item is expressed are not elaborated fully. For example, as pointed out earlier, point 16.2 states that 'In considering therapeutic goals, psychologists seek to ensure that neither their own values nor those of the institution or organisation in which care is provided, are unreasonably imposed upon the client', but we are given no guidance about what the unreasonable imposition of the values of the psychologist or the institution might amount to.

Point 16.3 recognises that psychologists '. . . are under no obligation to accept the client's values in determining the goals of intervention . . .'. In circumstances where she feels 'unable on moral or similar grounds to undertake intervention . .' it is stated that 'where it is considered appropriate, the psychologist assists the client to obtain access to care from an alternative source.' In relation to these points no indication is given of when it might be 'appropriate' to refer on to another psychologist a client whose aims in treatment arise from values that one does not share. Again there is an assertion that 'Psychologists do not condone, use or participate in the application of psychological knowledge or technique in any way that infringes human rights' (13.1) but no indication is given about what constitutes a 'human right' or a violation of one, or about what psychologists should do if they meet situations in which such rights are being violated.

In 7.6, discussing the relationship between a trainee psychologist and his supervisor, the *Guidelines* assert that

Where a trainee psychologist has legitimate reasons (on ethical or other grounds) for refusing to undertake a certain course of action as prescribed by the supervisor, the supervising psychologist, without prejudice, respects the trainee's right to do so. The legitimacy of such reasons may be established in consultation with a third party.

What might constitute a legitimate reason for a trainee's refusal to undertake actions prescribed by her supervisor? If these actions lie within the area of personal ethical principles then the matter might be considered to rest with the trainee's own chosen position. This would be analogous to the way in which attendance at abortions in gynaecological nursing is considered a matter of conscience. However, in some situations any legitimate ethical grounds for the student's refusal would also constitute an ethical reason for the supervisor's not prescribing such a course of action. In that case it would not be so much that the supervisor should respect the trainee's right to refuse to undertake the course of action in question, as that the supervisor would, as it were, have had his ethical sights changed.

Finally it is worth noting that the *Guidelines* share many of the weaknesses of the *Code of Conduct*. For example, in relation to the use of deception in psychological research, the statement 'Where deception or concealment has been necessary, revelation normally follows participation as a matter of course' (9.4) is not qualified by any indications about the kinds of instances where to withhold revelation might be considered acceptable.

ETHICAL CODES IN PRACTICE

If a code of ethics is to serve the purpose of assisting in the development of a thinking approach to the moral dimension of practice in any profession concerned with offering help, it should do more than simply present principles that seem to underlie that profession. To be helpful it needs in addition to relate these to practice in such a way that ambiguities and difficulties are pinpointed. Such an approach seems to be exemplified by the British Association of Social Workers 'Code of Ethics for Social Work' (BASW, 1975) which seeks to promote discussion of professional values among practitioners. The general approach of the BASW Code seems a fruitful one and has already led to a second step in debating social work ethics with the publication of a book of critical analyses of the code (Watson, 1985).

Although it has many faults, the approach of the BASW Code is to attempt to lay down some basic principles and in addition to discuss what these might mean in practice. The principles of practice in the BASW Code are thought provoking and cannot be easily taken for granted. They include, for example, considerations of the aims of professional social work and its relationship to the personal life of the social worker:

> He will respect his clients as individuals and will seek to ensure that their dignity, individuality, rights and responsibility shall be safeguarded.
>
> (BASW Code; *Principles of Practice, 1*)
>
> He will help his clients increase the range of choices open to them and their powers to make decisions.
>
> (BASW Code; *Principles of Practice, 4*)
>
> He will not reject his client or lose concern for his suffering, even if obliged to protect others against him, or obliged to acknowledge an inability to help him.
>
> (BASW Code; *Principles of Practice, 5*)
>
> He will give precedence to his professional responsibility over his personal interests.
>
> (BASW Code; *Principles of Practice, 6*)

The phrasing of the principles of practice in the singular 'He' serves to make them seem to address the professional worker personally, rather than making general statements addressed to the profession as a whole. The commentary amplifies and qualifies the principles such that the complexity of ethical issues is brought into focus. For example, in relation to point 6 above the commentary states:

> This principle recognises the opportunities for conflict between personal interest and professional responsibilities. It places upon the social worker an obligation not to pursue personal interests at the clients' expense. It does not imply that at all times the social worker must put his responsibility to a client above his other responsibilities, for example as a citizen or as a parent.' (BASW Code, *Commentary on Principle 6*)

Although less detailed than the BPS *Guidelines*, the strength of the BASW Code is in its open acknowledgment that matters of value and ethics are seldom simple. The BPS *Guidelines* by contrast at times seem to suggest that consultation with experienced or better qualified colleagues will offer solutions of an ethical kind. But unless such colleagues have particular expertise in ethical reasoning, or are themselves beyond reproach, morally speaking, it is questionable whether recourse to such a solution to one's ethical problems is likely to prove fruitful.

WIDER ETHICAL CONCERNS

It is impossible in a volume of this size for all the varieties of ethical issues encountered by clinical psychologists, therapists and those working in behavioural medicine to be discussed in detail. Many issues have been neglected to some extent including some relating to particular fields of work or client groups, such as forensic psychology, mental handicap and work with children; and others relating to particular treatments or interventions, for example group treatment, the use of token economies and rehabilitation.

The aims of the professional psychologist in clinical situations and in behavioural medicine form a cornerstone for much ethical superstructure. Hawks (1981) claims that prevention rather than cure should be a primary aim of psychology, enabling people to cope by themselves. In order to achieve the aim of prevention of psychological distress, Hawks states that other things, eg project type work, are more important than working in-one-to-one therapeutic situations. Prevention as an aim may be stated in terms of enabling people to cope without professional help and thus 'giving psychology away' to the client. This relates closely to the aspirations of Bakan:

> The value of understanding human functioning does not inhere in its application in the usual sense but in its possession . . . In order to help a person who is in psychological difficulties we work to enhance his understanding of himself and of his relationships to others. If we think in terms of traditional roles, then the significant place in society of the psychologist will be more that of the teacher than expert or technician (Bakan, 1967).

The aims of a psychological service translate practically into policy making. At this level many vital ethical issues may be conveniently summed up in terms of resource allocation, in particular deciding upon the optimal use of psychologists' time and energy. The way in which professional time, expertise and energy is used is one of the primary issues in resource allocation in all of the caring professions; indeed the justification of the way in which human effort is utilised is common to those who adopt a thoughtful stance in all of human enterprise.

Many larger scale ethical issues in behavioural medicine such as those relating to methods of health promotion are discussed in the chapters by Broome and Sanson-Fisher in this volume. However, much of behavioural medicine is concerned with improving interpersonal aspects of the care people receive from physicians; an example is the way in which psychology is used in training doctors and nurses in interviewing (Faulkner, 1984; Pendleton and Hasler, 1983; and Maguire, 1981). The possible benefits of such work are both physical and psychological. A doctor who relates well to his clients is more likely to elicit essential information in an efficient and friendly manner, both because he is clear in his requests for such information and because his client trusts him. It is also more likely that his clients will comply with his instructions about taking medication; of course he is also more likely to give such instructions clearly (Ley, 1977). These are important physical outcomes but perhaps the psychological benefits to clients of a good relationship with a doctor are more important still although harder to measure objectively. The extent to which use of psychological approaches and techniques to improve interviewing skills, rather than adding a superficial gloss of smooth communication, fundamentally changes the nature of the health professional-client relationship, is examined by Sanson-Fisher in this volume. Psychologists working in this area of behavioural medicine, by publishing their work and findings (Maguire, Fairbairn and Fletcher, 1986; Faulkner, 1986) are making clear to health professionals and clients alike, aspects of practice which may previously have been 'unexplored territory'. In doing this questions of professional values and competence are necessarily confronted. By adding on communication to other caring skills it may be that we change concepts of what it means to be a doctor or nurse interacting with clients (Tuckett, 1985; Armstrong, 1983.)

It might be considered that psychologists, working to extend the communication of health care professionals, are carrying out work that would inevitably lead to the aggrandisement of the power of the professional and to the reduction of the power of the client. However, programmes for the development of communication skills of health care professionals which take seriously concepts such as negotiation (Tuckett, 1985) and attending to the voice of the lifeworld (Mishler, 1984), might enable the client's own views of illness, treatment plan and prognosis, and the 'context of meaning' (Mishler, 1984) within which these are set, to be fully recognised and given validity. In this way the psychologist working in behavioural medicine may promote professional-client relationships which take account of the client's responsibility for her or his future and which uphold the centrality of an attitude of respect for persons.

In his examination of medical interviewing, Mishler (1984) emphasises the possible conflict of forms of discourse and provinces of meaning between the doctor and her patient. He is concerned to draw attention to the danger of the possible take over of ordinary language and values by scientific/technical jargon. He cites Habermas (1970): 'the absorption of ordinary language by technical language leads to the distortion and suppression of human values: it substitutes technical rational considerations for normative ones.' For Mishler, if the patient's 'lifeworld' is dominated by the framework of technical medicine the possibility for more humane treatment is severely limited. He therefore stresses the importance of placing the client's ordinary language and context of meaning, 'the voice of the lifeworld', at the centre of professional-client discourse. Mishler's comments seem equally pertinent for psychologists relating to their own clients and for psychologists studying other health care professional/patient interactions.

Another important dimension of ethical discussion that is not elaborated in any of the other chapters, is the location of ethical issues as being either primarily within the individual, or within the social, economic and political context (Arras, 1983). Contributors focus their discussions at various points along this continuum. Much of the foregoing discussion has centred on individual issues in clinical psychology. We want finally to examine some issues related to the context in which clinical psychology and behavioural medicine take place.

A number of issues arise in relation to the context in which therapy takes place. Statements such as, 'I can't stand working in this place any longer', may well reveal contextual as well as interpersonal ethical issues. For the psychologist working within the huge organisation of the NHS, control of and responsibility for the environment are likely to seem distant and removed from everyday considerations. The environment of the psychologist may not immediately seem to be ethically or therapeutically important.

The BPS *Guidelines* for clinical psychologists (BPS, 1983) address issues of context thus:

Psychologists seek to ensure that their services are provided in conditions that allow an adequate standard of psychological and physical well-being in respect of heating, cleanliness, privacy and other factors which may be relevant (6.5)

and further that when this is not possible that:

. . . they make every reasonable effort to bring about an improvement in these conditions including bringing them to the attention of the responsible health or other authority where appropriate (6.7).

In relation to the planning of treatment, the *Guidelines* indicate that psychologists should:

. . . .acknowledge the influence that environment has on human behaviour and. . . . .take account of this influence especially when involved in the planning or management of institutional care facilities (6.8),

and also state:

Psychologists are particularly sensitive to the rights of clients receiving care in an institution when the strategy of intervention involves the systematic control and possible restrictions of the client's environment, and psychologists ensure that their intervention does not infringe the basic rights of clients (16.8).

What the *Guidelines* do not do is recognise the extent to which the context of therapy may be an influential therapeutic factor rather than merely the possibility that adverse conditions may be anti-therapeutic. Canter and Canter (1979) set out the two extremes of a continuum by which an environment may be described as therapeutic. Firstly, this term may simply indicate the location at which the therapy occurs: its position in relation to other facilities. Secondly, it may indicate that the environment itself is considered as a significant therapeutic agent, as in the notion of a 'therapeutic community' or the therapeutic milieu (Cumming and Cumming, 1964). Many layers of context or environment surround the psychologist and her client from the small scale, that is the chairs and room within which the interaction occurs, to the large, including general policies of the health service and the extent to which health, rather than say defence, is a priority in the nation (Rowe, 1985). Some beliefs and practices within these layers of context are discussed in the chapter by McKechnie.

Canter (1977) indicates that we cannot fully describe a place without considering (a) the conceptions people hold of the place or the descriptions they give of it and (b) the behaviour or activities occurring or expected to occur there, as well as (c) its purely physical attributes. A complete description also takes account of interrelationships between all three parameters, expectations, conceptions and physical attributes. Hawks (1981) considers that too often psychologists, in dealing with the client in front of them, neglect to consider the wards from which they have come. Psychologists arguing for the refurbishment of long stay wards in a psychiatric hospital have to consider the possible cost effectiveness of their proposals in terms of therapeutic benefit. Holahan (1979) provides interesting examples of environmental changes in psychiatric hospitals, after which changes in behaviour of both staff and clients were recorded. For example, a greater amount of conversation took place in a dayroom in which furniture was arranged to promote interaction. Holahan uses Sommer and Ross's term 'institutional sanctity' to describe rigidly set and established patterns and expectations within an environment considered as practically unalterable by staff and clients. The editors would argue that if close attention is not paid to context for clients, then an important aspect of respecting them as people is being neglected.

Expectations are inevitably set up by the context within which the psychologist works; for example whether she works within a psychiatric hospital or unit on the edge of town or in a health centre close to the shops. These expectations relate to the perceived accessibility of the psychologist and to the nature of the clients and problems she will readily take on. Awareness of these aspects of her working environment may lead the psychologist to take action. Psychologists may seek to move their offices closer to the local shopping centre. It may be that if, like some health visitors, psychologists set up a stall at a local market in a deprived area (Booth, 1985), a different spectrum of clients and needs would be met and dealt with; ethical issues concerning decisions about resource allocation are involved here. Usually the psychologist sees a client away from her home environment; this divorce from customary environmental context when a client is being assessed may have profound effects in terms of the 'rights to display and masking of competence' which Harré describes in his chapter in relation to the social context.

CONCLUSION

Psychological practice is riddled with decisions, choices and practices which require justification not only in scientific or technical terms but also in moral terms. The psychologist working in a clinical setting practises within a framework of moral values including personal values and those of society as well as those of her profession whether implicit or explicit, as in the BPS Code of Conduct. Psychologists engage in decisions and practices all the time that are open to the question of whether they were 'good' or 'bad', 'right' or 'wrong' and not simply whether they were efficacious or cost effective: of course the question of whether a psychological intervention is efficacious or cost effective is in itself a moral one.

In making the book our aim has not been to produce a guide for moral decision making for those working in clinical psychology and behavioural medicine, but rather to draw the attention of practitioners to some areas of their work where moral problems are likely to arise. We do not seek to provide or endorse simplistic ethical solutions. Rather we want to encourage practitioners to notice the moral problems that arise in applying psychology in clinical contexts in order that they can be more aware in their practice that what they are about is a moral, as much as, if not more than, a clinical, scientific or technical enterprise. We want to encourage awareness that moral issues are important because whether we are conscious of them or not, they affect us as individuals.

All of the contributions to this book are concerned with questions of how it is appropriate to regard folk, to treat them, to relate to them. All contain, explicitly or implicitly, beliefs about what it is that is valuable about people's lives. All of the contributors in their individual ways attempt to make explicit some part of the complex of value systems that surround the attempt to facilitate psychological change. Our ambition is that the book should help to bring about a vociferous debate about moral concerns that have been addressed and provoke awareness of, and earnest reflection upon, many issues left untouched.

In her chapter Dorothy Rowe focuses on the way in which psychologists choose to care by attending to what she refers to as 'small issues' by which she means interpersonal issues, while in the main ignoring large ones, by which she means political issues, and in particular the issue of what they should be doing about the fact that men now have at their disposal unthinkable powers of destruction. We have considerable sympathy for Rowe's position and value the way in which she relates understandings gained in the interpersonal situation to global politics. The small issues are profoundly important because it is in our personal relationships that we can learn about the ways in which we conduct ourselves with others and also because if we cannot find it in ourselves to wish to act reflectively in our everyday personal and professional lives, then we cannot expect it of ourselves, or of anyone else for that matter, to want to act reflectively in relation to large-scale issues such as the future of the planet. We want to draw special attention to the importance of examining the small issues in more detail if psychology as a clinical discipline is to act with awareness and if psychologists as professionals and as caring people, are to care with awareness.

It is because each choice, each decision in clinical practice is unique that practitioners who wish to have regard for the ethical dimension of what they do should practise ethical thinking. It is because of the uniqueness of each moment in practice that reference to a simple rule book of ethics cannot in the end have any real place other than to draw attention to the ethical dimension in clinical interactions. The best way to become more ethical in one's actions and decisions is to study ethical problems in a detailed way, and to think carefully about what is involved in them. This is the case whatever one's ideological stance and whatever one's inclinations towards this or that ethical theory. Bringing all of one's experience of earlier problems and the results of one's actions in relation to those problems, to bear upon the moral problems one faces currently, can help to develop one's moral sense. And one must do this not only in terms of the consequences of one's actions in terms of their effects in the world, but also of their consequences on oneself as a person because it is only by being accountable to oneself that one can maintain integrity as a moral agent.

ACKNOWLEDGMENTS

We would like to thank Rachel Collingbourne, Rudi Dallos, Chris Winch and in particular Hazel Seidel for helpful comments during the writing of this chapter.

REFERENCES

Armstrong, D. (1983), 'The Fabrication of Nurse-Patient Relationships', *Social Science and Medicine*, vol.17, no.8, pp.457–60.

Arras, J. (1983), 'Preface to the second edition' in J. Arras and R. Hunt (eds) (1983), *Ethical Issues in Modern Medicine*, Palo Alto, California, Mayfield.

Arras, J. and Hunt R. (eds) (1983), *Ethical Isues in Modern Medicine*, Palo Alto, California, Mayfield.

Bakan, D. (1967), *On Method*, San Francisco, Jossey-Bass Inc.

Becker, M.H. *et al.* (1977), 'Selected psychosocial models and correlates of individual health related behaviour', *Medical Care*, vol.15, no.5, Supplement.

Bloch, S. and Chodoff, P. (eds) (1981), *Psychiatric Ethics*, Oxford, Oxford University Press.

Booth, K. (1985), Personal communication.

British Association of Social Workers (1975), *A Code of Ethics for Social Work*, adopted by the British Association of Social Workers, Birmingham, British Association of Social Workers.

British Psychological Society (1978), 'Ethical Principles for Research on Human Subjects', Leicester, BPS.

British Psychological Society (1981), 'Principles governing the employment of psychological tests', *Bulletin of the BPS*, vol.34, pp.317–18.

British Psychological Society (1983), *Guidelines for the Professional Practice of Clinical Psychology*, Leicester, BPS.

British Psychological Society (1985), 'A Code of Conduct for Psychologists', *Bulletin of the BPS*, vol.38, pp.41–3.

British Psychological Society (1978), 'Report of the Working Party on Behaviour Modification', *Bulletin of the BPS*, vol.31, pp.368–90.

Campbell, A.V. (1975), *Moral Dilemmas in Medicine*, second edition, Edinburgh, Churchill Livingstone.

Campbell, A.V., and Higgs, R. (1982), *In That Case*, London, Darton, Longman and Todd.
Canter, D. (1977), *The Psychology of Place*, London, The Architectural Press.
Canter, D. and Canter, S. (eds) (1979), *Designing for Therapeutic Environments*, Chichester, Wiley.
Cumming, J. and Cumming, E. (1964), *Ego and Milieu: Theory and Practice of Environmental Therapy*, London, Tavistock.
Faulkner, A. (ed.) (1984), *Communication*, Edinburgh and New York, Churchill Livingstone.
Faulkner, A. (1986), *Communication in Nurse Education: Research Project Reports 1–4*, Manchester, University of Manchester.
Glover, J. (1977), *Causing Death and Saving Lives*, Harmondsworth, Penguin.
Habermas, J. (1970), *Toward a Rational Society*, Boston, Massachussetts, Beacon Press cited in Mishler, E.G. (1984), *The Discourse of Medicine: Dialectics of Medical Interviews*, Norwood, New Jersey, Ablex Publishing Corporation.
Harris, J. (1985), *The Value of Life*, London, Routledge & Kegan Paul.
Hawks, D. (1981), 'The Dilemma of Clinical Practice – Surviving as a Clinical Psychologist', in I. McPherson and M. Sutton (eds) (1981), *Reconstructing Psychological Practice*, London, Croom Helm.
Heinz, S. (1982), *Ethical Problems in Psychological Research*, London, Academic Press.
Holahan, C.J. (1979), 'Environmental Psychology in Psychiatric Hospital Settings' in D. Canter and S. Canter (eds) (1979), *Designing for Therapeutic Environments*, Chichester, Wiley.
Kelly, G.A. (1955), *The Psychology of Personal Constructs*, (ed. F. Sanford), New York, W.W. Norton.
Konrad, G. (1975), *The Case Worker*, (trans. P. Aston), London, Hutchinson.
Ley, P. (1977), 'Psychological studies of Doctor-Patient Communication' in S. Rachman (ed.), *Contributions to Medical Psychology*, vol.1, Oxford, Pergamon Press.
Maguire, P. (1981), 'Doctor-Patient Skills' in M. Argyle (ed.), *Social Skills and Health*, London, Methuen.
Maguire, P. Fairbairn, S. and Fletcher, C. (1986), 'Consultation skills of young doctors I and II', *British Medical Journal*, vol.292, 14 June, pp.1573–8.
Middleton, D. (1985), 'Some issues of communication in multiprofessional assessment in clinical psychology and child development centres', *Division of Clinical Psychology Newsletter*, no.47, March, centre section pp.16–21.

Mishler, E.G. (1984), *The Discourse of Medicine: Dialectics of Medical Interviews*, Norwood, New Jersey, Ablex Publishing Corporation.

Pendleton, D. and Hasler, J.C. (eds) (1983), *Doctor-Patient Communication*, London, Academic Press.

Pilgrim, D. (1984), 'Some implications for psychology of formulating all illness as deviancy', *British Journal of Medical Psychology*, vol.57, pp.227–33.

Rowe, D. (1985), *Living with the bomb*, London, Routledge & Kegan Paul.

Shotter, J. (1974), 'The development of personal powers' in M. Richards, (ed.), *The integration of a child into a social world*, Cambridge University Press.

Shotter, J. (1975), *Images of Man in Psychological Research*, London, Methuen.

Singer, P. (1979), *Practical Ethics*, Cambridge, Cambridge University Press.

Smail, D. (1984), *Illusion and Reality*, London, Dent.

Smail, D. (1987), 'Psychotherapy – Deliverance or Disablement' in G. and S. Fairbairn (eds), *Ethical Issues in Caring*, London, Gower Press.

Sutton, M. (1981), 'Whose Psychology? Some Issues in the Social Control of Psychological Practice' in I. McPherson and M. Sutton (eds) (1981), *Reconstructing Psychological Practice*, London, Croom Helm.

Thompson, I., Melia, K. and Boyd, K. (1983), *Nursing Ethics*, Edinburgh, Churchill Livingstone.

Thorne, B. (1987), 'Ethical Confrontation in Counselling' in G. and S. Fairbairn (eds), *Ethical Issues in Caring*, London, Gower Press.

Timms, N. (1984), *Social Work Values*, London, Routledge & Kegan Paul.

Tuckett, D. *et al.* (1985), *Meetings between experts, an approach to sharing ideas in medical consultation*, London and New York, Tavistock.

Watson, D. (ed.) (1985), *A Code of Ethics for Social Work – The Second Step*, London, Routledge & Kegan Paul.

Watson, D., Leighton, N. and Stalley, R. (1983), *Rights and Responsibilities*, London, Heinemann.

Weiss, D.B. (1982), 'Confidentiality Expectations of Patients, Physicians, and Medical Students', *Journal of the American Medical Association*, vol.247, no.19, pp.2695–7.

Williams, C. *et al.* (1984), *Ethical Implications of Behaviour Modification with Special Reference to Mental Handicap*, British Institute of Mental Handicap, State Mutual Book.

Psychotherapy and 'Change': Some Ethical Considerations

David Smail

However obvious and tiresome it may be to do so, one must acknowledge at the start of any discussion of psychotherapeutic matters that there is no such 'thing' as psychotherapy, and that therefore generalizations about 'it' have to be made with caution. This is particularly the case in present times, when we are witnessing an explosion in psychotherapeutic and counselling procedures of all kinds. In much of what follows I shall be criticizing the conceptual basis upon which the – often implicit – claims for the effectiveness or value of various kinds of psychological therapy are made, and there is little doubt that such criticisms apply more to some varieties than to others; I shall not, however, differentiate between them unless I feel that any particular type of therapy (there are literally hundreds) merits special exemption from my criticism. I shall include under the banner of 'psychotherapy' even those approaches – for example the behaviour therapies – which have often been contrasted with the 'dynamic' and 'humanistic' approaches, since, while they may differ in many other respects, they all tend to share certain ethical as well as technical assumptions concerning the nature of psychological distress and its amelioration.

I am not for the purposes of this chapter concerned with what psychotherapy 'is' or how it operates in the sense of what correct scientific analysis of its processes and procedures might reveal. What I am concerned with, since they are clearly of considerable ethical significance, are the grounds, explicit or implicit, upon which therapists justify their activities, and the functions which, however unconsciously, the psychological therapies are coming to serve in our society.

There seems to be little doubt that the therapy industry is currently enjoying a boom. What was once a relatively esoteric set of procedures, practised by a small profession whose members were for the most part regarded by other professions and the public at large with, if not awe, then suspicion or amusement, has rapidly become a familiar and much more respected and 'credible' feature at all levels of the social scene. The jargon and the 'techniques' of therapy – much of them having spread from across the Atlantic – have penetrated the popular culture far beyond the more traditional field of mental health, so that, for example, spheres of business and management training, and even leisure pursuits (evening classes, etc.) have become saturated with ideas about psychological approaches to 'stress', 'relationship problems', and so on. Somehow or other, a demand for therapy has arisen which a small army of therapists, counsellors and consultants is falling over itself to meet. This is a matter of some surprise to those of us who struggled for years to defend psychotherapy against the hostile criticisms of a 'scientific' community which seemed never to give an inch. Suddenly, it appears, we are the victors in this war without ever having to our knowledge won a single battle. The explanation of this seeming paradox must lie, I think, in the fact that our battles were fought on the rational grounds of evidence, whereas the war has been won through a shift in the (largely economic) interests of society. It no longer suits anyone very much to question the scientific validity of the psychological therapies, while it is in the interests of most to assert their social validity as more or less self-evident.

It is, I think, indisputable that so far nobody has been able to demonstrate to anybody's satisfaction but their own that any form of psychotherapy 'works'. In other words, and despite prodigious efforts on the part of research workers and their production of a huge and voluminous literature (for a summary of some of which see Garfield, 1978), there is no consistent evidence that the individual who approaches a psychotherapist in the hope of losing his or her particular psychological burden will thereby be likely to do so. This fact is, surprisingly perhaps, not one which has been found unduly inconvenient or embarrassing by therapists themselves, who, as long as it seemed to matter, were able to find a number of reasonably convincing arguments to the effect that psychotherapy is too complex a procedure to be judged in terms simply of whether it works or not.

However, the fact that nobody can show consistently and to the satisfaction of the scientific community that psychotherapy works does lead one to ponder the grounds upon which it *could* be justified. The 'does it work?' question was fended off by the profession long enough for people to lose interest in asking it, so that now psychotherapists are able either to assume or to assert the effectiveness of their procedures without too much fear of contradiction, and indeed the sheer numbers of psychotherapists on the scene probably deter all but the boldest from asking so apparently naive a question; after all, if it didn't work, how could there be so many people making a living from it? However, there must be *some* rather more rational explanation for psychotherapy's success, if, as I am sure is still the case, that success is not based on its ability to 'make people better'. (I should point out at this stage that there *are* those who question seriously the possibility, and even the desirability, of psychotherapy's 'working' – eg Schafer, 1976 – but they are few and far between.)

My contention is that the success of psychotherapy is built upon a number of expectations, assumptions and beliefs which are subscribed to tacitly in our culture, as much by patients as by therapists, and which continue to support a belief in the *curative* power of psychotherapy in the absence of any objective evidence for it. The reason that such a belief continues to be sustained in the face of this lack of confirmation is because the assumptions and expectations which underpin it serve interests other than those which bear simply upon the effectiveness or otherwise of psychotherapy. Before discussing these tacit assumptions and expectations further, I shall first consider briefly the explicit justifications, such as they are, which tend to be put forward by psychotherapists for their practice.

The psychotherapy literature is not without its soul-searching aspects, but for present purposes it is, as it were, the public posture of psychotherapy which is of interest. Though some – perhaps even quite a few – psychotherapists may, in the comparative seclusion of the conference room or the pages of learned journals, be prepared to confess to doubts about the efficacy of their procedures or the validity of their techniques, they are scarcely likely to emphasize such doubts to their clients, to whom they present a much more confident front, if only by virtue of their very attachment to a professional institution. In fact, psychotherapists tend to justify their calling by means of two fairly distinct forms of rhetoric, the one technical, and the other professional.

I can think of no established and widely known school or variety of psychological treatment which does not appeal for its validity to an elaborated body of technical knowledge, and probably also an established technical procedure whereby that knowledge is applied to therapeutic ends. Psychoanalysis has its infantile fixations and complexes, its defence mechanisms, its transference neuroses and interpretations; behaviour therapy has its stimuli and responses, its contingencies of reinforcement, its procedures for desensitization, implosion, etc; Rogerians have their necessary and sufficient conditions for personality change; Kellians their construct systems and fixed role techniques – and so on, the list is virtually infinite. Any psychotherapist worth his or her salt will be able to offer you an account of your difficulties and what needs to be done about them in the concepts and language inculcated by the school to which he or she belongs. Since, as has been said, there is no compelling scientific justification for any of these approaches, one has to acknowledge the rhetorical nature of their conceptual language, at least as this is applied to therapeutic procedure, and it is surely no surprise that in just about every case the rhetoric is a technico-scientific one, for this is the form of rhetoric which has most 'credibility' in our culture. (I should state categorically at this point that I do not in any way wish to imply conscious charlatanism on the part of therapists, who for the most part are quite as, even if not more, gullible than their clients when it comes to being impressed by rhetoric.) The justificatory rhetoric favoured within any culture, where it is not supported rationally, presumably becomes no more than a kind of superficially plausible mask for the interests it serves; in this way the *technical* rhetoric of psychotherapy has, as I shall argue in a little more detail presently, more in common with magic than with a truly scientific spirit of enquiry.

The *professional* rhetoric made use of by psychotherapists is even more crudely persuasive, inasmuch as it relies for its effect upon an oblique appeal to what *ought* to be, but are not necessarily, professional virtues. Thus great emphasis may be laid on the thoroughness of training within a given school of psychotherapy, or the stringency of its selection procedures, or the impeccability of the qualifications it confers. The more exclusive the therapeutic club, so to speak, and the more rigorous the procedures through which one may be accounted a fully trained, paid up and approved member, the more confidence, one might reasonably think, might the public have in one's therapeutic prowess. Once again, however, this simply *assumes* the validity of the procedures in which therapists are trained. In the field of psychotherapy there are many different therapeutic schools with many, mutually incompatible theoretical allegiances, and many different forms of training. They cannot plausibly all claim the technical effectiveness their professional structure implies; the evidence, as far as it goes, is that none of them can.

It appears, thus, that the official rhetoric of justification for psychotherapy is far too thin to account on its own for the success of the therapeutic enterprise. What, then, does account for it?

Psychotherapy, in fact, serves a number of purposes. These are not only the purposes which can, as it were, be identified from within therapeutic theory and practice themselves, but include the wider social, moral, and political purposes which can be detected as maintaining the therapeutic enterprise from without. I do not intend to try in this chapter to give an exhaustive account of all the purposes psychotherapy serves, but to concentrate on two or three which have particular significance for the ethics of psychotherapy. These purposes, then, operate at different levels and in different contexts, and thus serve different ends. I shall argue that psychotherapy covertly, and partially, *fulfils a need* for love, by *making use of* a tacit expectation of cure (which in turn rests on a conscious but irrational faith in mechanism and an unconscious belief in magic), and *serves an ideological view* of human distress as arising out of the conduct and perceptions of the individual.

The interesting thing about all these purposes is that they are more or less inexplicit, as indeed are the interests of the therapists themselves (about which I intend to say no more here than is already implied in the discussion of justificatory rhetoric). It is a commonplace of individual psychology to observe that a person's account of his or her conduct need not and most usually does not bear any convincing relation to the actual reasons for it. On the whole, however, we do not extend the same scepticism to the official accounts given of their activities by professional bodies, especially those claiming a home within the scientific community. I suspect, though, that the accounts given by individuals and collectivities are extremely similar in being, often, rationalizations (persuasive rhetorics) of the barely perceived interplay of their own needs and interests in relation to those of the wider social context.

The principal service performed by broad-spectrum psychotherapy is in the provision of a commodity which is becoming increasingly scarce in our society – that is, love. (I have argued this point in some detail in Smail, 1984.) It would certainly not be fair to accuse all psychotherapists of performing this service entirely surreptitiously or covertly, and several therapists have avowed this aim and function quite openly, seriously and movingly (see, for example, Suttie, 1960). However, what they have not nearly so widely recognized is that by supplying love as a professional service they turn it into, precisely, a commodity. Therapists who write about the 'deeply meaningful' nature of the 'therapeutic relationship' tend to sentimentalize and obscure what is in fact a commercial transaction which has quite close parallels to that involved in prostitution. I use this analogy not to shock or denigrate, but merely to puncture humbug. I do not wish to say that psychotherapists should not provide loving attention to their clients, nor that to do so is dishonourable or unnecessary, nor that they should cease taking money for it. (Neither am I for the abolition of prostitution.) I merely wish to invite ethical reflection upon the nature of a society in which the provision of love becomes increasingly a matter for paid professionals.

A situation which practically all forms of psychotherapy offer is one in which the individual may, regularly and for reasonably long periods of time, receive the undivided attention and concern of someone who is solely concentrated on his or her life and the difficulties he or she experiences. Whatever the technical expertise claimed by therapists, they are inescapably involved as individual people in the 'therapeutic relationship' and most, nowadays, readily acknowledge the part played in therapy by their making available to their clients their own personal resources of concern and consideration. At a time when the battle between the sexes is raging as never before and families are, perhaps not entirely without reason, regarded by many as hotbeds of mutual hostility and rejection (see, for example, Lasch, 1980; Kovel, 1984), it is perhaps not surprising that therapists should find such a ready response to their offer of care and attention.

The most obvious ethical question to be asked about the therapeutic provision of love concerns the extent to which it actually is therapeutic. The ideal answer would be that the increase in the client's confidence and self-esteem which being the object of the therapist's attentive concern brings, enables him or her to take stock anew of the circumstances which necessitated therapy in the first place and to summon up the courage to tackle them. I would certainly not want to argue that people cannot be transformed by love (though neither am I sure that they can), but I would, without claiming it to be impossible, want to urge caution over extending such a possibility to therapeutic 'love', which is but a pale imitation of the kind of committed love which may transform, and, coming too little and often too late in the client's life, may simply prove addictive.

It may be that for many people in our society the only place where they can to some extent unburden their sorrows and find a sympathetic ear for the expression of the distress and despair of their lives is in the therapist's office, and many therapists count among their clients people they expect to be seeing for the rest of their lives for roughly this purpose. There is no problem about this as long as therapists are absolutely clear about what they are doing, and do not disguise it behind a mystifying technical rational or a grandiose programme of 'change'.

The provision of a kind of loving attention is not necessarily the only thing which psychotherapy may actually achieve; it may also be the case that in the course of therapy clients find that the nature of their predicament becomes clarified. Most of the more respectable schools of therapy do embody a theoretical psychology which to some extent informs their practice, and there is often involved in this an assumption that an aetiological theory automatically implies a therapy, ie that knowing what is wrong leads quite naturally to a technology of treatment or process of cure. It is this kind of assumption that I want to challenge here, since there seems to me in fact to be no reason to suppose that knowledge of cause leads automatically to prescription of cure, and one should not confuse a plausible or convincing – or even 'true' – psychology with an obvious programme for therapy.

The theoretical grounds of most 'dynamic' forms of psychotherapy, for example, strongly emphasize the importance of understanding symptoms of distress and experience of psychological pain or difficulty in terms of the client's personal history, and indeed it would be barely rational to deny that the way a person is now must depend to quite a significant extent on the course of his or her previous life and experience. On the other hand, there is absolutely no reason to suppose that laying bare the history of this experience will necessarily make any difference at all to the experience of psychological pain which it has engendered. Many therapists, of course, do recognize this, but even so the therapeutic potency of 'insight' is still something widely assumed.

A more obvious, but on the whole not frequently acknowledged function of investigation of the meaning of the client's distress in terms of his or her history is the *demystification* of 'symptoms', and it is presumably this that Freud meant when he talked of replacing neurotic misery with ordinary human unhappiness. However, not many patients, I submit, embark upon psychotherapy in either the hope or the expectation that they are about to swap one form of pain for another, and though my own view is that to do so is in fact not an unworthy ethical aim, it is one which should form an *explicit* part of the therapeutic procedure. To put the argument succinctly: the theoretical psychology informing many dynamic approaches leads to the demystification of symptoms, not to the cure of distress, and whether one regards this as 'therapeutic' or not is a question for ethical discussion and decision, but may not be assumed.

It is, then, perfectly possible to give a convincing theoretical account of how people come to be suffering the way they are without this having any necessary implications for what the individual may do about it. This may seem obvious, but in actuality most therapists and most patients do not seem to hesitate all that long at this logical hurdle. There are, I think, two reasons for this. One is the unquestioning confidence we have in technological solutions and our readiness to conceptualize ourselves as machines, and the other is an implicit belief in magic which is far more widespread than is usually thought. These two issues, in fact, may not be all that separable from each other: it may not be only in the popular imagination that technology *is* magic. For present purposes, however, I do not wish to attempt to substantiate this argument (a fuller treatment of which is to be found in Smail,

1984), but merely to address briefly each side of the equation in relation to psychotherapy.

The 'technological attitude' leads to the assumption that once you know what's wrong with something you can almost certainly put it right. As long as one is dealing with machines and mechanical systems (which is, of course, the proper province of technology) this does indeed seem a fairly warrantable assumption, for the obvious reason that machines are man-made, and, indeed, presumably made by men who *knew* how they made them, and therefore know how to repair them if they go wrong. It thus follows quite naturally that if psychologists and psychotherapists construct mechanistic models of human experience and conduct they will be able quite legitimately and without further thought to approach psychological 'dysfunction' with the same technical confidence as the electronics engineer approaches the faulty computer. And this, of course, is precisely what happens. Even those 'humanistic' therapies which loudly disavow a mechanistic approach, in fact almost without exception treat human beings as if they were mechanically constructed and understandable in terms of analogies with (depending on the history of the particular theory) steam engines, telephone exchanges or digital computers. In order to belong to the 'scientific' club it is virtually out of the question for psychological theorists to characterize people in any other way, and it is impossible to belong to any other club while expecting at the same time to gain professional 'credibility'. So saturated is our culture in a fundamentally mechanist world view that we can virtually not envisage any other which is not 'unscientific' and therefore invalid. Therapists must be experts in the mechanics of human nature. If we had to recognize that this is *not* the case, I suspect that our whole conception and understanding of therapy would change (for example, frighteningly regressive though the suggestion may seem, 'expertise' might have to give way to wisdom).

The upshot, anyway, is that human experience comes to be seen as being acquired mechanically, and as therefore in principle alterable mechanically. The 'program' can be replaced, experience erased and re-recorded in the manner of magnetic tape. It is in this kind of tacit belief that, for example, the plausibility of 'insight' lies.

Standing behind the 'expert' (and to some extent infusing him with his power) is the soothsayer or magical healer. Even very recently (within living memory) psychotherapists were more likely to be regarded (by the sympathetic) as possessors of essentially mysterious powers than as technical experts; the 'miraculous' and 'fantastic' achievements of technology have since transmuted and absorbed the magic of psychotherapeutic knowledge and given it new, technical form. But still there is the basically magical expectation (and every practising therapist meets it in his or her patients over and over again) that the patient will emerge from the therapeutic encounter *transformed*. In this sense, the therapeutic process, the 'talking cure' in which patient and therapist sit exchanging words in the emotionally charged sanctum of the latter's consulting room, begins to suggest a continuity with the incantations and spells concocted in the witch's parlour. In each case, the idea is that, without having *done* anything significant, and with no alteration to his or her world, the person emerges free of the burdens which prompted the initial consultation. There are, of course, also religious parallels – that of psychotherapy with the confessional being the one most frequently invoked.

These, then – our faith in technology and our belief in magic – are what support our confidence in the power of psychotherapy to cure our ills. What we actually get, if we are lucky, is comfort and demystification. I want again to emphasize as strongly as possible that I do *not* see comfort and demystification as unworthy or invalid goals for psychotherapy. I only want to point out that these are virtually never explicitly avowed as major goals by therapists, and never anticipated as the major fruits of therapy by their clients. I do not want to say that psychotherapy cannot promise or achieve anything, but only that too often it promises to achieve too much, ie more than it can deliver.

To say that psychotherapy does not 'work' in the way that it is by and large anticipated that it should is not to say that people do not or cannot change in the course of their lives, but rather that they do not change in the way that the practice of psychotherapy tends to imply. In other words, people do not change by contemplating their histories or shuffling the contents of their heads or sitting for specified periods of time in earnest discussion with therapists or learning to see things in a new light. Nor do people change by having flashes of insight, turning over new leaves or making resolutions. All of these activities may *contribute* to a process of change, but they do not in themselves *constitute* significant change.

People live in *bodies* which inhabit the *world*. It is essentially these two facts which therapeutic mythology tends to overlook. By treating people, at least implicitly, as consciousnesses (or indeed as unconsciousnesses), wills, sets of constructs or cognitions, or computer programs, therapeutic approaches tend to disembody the person, and hence to fail to take proper account of the *organic* nature of human psychology. The experience which underlies the development of symptoms of distress is acquired bodily, organically, and not abstractly or mechanically. In this way, new ways of feeling, perceiving or 'behaving' must be built on and grow out of old ways, which are themselves not erased by the acquisition of new experience. Rather than being repaired like machines, people have to be cultivated like plants. The terrifying sense of draining subjectivity which, for example, so often underlies the 'symptoms' of anxiety is a physical response learned in actual bodily engagement with the world and the other people in it. The roots of anxiety, in this way, are embedded in the living tissue of the body, and cannot be eradicated by purely mental or verbal activity; cannot, in fact, be eradicated at all. Thus the fundamentally anxious character does not through any process become fundamentally non-anxious, but, through further bodily experience of the world may come, with much effort and hard work, to learn new ways of dealing with the world. But the old ways cannot be forgotten any more than any other form of experience (for example of language or other learned abilities and competencies) can be forgotten. Magical rebirth is not a possibility from a psychological standpoint, whether through psychotherapy or any other process.

Just as therapeutic mythology tends to disembody people, it tends also to dislocate them, ie it conceptualizes them as essentially out of relation to a world, with the result that a tremendous overvaluation is placed on the role of 'mental' operations in the explanation of conduct. Recognition of this kind of difficulty for psychology more generally was of course the main contribution of behaviourism, which, in developing the concepts of behaviour as response to stimulus, the 'contingencies of reinforcement' entirely outside the individual's skin, etc. tried to redress a situation in which psychology threatened to cut the person off from the world altogether. But, of course, in taking this line, behaviourism attempts to solve the dualist dilemma by embracing too tenaciously one of its horns and becoming so purely physical that it can offer no account of the kinds of concepts (intention, meaning, interpretation, etc.) it has banished along with mentalism. In the therapeutic arena, the difficulties caused by attempted solutions of a fundamental dualism are evidenced in the observation that behaviourists seem to leave out of account the fact that the world is experienced, while the cognitivists make the mistake of concluding that experience is not experience *of* anything.

In fact, though a person's distress will of course be interpreted in the context of his or her 'organic history', many of the reasons for it are to be located and understood in the social, moral and physical environment in which he or she is situated. Psychotherapy may, as part of a legitimate function of demystification, uncover the extent to which a person's unhappiness is the result of circumstances and events beyond his or her immediate control, but it cannot thereby remove them.

In so far as psychotherapy places an at least tacit emphasis on the eradication of distress as a function of purely personal 'change', it adopts an extremely demanding moral position, since it implies both that individuals are in some sense accountable for the ravages of a world beyond their control, and that to the extent that these ravages *are* attributable to the personal stance they have developed towards the world, they have somehow to reach inside themselves to transform their organically acquired experience.

There is nothing wrong with being morally demanding, as long as, alongside the provision of an intellectual context in which such demands can be understood, there is provided a practical one in which they can be met. Though some approaches to psychotherapy have the beginning of a theoretical psychology in which the origins of human distress can at least to some extent be traced, none so far has an adequate conceptualization of how changes may be made, and most vastly over-emphasize the possibilities for change which are open to people purely through their own efforts. Moral demands become, in my view, immoral demands if the only context they offer for their solution is basically a magical one. An even greater danger is the opportunity that what one might call the 'psychotherapeutic ethic' offers to those seeking support for an ideological view of social ills as personal responsibility; it is all too easy perhaps through the use of a version of the recently expressed 'on your bike' philosophy, to foster a view that social constraints (like high unemployment) are really personal shortcomings (like 'laziness'), and it is but a step from here to suggest that such shortcomings may be 'treatable'.

The professional interests of a rapidly growing army of therapists and counsellors, most of whom entertain no other conscious aim than to help alleviate the pain of people's lives, threaten in this way to mesh with the ideological interests of a fundamentally repressive political order which seeks to promote a view of, in particular, economic failure, and the distress it gives rise to, as personal inadequacy.

I am afraid that I shall be misunderstood, on the basis of the foregoing, as arguing a number of things which in fact I am not. I am not saying, and I think have not said, that psychotherapy is useless, or immoral, or politically repressive. I am suggesting that, through becoming unthinkingly over-extended, it is in danger of being ethically misused or abused. In order to guard against such misuse, psychotherapists must beware of slipping into the role of established and technically sound professional experts, must rigorously examine the intellectual basis of their theoretical position, and above all question the grounds upon which they conceptualize the process of change.

REFERENCES

Garfield, S.L. (1978), *Handbook of Psychotherapy and Behaviour Change*, New York, Wiley.

Kovel, J. (1984), 'Rationalization and the Family', in B. Richards (ed.), *Capitalism and Infancy*, London, Free Association Books.

Lasch, C. (1980), *The Culture of Narcissism*, London, Abacus.

Schafer, R. (1976), *A New Language for Psychoanalysis*, New Haven and London, Yale University Press.

Smail, D. (1984), *Illusion and Reality: The Meaning of Anxiety*, London, Dent.

Suttie, I. (1960), *The Origins of Love and Hate*, Harmondsworth, Penguin.

Deception, Self-Deception and Self-Determination

Don Mixon

Ethical issues in behavioural medicine, like ethical issues faced by all modern professionals, are connected with the characteristic disparity in power and often in status between professional and subject and professional and client. Such power is buttressed by the possession of exclusive expert knowledge and can lead professionals to disregard the inexpert viewpoints and even the rights of subjects they use or clients they 'serve'. Compared to the situation in, say, the legal profession, behavioural medicine's exclusive expert knowledge has the added prestige of being scientific.

One way of addressing some of the ethical issues in behavioural medicine is to show that scientific answers are not available for some of the most basic questions professionals face and that the status of much of the research that makes up their exclusive and privileged knowledge is less than scientific. I assume that the more confident professionals are of the validity and certainty of their expert knowledge, the more likely it is that they will believe that they and only they know what is best for clients or subjects – and that they will claim the special dispensation from ordinary moral obligations that is thought to go with privileged and exclusive knowledge. I could argue that possession of valid, scientific knowledge does not grant a special ethical dispensation, but if I can show that the status of knowledge in the behavioural sciences falls considerably short of being valid and scientific, then special dispensations become less thinkable. A realistic humility about the status of their expert knowledge might encourage those behavioural professionals who need such encouragement, to give consideration to the viewpoints and rights of their subjects and clients.

Because the subject matter of behavioural science is behaviour, lacunae at the heart of science affect behavioural science in a special and peculiar way. Statement of the problem should point to the moves we must make before solutions become possible.

I think it is safe to say that most empirical scientists believe that they are involved in determining and describing what some part of the world is like, but that they cannot say whether or not the part of the world described is good or bad. 'When it comes to describing the universe, we must take the empirical scientitist's expert opinion; when it comes to evaluating it, however, his judgment is no more authoritative than anybody else's' (Harrison, 1967, p.69). In this view, since the aspect of the universe that behavioural scientists describe is behaviour, it is not part of our task – we have no scientific warrant – to say whether or not particular behaviour is good or bad. However necessary it is in the course of our work to make such judgments, we have no scientific warrant to do so. We may be behavioural experts, but our chosen means of acquiring knowledge does not make us moral or ethical experts.

Even though science appears to bypass morality, science would not be science, or indeed be possible, if it were not for ethics embedded in its practice. One of the missions of science is to replace authority with explanations based on natural processes, explanations supported by evidence of the senses (or the senses extended by the devices of science). An assumption essential to the practice of science is that scientists must be free and unfettered to practise as they choose – free from authority or from any kind of hindrance or check on imagination, intellect, or behaviour. On the surface such freedom seems a prescription for scientific licence and an invitation to fraud. But the very method used to detect error and fallibility and to certify science's product regulates the behaviour of scientists. The method is replication, the product: knowledge.

To have confidence in a discovery, I must in my laboratory (or with my telescope, etc.) be able to duplicate the findings of colleagues elsewhere. When the necessity to check on or replicate findings is recognised and practised the detection of fraud becomes inevitable. Strictly speaking there is no knowledge until a finding is reliably duplicated by someone else. Honesty becomes not simply the best policy, but the only policy. Police, courts and prisons are not needed to regulate the conduct of scientists one to another.

Morality embedded in scientific practice has worked so well in the past that Kropotkin used the self-regulating behaviour of the international community of scientists as one of his strongest arguments for anarchy, for the possibility of a world community free from coercive power of the state.

Unfortunately, the ethic which regulates the behaviour of scientists toward each other and makes possible the remarkable joint efforts of the international community of scientists is silent concerning the relationship of scientists to the objects, creatures, or people they study; is silent concerning relationships between those who apply the findings of science and their clients; and is silent concerning the consequences of the practice of science for the world community. As might be expected, ethical problems in behavioural research and practice are in the areas about which the scientific ethic is silent.

How do we determine the way we should behave toward the creatures or people we study or toward the clients we serve, or toward the effects of our theories and practice on society? Put baldly, the question may be a bit bewildering at first. Behavioural scientists are accustomed to using empirical means to find the answers to questions. At the same time most scientists believe matters of right and wrong cannot be determined empirically. A few philosophers disagree. John Dewey, for example, thought that it is a fundamental mistake to hold that scientific knowledge is different from moral, philosophical, or religious knowledge. He held that there is only one kind of knowledge and one way of attaining knowledge – the experimental method. Later in the paper I shall suggest a way experimental method potentially can make a contribution to ethics. But until and unless psychology is conceptually transformed, behavioural scientists must look elsewhere for answers, must look where anyone else must look: to conscience, to moral philosophy, to religion, to social rules and conventions. In line with what I have just said, I can, of course, claim no scientific warrant for the ethical statements I have made and am about to make. I can only hope readers share ethical principles or values, or that I can persuade them that I have identified ethical issues and the obstacles in the way of their solutions.

A basic contention of this paper is that the freedom which is essential to the activity of producing scientific knowledge, the freedom regulated by science's social, empirical, non-authoritarian manner of practice, does not transfer, does not naturally regulate, when it comes to the relationship between scientist and 'subject', or practitioner and client.

A clear example of the harmful effects of leaving behavioural scientists free to treat their subjects as they please can be found in social psychology. Social psychologists lie to people taking part in experiments. This may surprise some readers, for honesty is so strongly associated with science that a lying scientist seems a contradiction. But social psychologists are not lying to each other about data (so far as we know), they are lying to 'subjects', a practice that falls outside the self-regulating ethic of science. The qualifying clause, 'so far as we know', is necessary because we cannot know whether or not they lie to each other about data. We cannot know because, quite simply, social psychologists seldom bother to replicate experiments and so fail to take advantage of science's built-in lie detector. Technically speaking, there is little knowledge in experimental social psychology because a finding does not become knowledge until it is reliably repeated.

Why do social psychologists lie? We cannot be sure. For social psychologists have never coherently justified the practice of lying. Individual liars appear to assume that the need to lie to participants is intuitively obvious to anyone familiar with experimental methods. Not that they claim lying is good. I have never talked to, or read a lying experimenter who was not happy to affirm that lying is bad – but in the next breath to affirm that no matter how bad lying might be, the practice is justified by the value of the knowledge so produced.

Ignoring for a moment the fact that unreplicated experiments do not produce scientific knowledge, I wish to examine the justification. I think it is quite simply the expression of a belief central to the practice of modern science: that the product resulting from the practice of methods deemed scientific are good. The belief is so central and unshakable that I can think of no demonstration that could convince the community of scientists of its falsity. For if products of scientific research are good, then nuclear weapons must be good. If the fact that this particular fruit of scientific practice has made seemingly inevitable the destruction of civilisation and of science itself does not convince, what can? The assumption of the goodness of scientific practice is an essential part of the nature of modern science. Should scientists begin to believe that they might not be doing good by practising science they would no longer be modern scientists, but something else.

It is one thing to claim that a particular end is good, but another to say that it justifies doing something that we admit is bad. Do those who claim that the fruits of lying justify deceit demonstrate their claim? No. Evidently they see no need. Once again we have come up against a belief or an article of faith. Social psychologists do not and probably cannot demonstrate that the results of a single experiment or even of all social psychological experiments ever done outweigh in value the harm done by lying. For them, it simply must be so – because the fruits of lying are 'scientific', and by definition, by belief, by faith, science's products have the highest value. That lying can be harmful is a mere social convention, part of a different, if not lower, realm altogether.

However, even true believers in the goodness of scientific knowledge have a couple of ethical issues to face. Whereas replication as a means of certifying knowledge is a matter of epistemology, the claiming of scientific status for unreplicated experiments is a matter of ethics. Experiments that have not been successfully repeated do not provide scientific knowledge and therefore are not covered by the belief in its goodness. To identify the results of unreplicated experiments as scientific knowledge is to make a false claim. In addition I have shown (Mixon, 1985) and Siu Chow (1985) has shown that typical social psychological 'experiments' are not even experiments. To qualify as an experiment it must be possible to control for plausible alternative explanations of the obtained results. Social psychological deception 'experiments' cannot in principle control for alternative explanations. Arguments needed to demonstrate the basic incoherence of the deception strategy would take me far too far afield and are available elsewhere (eg Mixon, 1977, 1979). I can make a more general point by demonstrating the social effects, the effects on psychological research, of the practice of lying.

If a group of psychological experimenters habitually lie to the people who take part in experiments they will in time gain a reputation for lying. If experimental participants cannot distinguish between psychologists who lie and those who do not, all psychological experimenters will gain a reputation for untruth. In order for liars to deceive successfully they must not be identified as liars. Each time social psychologists exercise their scientific freedom to do as they choose – to lie – they strengthen psychology's reputation for untruth and make it more likely that their lies will not be believed. Furthermore, since to most participants a psychologist is a psychologist, the reputation for untruth will stick to those who have done nothing to deserve it. Lying experimenters make it more likely that the statements of their truthful colleagues in the fields of perception, learning, and memory will not be believed. Individual decisions to lie undermine the entire social project of experimental psychology.

Researchers in general experimental psychology have been aware of the situation for some time. A former colleague, Steve Schwartz, who does experiments in problem solving, told me in 1973 of the difficulties he was having in getting participants to believe he was telling them the truth. If participants do not believe experimenters, how can we know what they *do* believe? If we cannot know what they do believe, how do we interpret experimental results? A minimum condition for good experimental practice with humans is that participants believe what the experimenter tells them and do not engage in private interpretations of instructions based on the assumption that they are lies.

Why don't experimenters in general psychology do something about the way experimental social psychologists are interfering with their work? One of the several reasons I can think of is of particular interest, because we will see it again when I discuss clinical practice. The reason stems from the belief discussed earlier: that scientific investigators must not be interfered with, must be free and unfettered. I (as a scientist) strongly believe that no one should tell me what to study or how to study what I wish to study. Therefore I will not interfere with the practice of fellow scientists. Even when their practice interferes with my own work.

In order to solve ethical issues connected with research on animals and humans it is necessary to assume that the intellectual freedom needed to do science does not licence scientists to treat their animal or human subjects as they choose. Even for scientists who believe that the knowledge produced by scientific practice is generally good, that does not issue a general warrant for harmful means. If the pursuit of a scientific end is accomplished by harmful means it should be on the shoulders of those engaging in harm to demonstrate both that other means cannot be used and to demonstrate the overriding value of their activity. I doubt in most cases that they can. I know social psychologists cannot. It is time we stopped assuming scientific ends to justify the means scientists employ. The assumption prevents debate and deadens moral sensitivity.

The deceivers deceive themselves. Experimental social psychologists have created an ethical problem because they fail to understand the logic of experiments and fail to certify their results by replication. Replication is so often and so easily ignored that an early example of its need may prove instructive. In the winter semester of 1890–91, Lincoln Steffens, the man who was later to become one of America's most distinguished reporters, went to Leipzig to do graduate study with Wilhelm Wundt. While he and some other students were looking at the laboratory records of an American student who had gone home to a Professorship and eventually to the status of 'one of the leading men in American science and education' (Steffens, 1931, p.150), they found that the student's PhD data at first

> confounded one of Wundt's most axiomatic premises. . . .; he must have thought, as a psychologist, that Wundt might have been reluctant to crown a discovery which would require the old philosopher to recast his philosophy and rewrite the published volumes of his lifework. The budding psychologist solved the ethical problem before him by deciding to alter his results, and his papers showed how he did this, by changing the figures item by item, experiment by experiment, so as to make to the curve of his averages come out for instead of against our school. After a few minutes of silent admiration of the mathematical feat performed on the papers before us, we buried sadly these remains of a great sacrifice to loyalty, to the school spirit, and to practical ethics (p.151).

For scientists who appreciate its importance, failure to replicate can rouse strong feelings. Pavlov, upon failure to duplicate an experimental result reported by a student of his rival Bechterev, became convinced that Bechterev was 'debasing science' (Miller, 1962, p.184).

Only true experiments provide the closure and the controls necessary to make precise duplication possible. The bulk of data drawn on by practitioners of behavioural science is quasi-experimental at best. Even when done honestly and without error, less-than-experimental research offers at best only modest certainty of causal inference. With such research science's built-in lie detector, even on the occasions when attempted, is insufficiently sensitive. For example, the nature of the data in Cyril Burt's twin study were such that strict duplication was not possible. His creativity with numbers could be detected only by someone with a strong motive to look closely at the data. In Burt's case the moral and political implications of his data provided the motive. Since the masses of unreplicable research data upon which clinical practice is based do not receive the scrutiny given to Cyril Burt's work, we cannot be confident of its status, of its validity.

In summary, science as ordinarily conceived and practised disqualifies itself from producing answers to the most important question a client can ask: What *should* I do? Further, I have tried to show that the intellectual freedom required to do science does not warrant incompetence, does not justify treating animals or people as individual scientists choose. The claim that one is engaged in doing good (science) does not and cannot justify the use of harmful or immoral means.

The honesty and certainty associated with duplicated experiments cannot be claimed by either unreplicated experiments or unreplicable less-than-experiments. Empirical science has a moral mantle, but the parts of scientific activity covered by the mantle are limited and have been identified.

By showing that producing scientific knowledge is not an end that justifies immoral means, I hope to convince that practice based on scientific knowledge has even less claim to justify dubious means. The ethical/epistemological problems connected with doing research are directly linked with the status of the various kinds of knowledge in behavioural science. The status of much of the 'scientific' knowledge practitioners draw on is uncertain at best and whereas it cannot warrant a special dispensation from ordinary moral obligation it can engender an attitude of realistic humility.

Those who practise or employ behavioural science have many titles and come from several fields. I shall use 'therapist' to stand for all. Therapists share ethical problems with other modern professionals. The professional expert has increasing power, is coming to be seen as more and more essential to modern society. To the extent that we come to depend on expert professionals, whether they be lawyers, physicians, accountants, or therapists, they have power over us. To the extent that the dependence is on professionals to do what once we all could do for ourselves, the professions are 'disabling' – to use Ivan Illich's term (1978). To the extent that profession create dependence and disability, they create a serious social and ethical situation. Even though professionals may be in a 'helping' profession, often they end up helping those who once could help themselves. The creation of disabled dependants is part of a general social process connected with the increasing specialisation of modern life, a social process outside the effective control of any single professional or profession. Nevertheless, if professionals looked at and understood the historical process of which they are a part it might help dampen the arrogance and self-deception that often clothe those who believe themselves possessors of expert knowledge. It is hardly unambiguously virtuous to help people who, in other times and places. could look after themselves.

As might be anticipated from earlier comments, behavioural professionals face a special problem, for they are experts in behaviour. It is inevitable that the expert advice, guidance, and help sought will involve, at one level or another, how one *should* behave. Since the scientific methods that make behavioural professionals expert are silent when it comes to *should*, their position *vis-à-vis* clients is a special one. Behavioural professionals cannot avoid giving advice, guidance, or help in questions involving *should*. Nor should they. But they should take care to be clear, particularly to themselves, about where the advice is coming from. It does not come from empirical science. It comes from their own experience, sensitivity, perspicacity. To believe that their advice is objective, is scientific, would be to practise self-deception. To describe the moral advice as objective, as scientific, would be to practise fraud.

Ethical issues for behavioural professionals are magnified by the fact that the people they serve often seem so clearly in need of expert help. When one is obviously engaged in doing good, the harm that attends doing good can become invisible. Although we easily deceive ourselves in such matters, it is not difficult to look back and to recognise and understand the moral blinkers of helpers in times past. To cite only one of the better known cases: anthropologists can clearly see the serious harm done to communities by missionaries introducing change in traditional practices. Yet the missionaries were doing what appears to them the highest good – saving souls and introducing civilisation. And with the vantage point of time it is now possible to see the harm done to native communities by *anthropologists* who themselves were guided by their own notions of good – the higher good of doing science. The point is an ancient and obvious one. Good intentions do not necessarily produce good results. People engaged in helping professions cannot be too aware of the fact that our own good intentions tend to blind us to the complexity of the consequences of our help.

Although good intentions may blind us to the consequences of our own help, we can often see clearly the unfortunate consequences of a fellow professional's help. However, perceiving harm does not necessarily lead to action. A recurring difficulty in enforcing codes of ethical conduct is the reluctance of one professional to interfere with the actions of another. One professional may clearly see the harmful, even disastrous, effects of another's helpful (sometimes malevolent) 'service' and feel helpless to do anything about it. Many reasons for this might be given: a belief in freedom of practice, loyalty to a group member, fear that we may be wrong, compassion for a colleague, not wanting to appear an informer, fear that someone may interfere in our own practice. Some of the reasons are quite creditable. None the less, it is clear that most of the time we are more able to see the harm produced by another than the harm we ourselves produce.

If professionals wish to protect their clients from harm they must work out some way of interfering (to put it bluntly) with the activities of fellow members of the profession. It is an unpleasant thought – something which goes against the grain of most professionals. Physicians, for example, are notoriously reluctant to testify against colleagues, even when they know them to be dangerously incompetent. We in the teaching profession do no better. All of us know colleagues who should not be let near students, yet we seldom do anything about it. The reluctance of professionals to judge or interfere with the activities of colleagues is understandable. The more we know, the less certain we are of our own competence. The thought of colleagues watching and judging is enough to bring to a halt notions of reform, enough to set us thinking that *we* not our powerless clients, need protecting. Yet, if we as individuals are so little able to see the harm we ourselves produce, are so vulnerable to self-deception, how are we to protect those we serve unless we can put the welfare of our clients above the welfare of our colleagues, unless we can create some social means to effectively keep watch?

Illich, with considerable warrant, has called the present time 'the age of disabling professions'. I cannot escape the unease as being a member of a disabling profession by claiming that I am a lecturer, nor a therapist: for in Illich's terms one of the chief disabling professions is the teaching profession. Besides, I think that to the extent that psychology disables, responsibility lies more with the academic, the scientific, side of psychology than the practising side. It has to do with the ways in which we have conceptualised our research task. For example, behaviourists since Watson have ritually incanted that the scientific task of psychology is to predict and control behaviour. They, by definition, have placed control outside the individual and, even though modern behaviour therapists write of 'self-control', they can do so only by contradicting their own basic assumptions. The determinism that nourishes behaviourism denies the possibility of self-determination. Behaviourism is simply the most obvious exemplar of determinism. Depth psychologies, although they deal with matters internal to the individual, seldom do better. In a recent defence of psychoanalytic theory John Maze (1983) states the case clearly: 'abandon any understandable conception of causality and propose that such an entity has the power of changing itself – a kind of event which, if it should ever happen, would be blankly incomprehensible' (p.58). Maze is right. Given the notion of cause that goes with the philosophical creed of determinism and which undergirds most psychological theories and systems, it *is* blankly incomprehensible that people can change themselves, that people can guide or direct their own behaviour, that people can be responsible for what they do. Or that this ethical discussion makes any sense. (If we cannot be moral agents it is absurd to engage in ethical comment.) Psychology (and the other behavioural sciences) has taken as its model traditional science, which treats things as passive substances. In such a science people, by definition, are passive things. I cannot imagine anything more basically disabling than the 'scientific' belief that people are passive things that can only be acted upon, that can only do what they do. Such a 'science' contradicts the belief people have always had of possessing abilities or powers that can enable them to be responsible for what they do. In ethical discussion, any notion of *should* is incoherent unless to some degree we can become responsible for our actions.

Ironically, *modern* science treats things as individuals with powers (Harré and Secord, 1973). Psychology has only to join modern science to become, potentially at least, enabling. Research in the fields of learning, perception, and memory already is cast in a form compatible with a power's conception (Manicas and Secord, 1983). What Thomas Reid (1788/1977) called the speculative powers 'The powers of seeing, hearing, remembering, distinguishing, judging, reasoning' (p.12) are being studied by psychologists. No doubt they could be studied more fruitfully if psychologists conceptualised them as powers. But it is a start. What needs most to be done if psychology is to become enabling is to conceptualise and study what Reid termed 'active power' (p.12). In other words active power is the power to do – or in a broad and non-behaviourist sense, to behave. Reid's 'active powers' in modern terms would be called 'behavioural powers'.

If modern physical scientists can conceive of the things they study as individuals with powers, surely behavioural scientists ought to be able to do the same. People, in spite of behavioural science, usually think of themselves in this way. Conceiving their subject matter as individuals with powers, psychologists could set themselves the task of determining what augments and what limits the powers they study. Potentially we could discover how to enable or empower people. We disablers might become enablers.

In simple terms a change from the study of behaviour to the study of behavioural powers would mean a shift from studying what people do to studying what people can do. This seems to be precisely the kind of information a therapist needs. Any therapist can tell you that it does no good to tell clients what to do if they cannot do it. Doing something is not simply a matter of advice, or of motive, or of environmental stimuli – as any actor can tell you. Successfully doing something on stage depends upon acting skills. Analogously, successfully doing something in everyday life depends upon behavioural skills or powers – or what elsewhere I have called 'habits' (Mixon, 1980) or 'expressive skills or powers' (Mixon, 1985).

I hope that the following passage from Hubert Dreyfus' enlightening book on computers will help clarify the advantage to therapists of seeking to understand the skills or powers upon which behaviour depends.

A skill, unlike a fixed response or set of responses can be brought to bear in an indefinite number of ways. When the percipient acquires a skill he does not weld together individual movements and individual stimuli but acquires the power to respond with a certain type of solution to situations of a certain general form. The situations may differ widely from place to place, and the response movements may be entrusted sometimes to one operative organ, sometimes to another, both situations and responses in the various cases having in common not so much a partial identity of elements as a shared significance (Merleau-Ponty, quoted in Dreyfus, 1972, p.161).

Strictly speaking current behavioural knowledge deals with responses or behaviours. Changing a response or behaviour may be of some limited benefit to clients, but the possibility of acquiring or augmenting behavioural skills seems to be both what clients would seek and what therapists would like to be able to offer.

A further advantage of studying behavioural skills or powers lies with the increased certainty of knowledge that would ensue. For the closure needed to conduct a true behavioural experiment is possible only if powers or skills are being studied (Manicas and Secord, 1983; Mixon, 1985). That is why the fields of perception, memory, and learning have a solid experimental base and most of the rest of psychology does not.

But what of my notion that humility concerning the knowledge upon which their advice is based would go some way to alleviating ethical issues behavioural professionals face? Would not the relative certainty of knowledge which would accompany experiments on behavioural powers militate against humility and thus increase ethical problems? It would – to the extent that humility is the only solution. However, in time the study of behavioural skills or powers could make a major contribution to the understanding of ethics. For ethical judgments must be based ultimately upon what people can do. Injunctions to do something one cannot do or not to do something one cannot avoid doing are both futile and fatuous. The relationship of *is* to *ought* has long been debated. The relationship of *can* to *ought* is waiting to be established. A psychology which studies behavioural powers and skills might in time be able to map the powers we must have before in truth we can take responsibility for a line of action, the powers or skills necessary to a moral agent. Questions of *can* are intimately related to questions of *should* and thus have direct bearing on ethics. Such a science, such a psychology, might one day have something to contribute to discussions such as this.

REFERENCES

Chow, S.L. (1985), Social psychology of psychological experiments revisited, manuscript submitted for publication.

Dreyfus, H.L. (1972), *What computers can't do*, New York, Harper & Row.

Harré, R. and Secord, P.F. (1973), *The explanation of social behaviour*, Oxford, Basil Blackwell.

Harrison, J. (1967), 'Ethical naturalism', in P. Edwards (ed.), *The encyclopaedia of philosophy*, vol.3., New York, MacMillan & The Free Press.

Illich, I. (1978), *The right to useful unemployment and its professional enemies*, London, Marion Boyars.

Manicas, P.T. and Secord, P.F. (1983), 'Implications for psychology of the new philosophy of science,' *American Psychologist, 38*, pp.339–413.

Maze, J.R. (1983), *The Meaning of Behaviour*, London, George Allen & Unwin.

Miller, G.A. (1962), *Psychology: The Science of Mental Life*, New York, Harper & Row.

Mixon, D. (1977), 'Temporary false belief', *Personality and Social Psychology Bulletin, 3*, pp.479–88.

Mixon, D. (1979), 'Understanding puzzling and shocking conduct', in G.P. Ginsburg (ed.), *Emerging strategies in social psychological research*, New York, Wiley.

Mixon, D. (1980), 'The place of habit in the control of action', *Journal for the Theory of Social Bchaviour, 10*, pp.169–86.

Mixon, D. (1985), Pretending, certainty, and psychological experiments, Manuscript submitted for publication.

Reid, T. (1977), *Essays on the Active Powers of Man*, New York & London, Garland. (Originally published 1788.)

Steffens, L. (1931), *The Autobiography of Lincoln Steffens*, New York, Harper & Row.

Rights to Display: The Masking of Competence

Rom Harré

In this chapter I hope to bring out one of the most dangerous deficits of contemporary empirical psychology. I hope to show that the very methods by which psychologists explore the nature of human beings serve to conceal and thus falsify the phenomena which they are ostensibly studying. We shall see that this arises through a systematic neglect of the moral framework within which human action occurs.

There are various ways of bringing out these issues. In other studies I have described the morally sensitive psychologies which are in the process of construction (Gergen, 1982; Shotter, 1984). One can contrast these with the amoral technologism which has been the political background to much psychology that has had its origin in the United States. It is characteristic of American psychological thought that there should be a systematic translation of moral issues into technical problems. The failure of the technologistic way of conceiving human life is only too evident, and in this paper I shall take it for granted that the technologistic attempt to eliminate the moral dimension from psychological studies can be taken to have failed. My aim, then, is to show that by neglecting the differential rights of people to act in framing their contributions to collective human action, there is a mask which effectively prevents an investigator from making any reasonable assessment of the relative competence that people have in themselves.

THE PRIORITY OF THE PUBLIC-COLLECTIVE ASPECTS OF HUMAN INTERACTION FOR UNDERSTANDING SOCIAL ACTIVITY

The traditional conceptual framing of psychology owes a great deal to the Cartesian way of marking off the mental and the physical. The idea that the mind and the body are both substances with logically incompatible properties is the ultimate source of the sceptical stance which has affected attempts to create a mental science. This is usually framed in terms of the two distinctions, inner-outer and subjective-objective, which are run together in contemporary Cartesianism. Behaviourists, rightly sceptical of the scientific status of introspective reports of the alleged inner and subjective goings-on of the mind, tried to construct a science based entirely upon reports of the outer and, it was naively supposed, objective, behaviour of individual human beings. The result was disastrous. The very phenomena which behaviourists set out to study were dissolved in the process of setting up the conditions under which this methodology could be used. This point has been reiterated so frequently that it is hardly in point to reassert it. Phenomenological psychologists, on the other hand, rightly sceptical of the scientific pretensions of an externalist account of human action, persuaded themselves that a systematic description of the inner life of human beings would be an adequate foundation for a psychological science. Reflection on this programme led to the realization of the well known difficulties that beset the Husserlian epochs. As Schutz (1972) pointed out, it is impossible to reconstruct the ordinary world of human relations once our common sense knowledge upon which that world is based has been hypothetically suspended from use.

If one has lost one's faith in the original Cartesian dichotomies and one is still determined on the creation of a science of human thought and action, one must look around for some other way of conceiving of the mental life of individual human beings. The view I wish to present sees individual minds as secondary formations, as partially privatized versions of the public conversation (Harré, 1983). The notion of conversation is fundamental to the point of view I am developing in this chapter. In its literal use conversation is the name for a largely verbal phenomenon, comprising the speech-acts of the members of the community who mutually understand and take account of each other's intentions. But I wish the notion to be understood in a somewhat wider sense to include various other forms of symbolic interaction, including gestures and other kinds of semiotic displays. My thesis, then, is that in the last analysis it is the conversation that is prior and individual minds which are abstractions or appropriations from it.

An immediate consequence of this move is a reconsideration of the taken-for-granted nature of many psychological processes. For example, it has been characteristic of contemporary psychology to suppose that reasoning, the interpretations of feelings as emotions, the identification of a recollection as a memory, and so on and so on, are properly to be located in individual human beings. Cognitive science, for example, would like to be able to treat these phenomena as the expression of the results of the workings of information processing modules, the components of individual minds. The shift to the point of view I am advocating directly challenges these assumptions.

There are two kinds of cases. First, there is the question of the logical priority of the public and collective, or social activity of conversation over the individual activity of, say, interpreting feelings as emotions. By logical priority I mean something like this: That it would not be possible for an individual human being to interpret a bodily perturbation as a particular emotion without making use of certain social – that is public and collective – features of local cultures. In particular I have in mind common sense theories as to the causes of bodily perturbations which, as the work of Moscovici (1976) and others has shown are, at least in many cases, what the French call 'social representations', ie depend upon socially maintained and promulgated versions of scientific theories. But more importantly from the point of view of this chapter, is the idea that emotions are not only defined by the identification of the causes of a bodily feeling, but also through the moral qualities both of the feeling and the conditions which bring it about. An emotion like sadness is not just a feeling, it is also a moral stance, and furthermore is itself morally required. Emotions are not just passive responses to stimuli. They are crucial parts of *particular*, contextually relative, patterns of action.

A full-scale theory of the emotions involves not only a study of the physiological effects of various kinds of stimuli, but also of the moral orders of the societies in which this or that emotion has a place. For instance, one of our uses of the word 'fear', though not the only one, is for the emotion associated with the bodily perturbation that is occasioned by the appearance of some dangerous or threatening object. But the emotion of fear, for people of our sort, is embodied in a very complex set of moral assumptions in which the notions of courage and cowardice play an essential part. For us, fear is something which should be overcome. We are expected to 'stand up to' the fearful object. The anthropologist Catherine Lutz (1982) has shown how, among the Ifaluk, the bodily perturbations occasioned by the appearance of threatening objects or people are located in a wholly different moral universe. The emotion *metagu*, which is an Ifaluk interpretation of the flush of adrenalin, is associated with a conception, the inverse of ours, as to what is morally proper on such occasions. The Ifaluk praise those who flee, and so far as we know punish and abuse those who display what we would call bravery. Now in these sorts of cases the logical priority in the theory of emotions must go to the local moral order rather than the universal flush of adrenalin. *Metagu*, seen in this analytical framework, is not a species of fear. There may even be societies in which that particular perturbation has no place in the system of emotions, and indeed there are many bodily perturbations which, though situational in character and origin, do not count for us as emotions at all, for instance pangs of hunger, nervous inflammation of the bladder, etc.

The second way in which the social or public and collective world realized in the human conversation has priority over individual mental phenomena, is what I might call 'temporal priority'. That is, in the development of individual beings the phenomenon in question, such as the capacity to reason logically, first of all appears in conversation, and only at some later stage does it become part of the skill of an individual human actor. The most striking example is rationality. By rationality, I mean doing or saying what one does for a readily avowed reason. It seems that on most occasions the assumption that the rationality of some human product, some contribution to the human conversation is the effect of, or the public manifestation of, rational individual cognitive processes is mistaken. There have been many recent interesting studies which have looked at the matter of rationality in a wholly different fashion. For example, the studies of the rationality of scientists which have been undertaken by Bruno Latour (Latour and Woolgar, 1979) and others, have shown that the way in which rationality is created in a scientific paper (a contribution to the scientific conversation) is not to be understood as a public manifestation of the workings of a private logic machine. It seems to be the result of a long series of social interactions in which rationality is put into scientific thought for the purposes of persuasion and the debate to which much scientific work is subjected. Rationality is a feature of certain contexually required rhetorics and not a feature of the cognitive processes by which conversational contributions are produced. Now this idea is in flat contradiction to many of the assumptions of the cognitive science movement, in particular the assumption that underlying all human mental processes is some sort of computational logic. The collectivist view would hold that the mental processes of human beings are characteristically non-logical, indeed it is well known that in many cases the best logical strategies are short-circuited or abandoned in favour of analogical and other forms of reasoning involving content. So the problem of the source of the logic of scientific and other forms of discourse cannot be solved, it seems, by reference to the cognitive processes of individual human beings.

The social-collectivist idea is, it seems to me, a successful solution to the problem of where the rationality comes from. It is nothing but a social convention. Of course, this idea is fatal to the Piagetian conception of a universal ladder of human development from the concrete to the abstract and from content-related forms of reasoning to abstract logical. From the social collectivist point of view, the Piagetian ladder must be a projection onto psychology of the social priorities given in francophone communities to different kinds of public displays of rationality. Of course, it is obvious that what is fashionable and seen to be morally worthy in the way contributions to a conversation are valued, will lead to rehearsals of certain kinds of ways of speaking. It would indeed be astonishing if those, whose conversation was valued according to the principle that logical coherence is to be preferred to all other forms of rhetoric, did not prepare for such speech and the challenges that are likely to be made to individual contributions to it.

But doesn't this presuppose a kind of meta-rationality? It may be individually rational to make public displays of rationality. But most people are not so machiavellian, merely living out the collectively maintained conversational conventions of their several social worlds.

THE CHALLENGE TO PIAGET

Doubts about the Piagetian framework, once they have been admitted, tend to go much deeper (Harré, 1985). Following the lead of Vygotsky (1962, 1978), whose work is now largely available outside the Soviet Union, it has been suggested that most individual psychological processes are extracted for personal use from what are essentially social processes which are functionally equivalent. Now this lays challenge to almost all the basic Piagetian ideas, not only the location of rationality as the top floor in the edifice of cognitive development.

Vygotsky's most important contribution to this debate was his challenge to Piaget's theory of egocentric speech. It is worth remarking parenthetically on the amazing resistance of Piagetian dogma to empirical and logical criticism. To the uncommitted outsider, Vygotsky's criticisms of the Piagetian theory of egocentricity which were formulated and published in the 1930s are devastating, and yet it is still possible, fifty years later, to find the theory of egocentric speech *à la* Piaget being promulgated by people who ought to know better. According to Piaget, the fact that young children preface a great deal of their speech with 'I' is a sign that they are locked into a self-centred universe and are unable to comprehend the point of view of others. Vygotsky showed, and I use that word advisedly, that the prefacing of contributions to a discourse with 'I' is no more than the ordinary mark of intentional mental activity and has nothing at all to do with point of view. A small child does most of its cognitive work in public, that is it speaks its mind out loud. The 'I' which prefaces so many childish contributions to the conversation is an indexical marking of an unproblematic performative which simply indicates that the intention on display is that of the speaker. It has nothing whatever to do with whether the speaker can take the point of view of somebody else. Thus, for Vygotsky, the disappearance of egocentric speech is not to be explained by the sudden realization that there are other human beings in the world, which is roughly the Piagetian claim.

Rather, it is the mark of the moment at which the developing human being learns to do thinking in private. Egocentric speech simply goes underground and becomes the ordinary commonplace thought processes for planning, intending, wanting, etc. This further emphasizes and confirms the general theory of social constructionism that individual minds are appropriations from the public conversation. The mind of a small child is not fully detached from the public conversation because a great deal of his or her cognitive activity simply is public speaking.

APPROPRIATION FOR PSYCHOLOGICAL SYMBIOSIS

In the Vygotskian point of view (which is echoed in many of the later ideas of Wittgenstein) the process by which the young person comes to speak and makes contributions to public conversation, moves to the centre of our interest. The privatization of public speech, though enormously important in the actual development of an individual mind, seems to me to be psychologically unproblematic. But it is the process prior to that, the step by which the beginnings of cognition appear in public activity, that are intentionally performed, to which we must pay the most attention. We owe to Shotter and Newson (1974), who borrowed a term from Spitz, the idea of psychological symbiosis. This is a name for the kind of relationship which obtains between mothers and infants, through which the infant's mind is created. This is an idea I believe of enormous psychological importance. When a mother, or any other intimate, interacts with an infant, it seems clear that the 'other', the adult or older child, does not interact with the infant as such, but rather interacts with a composite being which has been partly created by the contribution of that very 'other'. So mothers react to their babies not by virtue of what the baby actually does, but rather to the further interpretation and complementation of that action which, characteristically, is achieved by what the mother says and does.

Mothers attribute high level psychological processes to newborn infants, such as intentions, wants, and even moral responsibility and sensibility. What is going on? Well, from the study of mothers' speech and the speech of older siblings, it seems that the speech acts of such persons serve to supplement the infants' activities and interpret such behaviour as is visible, to compensate for any psychological deficits that the child may have by virtue of its infancy. In this way, the mind of the infant is collectively created by those who interact with it. In short, the infant appears on the social scene, not only as a distinct human individual, but also as a person. The mind of an infant, then, is not the possession of that infant as an individual, but rather is created in the circumambient conversation surrounding that infant and to which the others react. The child is presented to the world not as it is in itself, but as it is complemented by the other members of its social collective. This idea is of quite central importance to the social constructionist point of view, and for the rest of this chapter I want to bring out the enormously important consequences that follow from taking it up.

This said, how does development occur? There seem to be two primary phenomena involved. Very young infants seem to be 'programmed' to produce a certain range of public behaviour which is just what is needed to set going the symbiotic activities of those with whom the infant interacts. It is as if very small children were constrained in some way to produce in others the very kind of reciprocal behaviour which they need to appropriate in order to become fully human.

The second aspect of development concerns the psychological processes which must be called upon to explain how the transfer of cognitive competence from mother, father, sibling, etc. to infant occurs. It is clear that by about the age of five most children have acquired those conversational skills which will last them for the rest of their days. How has it come about? Vygotsky coined the phrase 'Zone of Proximal Development' for the preparatory stages that lead to a developmental step. The process of transfer of cognitive skills from eg mother to infant occurs in a stepwise fashion. Later acquisitions depend not only upon earlier acquisitions but upon restructurings. It is these that lead to quantum leaps in competence. This is one of the few developmental concepts that Vygotsky shares with Piaget.

I believe that the process is essentially simple and that no other more mysterious psychological process than imitation is needed to understand it. My speculation goes something like this. Children from the very young to the adolescent, and maybe beyond, are extraordinarily imitative. In the first instance they imitate the activities, conversational and otherwise, of the people who surround them. But these activities are imitated, so to say, piecemeal and perhaps, even, in a random way. Bits and pieces of the conversation are imitated by the infant, accumulating a rag bag which is a mere aggregate. However, once all the necessary components of a structure have been acquired, then without further ado they form up into the only kinds of structures of which they are capable. This kind of phenomenon is common throughout the biological scale. It is found in the development of motor skills by the accumulation of fixed fragments of routines. It occurs in the folding of proteins created by RNA synthesis by the assemblage of the usual twenty-fold set of necessary amino acids. Structure can arise, and usually does arise from the mere co-presence of the totality of required components. No additional template is usually necessary. This commonplace biological idea can, I think, take the mystery out of what goes on in the zone of proximal development.

So far I have concentrated almost entirely on the world of psychological symbiosis in infant development. And of course this is a necessary step in order to defend the idea that individual human minds are appropriations from, or privatizations of, aspects of human conversation. However, it is important to realize that psychological symbiosis is not confined to infancy. I believe that it is a typical feature of human association throughout life. Let me illustrate this with some examples. David Pendleton (1983) has shown how in a medical consultation the interaction between doctor, mother and daughter is dominated by the shift of attention from child to mother as the interlocutor of the doctor's diagnostic questioning. The deficits, both social and intellectual, of the child, are made up by contributions from the mother. It is important to notice that the deficits are frequently social. In looking at Pendleton's transcripts with this idea in mind, it is both amusing and instructive to notice that the mother begins to chip in to the conversation when the family's image is in some way being let down by the child's revelations. Certain kinds of complaints, such as 'boils on the bottom' are, so to say, derogatory of the family's conception of itself. They have to be played down and reworked in various ways. This brings out the further point that psychological symbiosis is not only a matter of supplementing skill but also of correcting social presentation. To put it in sociological terms, psychological symbiosis is not only an activity in the practical order supplementing skills of reasoning or physical capability, but is also to be found within the expressive order, where matters of honour and virtue are at stake.

This takes me to the next example. Goffman pointed out that waiters sometimes engage in psychological symbiosis, in that they supplement the inadequacies of clients by subtly coaching in choosing from the menu and wine list. And the point of it all is to make sure the restaurant has the kind of client which fits with its conception of itself. One can also observe psychological symbiosis at any dinner party, at any doctoral examination, and I dare say in all sorts of other milieu where that peculiar combination of practical skill and expressive display that typifies so much of human conversation, is to be found.

THE ISSUE OF RIGHTS

So far I have not considered the internal structure of those psychologically symbiotic dyads by which the conversational contribution to mankind are organized and their level maintained. Like any other human groups, those which exist to complement each other's cognitive skill and moral standing will have their own social structures ordered according to such principles as relative power, status, rights and so on. This raises the issues of the role of local moral orders in psychology from another direction. The question to which I wish to address myself now is how far the displays that an *individual* can make in any given social milieu are determined more by the local system of rights and obligations to display than the competence in the necessary skills that that individual may have as such.

Let me illustrate this first of all with a very simple example. When studying the social order in a kindergarten, I was much struck by the difference in certain social rights that this or that particular child had, depending on whether it was in symbiosis with its mother or its father. Characteristically, when with its mother, a child of three years old was socially ignored by other adults. For example, the greeting and farewelling was directed to the mother. However, on other occasions, in which the very same child was with its father and interacting socially with the very same adult, the child was treated as a social individual and farewelled and greeted as a socially distinct person. It seems clear that what I was observing were differential rights of display. The three-year-old child was manifestly competent to perform the social rituals required but did not have the same right to carry out those performances when it was with its mother.

We can take this idea very much further. The whole of the conversational matrix within which human beings engage each other is shot through with rights and conventions of display. These are not only differential rights to greet and farewell, but even of the right to speak. The roles people occupy with respect to certain forms of social interaction, determine not only what they can do, but also which speech acts they can perform. Furthermore, there are obligations to listen, and even in some cases there are rights to eavesdrop. Now all of this means that when we come to look at psychologically symbiotic groups we must take account not only of the differentiation of competence between the members, but also what rights of display they have.

The most striking case of the failure to take account of differential rights of display is the moral development theory of Kohlberg. The empirical work upon which it is based is, one can only say, peculiar. If I may remind the reader, the characteristically Kohlbergian technique is to present a person with a written story which describes some kind of moral dilemma. The person, and I emphasize the individuality of the respondent, is then usually required to write a little essay in which their version of how the dilemma should be resolved is set out. The answers are analyzed, again I emphasize individual answers, according to an interpretative code. The result is a determination of the level of cognitive competence with respect to moral reason.

This is indeed a bizarre state of affairs. First of all, it could hardly be more obvious that that is not how moral reasoning takes place. Most people make their moral decisions in the course of conversations with others. Most moral decisions I would claim are in that way collective rather than individual. This has been demonstrated by the pioneering work of Kitwood (1980) on the way in which adolescents make moral decisions. Furthermore, Kohlbergian, or for that matter Piagetian investigations of cognitive capacities, whether moral or otherwise, simply take no account at all of whether there are differential rights of display involved. It may be that children subscribe to certain conventions as to what it is proper or even advisable to argue out with an adult. If this is true, and it is also the case that cognitive competence is largely displayed in speech, the systematic confusion between the lack of a right to display for a certain level of competence, and a lack of the competence to display is only too likely to lead to fundamental confusions in various fields. This confusion, as I have suggested, has been to my mind fatal in the efforts to establish that there is a *scala natura* of moral reasoning which can be interpreted developmentally. The alleged levels of moral reasoning which Kohlbergians claim to have discovered seem on unprejudiced examination to be different moral theories. Kitwood, and more recently Davies (1982), have both shown that far from it being the case that children move through a growing competence in moral reasoning from concrete and narrowly local ideas of prudential morality, to Kantian transcendental deductions, children, even at a tender age, seem to be in command of a wide range of ways of moral reasoning. And they are also in command of a very detailed theory as to the appropriateness and strategic utility of the display of each kind of moral reasoning. Davies has illustrated, in a way that complements Kitwood's work, how different kinds of moral theory are invoked strategically. If they are losing an argument at a 'high' cognitive 'level' they quickly revert to lower 'levels' of the Kohlbergian scale. They use this device to trap the adults into feeling uneasy for treating them as 'just children', in a meta-morally unacceptable way, ie as if they really were adults. The reported conversation published by Davies in the *British Journal of Sociology of Education* (1980) is a fine illustration of this particular strategy.

Now what this shows is that the attribution of levels of competence to human beings, by virtue of a study of their performances in concrete situations, is systematically fraught with the possibility of error. This is because what appears in a performance is a display of what such a person has a right or duty to display. It does not show the extent of the underlying skill or knowledge upon which that display is based. Further, it should be obvious that amongst those skills is a profound grasp of the social conventions in accordance with which various kinds of conversation are to be carried on. So it is literally impossible to deduce a level of competence from a level of public display. Can this be remedied? Well of course it can, and it comes out most obviously in what I have been saying. If one pays attention to the moral order within which a particular conversation is being carried on, it is possible to discover, as Davies, Kitwood and others have done, just what is the system of rights, obligations and duties that is at work in that *particular* occasion. Once this step has been taken, it is then possible to divide out by the moral order, and come to some more just assessment of the level of competence. One must acknowledge, too, that the skillful management of one's conversational and other acts in accordance with one's rights and duties *is also a competence*. A remarkable result emerges. The Piaget-Kohlberg ladders of competence don't seem to exist. That is, once children have passed through the Vygotskyean zone of proximal development and have emerged at the age of five as reasonably competent speakers of the language, they are to all intents and purposes cognitively mature. Of course there are many things they don't know. And, most important of all, there are many rights that they do not have. So they do not do what adults and older children do, at least not in the presence of their elders and betters.

APPLYING THIS IN OTHER CONTEXTS

I have concentrated in the last section on the issues of rights and competence and how realization of its importance affects our understanding of children. But of course my earlier claim that psychological symbiosis is typical of all forms of human association must lead one to wonder whether the muddle between competence and rights is ubiquitous.

I can illustrate the point by referring to the marvellous ironies that abound in the writings of Jane Austen. One of the major psychological preoccupations of her works, and in particular *Pride and Prejudice*, is the manifest difference between the kinds of reasoning that women can display when conversing with women, compared with those that convention allows them to display when conversing with men. In *Pride and Prejudice*, Elizabeth, the archetypal Austenian heroine, is shown in a wide variety of different social milieu. Her conversational interactions with her father and Mr Darcy are markedly different from those in which she engages with her mother and her sisters. The psychological plot seems to me to centre round that contrast. Jane Austen brings out the power of Elizabeth's intellect and the sensitivity of her moral intuitions in those conversational occasions in which she is dealing with her silly mother and in different ways with the differing levels of cognitive competence and moral responsibility that are manifest in her sisters. The irony emerges in the ways in which she is forced to deal, according to the conventions of the age, with her father and the man who later becomes her husband. In those interactions she strategically invokes what one might call women's intuition and feminine wiles. The most significant conversation in the entire book, I believe, is with Mr Darcy when she is staying with the Bingleys on the occasion of her sister's illness. I believe that novels by writers of genius are more valuable as textbooks of human psychology than most of the works emanating from the university presses of this world and it is in those conversations and the ironical inversions of relationships that we see the genius of Jane Austen as an observer of psychological complexities of mankind. It is an ironized example of the way lack of rights to display can mask competence.

Bringing the story up to date we have to ask now about the role of the written examination, the psychiatric interview, and so on, in which one person is assessed by others, in particular assessed for levels of intellectual competence and for the skills needed in various aspects of social and intellectual life. If human life is normally lived in conditions of psychological symbiosis, and if the ways in which people exercise and display their competence is crucially dependent on the local moral order which, role by role, determines rights of display, then neither the written examination nor the psychiatric interview is likely to be of much value in telling us how a person actually lives. And this is for two complementary reasons. If I am right about the ubiquity of psychological symbiosis, then the way in which written examinations and psychiatric interviews, and such other typical modern events, extract the hidden human being from the normal milieu of others, can give us no idea whatever of the roles that person occupies and how his or her thoughts, decisions, moral judgments, etc. are created in the symbiotic groups to which he or she belongs. Secondly, written examinations and psychiatric interviews, etc. are themselves social events in which certain conversational rights are implicit so that obligations, duties and prohibitions of certain kinds of contributions to the conversation are at work in those situations too. The isolation of the individual from the rest of the people who are involved in the sustaining of that particular mind may lead to further distortions of our assessment of competence just because certain kinds of displays are forbidden by virtue of the conventions of the examination and the interview. For example, in a written examination there is no place for the drawing of pictures, the making of jokes, and so on. I am not sufficiently experienced in the minutiae of the psychiatric interview to identify its characteristic features, but the theory expounded in this chapter would suggest that such an intimate human social interaction can hardly be different from others of the same sort in which the differentiation of rights and obligations is so highly marked.

The conclusion I wish to draw is both practical and methodological. From the practical point of view the theme of this book must surely require attention be paid to the moral order that is at work in the very events which constitute clinical psychology and behavioural medicine. How little we know about these matters. The work of Pendleton does suggest that the moral order that obtains within a medical interview, and the psychological symbiotic relationships that develop within it are absolutely crucial to our understanding of what is going on in the event and to our assessment of its value. From the methodological point of view, the next step in the study of human psychology, in both its normal and its pathological manifestations, must surely be the detailed and fine-grained analysis of the kinds of moral principles that are at work in the building up of a human mind in the day-to-day interactions through which it is constructed and maintained.

REFERENCES

Davies, B. (1980), 'An Analysis of Primary School Children's Accounts of Classroom Interaction', *British Journal of Sociology of Education*, vol.1, no.3, pp.257–78.

Davies, B. (1982), *Life in the Classroom and Playground*, London, Routledge & Kegan Paul.

Gergen, K.J. (1982), *Towards Transformation in Social Knowledge*, New York, Springer Verlag.

Harré, R. (1983), *Personal Being*, Oxford, Blackwell.

Harré, R. (ed.),(1985), *Oxford Review of Education*, vol.10, no.1.

Kitwood, T. (1980), *Disclosures to a Stranger*, London, Routledge & Kegan Paul.

Latour, B. and Woolgar, S. (1979), *Laboratory Life*, Los Angeles, Sage.
Lutz, C. (1982), 'The domain of emotion words on Ifaluk', *American Ethnologist, 9*, pp.113–28.
Moscovici, S. (1976), *La Psycholoanalyse: son image et son public*. Paris, Presses Universitaires de France.
Pendleton, D. (1983), in D. Pendleton and J.C. Hasler (eds), *Doctor-Patient Communication*, London, Academic Press.
Schutz, A. (1972), *The Phenomenology of the Social World*, (trans. G. Walsh and F. Lehrer), London, Heinemann.
Shotter, J. (1984), *Social Accountability and Selfhood*, Oxford, Blackwell.
Shotter, J. and Newson, J. (1974), 'How babies communicate', *New Society, 29*, pp.345–7.
Vygotsky, L.S. (1962), *Thought and Language*, Cambridge, Massachussetts, MIT Press.
Vygotsky, L.S. (1978), *Mind in Society*, Cambridge, Massachussetts, London, MIT Press.

On the Ethical Basis of 'Scientific' Behaviour Therapy

Peter Trower

The behaviour modification and therapy movement has produced many innovative treatment techniques in a comparatively short time (Agras, Kazdin and Wilson, 1979). Some of these have had a beneficial effect on many different problems (Bellack, Hersen and Kazdin, 1982). However, the radical criticisms of the moral basis of such techniques (eg Smail, 1978, Ingleby, 1981) have remained very much on the periphery of considerations. Among these criticisms, as I understand it, is the charge that the guiding parameters of 'scientific' behaviour therapy are potentially and actually detrimental rather than therapeutic, and where their pursuit is carried out mindfully, amounts to unethical practice.

There are at least three views on this question among behavioural therapists – practitioners and researchers: (a) the criticisms are wild and irrational, unworthy of serious discussion, since they attack the very basis of behaviour therapy – its status as an objective and value-free science; (b) if valid at all, they apply to psychiatry and not to behaviour therapy, which is after all 'liberated' from the medical model; (c) the critics are attacking a 'straw man' since, following the 'cognitive revolution', most behaviour therapists are eclectic and no longer adhere to 'behaviourism'. In this chapter I shall argue that there are sound reasons for thinking the critics' charge may be substantially valid, and that we should take it very seriously, for it replaces the reassuring picture most of us have with a far more disquieting one.

The argument can be divided into two main points. The first point is that the practice of behaviour therapy, because of rather than in spite of its espoused status as a value-free, applied science, tends to devalue and thereby dehumanize its clients. It does so by treating people for 'scientific' purposes as if they were 'organisms' rather than 'agents' who are helpless victims of forces outside their control. Behaviour therapy has to be included along with, rather than against, medical psychiatry and classical psychoanalysis, the only difference being that the controlling forces lie in environmental contingencies and, more recently, dysfunctional cognitive mechanisms rather than organic abnormalities or intra-psychic entities.

The second point is that clients believe or soon come to believe – given the overwhelming 'scientific' ethos – that they are abnormal organisms (deficient, ill, etc.), and that they are not only helpless but worthless, because that is part of the culture-wide stereotype of 'mental illness' and allied terms, as the literature shows (eg Farina, 1982).

There are disturbing political and social implications, as Ingleby (1981) and others have argued. But there are also direct therapy implications. Behaviour therapy may, like medical psychiatry, make clients worse to the extent that they convince those clients that they are abnormal or maladapted organisms, with the stereotyped attributes of helplessness and worthlessness. The constructive answer to this problem is to do therapy which helps people regain their sense of agency and worth, not help them lose it quicker.

WHY AND HOW 'SCIENTIFIC' BEHAVIOUR THERAPY DEHUMANIZES

Few behaviour therapists would want to deny that behaviour therapies are based on, and indeed distinguished by, the 'scientific' method. Arguments are made about the status of private events and feelings, theories are modified, methodologies revised and distinctions made between different forms of behaviourism (eg methodological versus radical). But the same, so-called 'scientific' paradigms remain, and have so far substantially resisted the challenge from within the movement – the 'cognitive revolution' – by simply absorbing it within the old behavioural paradigms (see below).

But then, is there really any option? Who would want to

challenge the principles of science? Are they not self-evident? Isn't this the best possible basis for practice? The trouble is that along with such self-evident truths as theory-building, and testing, reliability, validity, replicability, systematic observation and comparison etc., a number of further, highly contentious sacred cows are imported under the name of 'science'. These have already been widely referred to, but bear repeating here. To quote from Harré and Secord (1972) they are:

> A mechanistic model of man, a Humean conception of cause that places stress on external stimuli and a related methodology based upon the logical epistemological theories of logical positivism (p.29).

The conditioning theories – classical and operant conditioning – are the paradigm examples of mechanistic models, where the organism is under the control of various forces. A number of recent variants of these models have been developed (eg Levis, 1982). The nature of the connection between behaviour and its controlling stimulus is explained by Hume's conception of cause, ie a simple association or continguity. The overall framework for these events is logical positivism, in which all complex phenomena can be reduced to simple variables that interact in these mechanistic ways.

The implications of these paradigms are also well known but commonly misunderstood. Some of these are:

1 On the one hand scepticism towards, and on the other reification of, mental phenomena. In brief, the two main divergent views are that mental events are epiphenomena and do not have a causal role, and the second is they do have a causal role but as mental versions of Humean billiard balls (eg reified dispositions, intra-psychic entities and the like). What is decidedly omitted – rejected or overlooked – is the notion of the intentional nature of mental events (Searle, 1982).

2 Rejection of freedom and allied concepts of choice and responsibility which underlie morality. These are incompatible with the Humean account of cause and therefore outside the remit of a science-based therapy. Taken to its extreme, moral considerations would not enter into assessment and treatment of a client.

3 Rejection of the ordinary layman's epistemology or 'ordinary explanations' (Antaki, 1981), where meaning lies in the relation between events in complex, rule-bound structures, figures against contextual grounds etc., and its replacement with positivist

epistemology where meaning is reduced to the level of discrete phenomena.

THE COUNTER-ARGUMENTS

In considering the counter-arguments, we should clarify what is at issue. There are in fact two different issues which have become intertwined and confused (for these observations I am indebted to the philosopher Greg McCulloch).

1 Is behaviourism the only properly scientific methodology for *understanding* psychological reality?

2 Are therapeutic interventions in clinical practice best construed (by the therapist) as disinterested proddings of a scientifically viewed object (ie passive organism)?

The answer to 2 could well be 'no' even if the answer to 1 is yes. In other words the 'scientific' approach, even if valid, may not be the best approach in practice. Conversely the effectiveness of a 'non-scientific' practical procedure would not disprove the 'scientific' approach.

We are now in a position to consider the issues to be tackled in this chapter. The issues can be summed up by considering the following propositions:

1 A naturalistic conception of human beings (ie a view that sees human beings as physical systems) is scientifically correct.

2 Clients should be treated in a 'scientific' manner for clinical purposes (the manner determined by 1).

3 One aim of therapy is to prevent clients from behaving 'like passive organisms'.

4 Clients be treated, for clinical purposes, as *agents*.

In this chapter I am asserting that 3 and 4 are true. I am claiming, however, that behavioural practitioners (mindfully or otherwise) not only believe 1 is true, but that 2 necessarily follows from 1, which defeats the aim 3 and rejects 4. However, we have seen that 2 does *not* follow from 1. In fact 3 is perfectly compatible with naturalism, and, we claim, is best achieved by 4.

To restate this briefly, just because people are physical systems does not imply they should be treated, when they are clients, as if they are passive organisms, and indeed it is just as compatible, and empirically testable, to treat them (more effectively) as agents. In other words, the counter-argument is that we do not have to endorse contentious assumptions like 2 above in order to be 'scientific'. Counter-arguments of this kind have been made from the point of view of philosophical psychology, social psychology and radical sociology (Smail, 1978; Douglas, 1977; Mischel, 1973; Harré and Secord, 1972; Szasz, 1961). They have also been made, with varying degrees of sophistication, by alternative model builders within the cognitive behaviour therapy movement.

Indeed some would go so far as to say that the argument has already been won, the 'cognitive revolution' has taken place and the majority have endorsed what I have termed the 'agency' paradigms and abandoned the behaviourist ones. Certainly this might be the impression gained by a casual reading of Mahoney (1984) reporting on an apparent convergence of thinking between the behavioural and cognitive schools. However, there are a number of arguments and various pieces of evidence to suggest that such an impression is false. These are as follows:

1 The apparent eclecticism reported by Mahoney (1984), Franks *et al.* (1982) and others may really only represent muddled thinking. Liotti and Reda (1981) point out that the two approaches (in their terms associationism versus rationalism) are of incompatible philosophical natures, and an eclectic mix of the two merely produces conceptual confusion. This impression is gained from Schwartz's (1982) review, and from Mahoney's survey of attitudes of leading protagonists (Mahoney, 1984), where there is as much variation within camps and indeed within individuals as between the groups. One of the things they did mostly agree on was not being satisfied with the adequacy of their current understanding of human behaviour.

2 Leading behaviour therapists of the ABA (applied behaviour analysis) school certainly still adhere to traditional behaviourism. In a recent authoritative policy statement on applied behaviour analysis, Baer (1982) says 'private events' (ie thoughts) are simply behaviours subject to environmental control and in no sense autonomous causes of observable behaviour.

Orthodox behaviour therapists in Mahoney's survey endorsed such items as 'human learning is basically governed by principles of operant and classical conditioning.'

3 Behaviour therapists of the neobehaviouristic mediational S-

R school (Wilson, 1978), ie those based on classical conditioning theories, interpret internal events in a way essentially similar to the ABA school, ie as covert equivalents to overt behaviour, susceptible to the same laws – Mahoney's (1974) mediational model 1. In other words they adhere to the passive organism paradigm. Mahoney's orthodox behaviour therapists endorsed the item 'thoughts and mental images are probably conditioned mediating responses that act as stimuli for subsequent behaviour.'

4 It may be assumed that those who identify themselves as 'cognitive-behaviour therapists' endorse a revolutionary, agency approach, but there is much evidence against the assumption. After reviewing the cognitive behaviour therapies, Latimer and Sweet (1984) conclude 'the more recent development of cognitive therapy is an elaboration or embellishment of an existing paradigm within the broader field of behaviour therapy' (p.12). Schwartz (1982) notes that most research in the 'cognitive' area is more of a mediational behaviouristic than truly cognitive type, and Coyne (1982) makes a similar point. In fact in many ways some cognitive-behaviour therapists, by adopting a muddled eclecticism, have made the task of distinguishing the organism and agency paradigms even more difficult.

HARMFUL PARADIGMS

Despite the prevalence of the organism approach, it cannot be said that ordinary practitioners of behaviour therapy are particularly aware of the paradigms they assume, nor even that they have paradigm assumptions – somehow it all seems self-evident. The harmful consequences therefore need to be made explicit. I have elsewhere attempted to make them so in the context of SST (Trower, 1984), including the rejection of the intentional nature of mental events, of freedom and responsibility and lay epistemology (referred to earlier), and the endorsement of a mechanistic notion of cause.

Perhaps the last of these – the mechanistic notion of cause – is the most harmful single paradigm embedded in the positivist version of science. As Ingleby (1981) says, in claiming that behaviour or a state of mind is caused (determined) by a particular event, advocates are in fact making a subtle claim about the nature of that mental state '. . . for they imply that the person who has it is essentially not a rational agent. Their claims are about "what makes people do things" rather that "what people do".' Organisms are bound by causal laws, agents can choose to obey or disobey rules of conduct. Positivist science as applied to people in behaviour therapy and psychiatry seeks to either ignore or convert the human order into the non-human, where there are no successes or failures, and no moral judgments, but simply organisms – in this case faulty or diseased or malfunctioning organisms, and the accompanying symptoms. For example, common problems which fallible and vulnerable beings suffer in day-to-day life are converted into symptoms of the organism. Thus the Laingian schizophrenic is not responding to intolerable family dynamics, the depressed housewife is not reacting to inhuman housing-estate ghettos, but merely malfunctioning. Further, the various forces, such as conditioning, take responsibility for, and indeed the possibility of, intentional action out of the hands of the individual sufferer, hence the meaning of 'helpless'. Finally, the problems of the client are entirely to be explained in terms of mechanical causes and effects (including cognitions viewed simply as mediating causes and effects), and not in terms of values. Hence the client's 'emotive' language, couched in positive and negative evaluations, has its normal psychological meaning translated into 'scientific' language, and is seen as a conditioned response or symptom. To take such words at face value runs the risk (for the novice therapist) of being regarded as unprofessional, behaving like a layman and not being a proper practitioner-scientist.

So, the task of the practitioner-scientist is (1) the identification of behaviours, and perhaps (if trendy) cognitions and (if even more trendy) emotions which are problematic; (2) the identification of the antecedent and consequent events and other organismic variables which control those behaviours; (3) the rearrangement of such events to produce changes in behaviours, cognitions and emotions (suitably reified). In the case of SST, trainers are expected *qua* practitioner-scientist, to view their patients 'objectively' (ie uncontaminated by either their own or their patients' subjective experiencing), as a behaviourally and (now) cognitively dysfunctional organism (called problem identification), which needs to be modified (treatment goal). In practice, practitioners examine patients for these deficiencies (behavioural assessment), apply a treatment (SST) which is designed to institute the missing or deficient 'response component skills' and plug in new, functional cognitions.

While this is a different terminology from psychiatry, the basic underlying paradigms are the same. Behavioural approaches 'tend to be championed by those, such as social workers or clinical psychologists, who feel psychiatry's defects are basically due to the stranglehold of the medical profession,' argues Ingleby (1981, p.39). However, he adds, to adopt them is to 'jump from the frying pan into another frying pan – since they all adhere to the same paradigm of explanation as the medical model itself', and paradigms guide our clinical practice, as we have seen.

The problem lies in the very same adherence to a positivist model of science. One of the chief aims of such a 'science' is the eradication of subjective meaning and all that this entails. The entire spectrum of experience associated with woolly subjectivity, including ethics and politics, is disallowed. Indeed, as I have already intimated, the aspiration is for a value-free science which is amoral and apolitical, and there is, therefore, an ironic truth in the assertion that behaviour therapy and its sister disciplines strive to *de*value, *de*moralise and *de*humanize people into organisms. Organisms, of course, are much easier to deal with than suffering, protesting people, and we the 'professionals' and the institutions we work within, are much less exposed to ethical decisions and dilemmas.

THE EXPERIENCE OF SCIENTIFIC BEHAVIOUR THERAPY FOR THE CLIENT

ORDINARY EXPLANATIONS OF PROBLEMS

The ordinary lay person's accounts of daily life have two particular features of interest to us at this point. One is concerned with ordinary *explanations*, the study of which is attribution theory (Antaki, 1981). The second is concerned with people's *evaluations* of events.

Firstly, explanations. In the physical world it is a comparatively straightforward matter deciding on the identity of objects and their causal relations. However in the *social* world there is much more scope for disagreement, negotiation and change with regard to the identities of social objects and their causal relations. The most prominent 'objects' in society are people themselves, and the labels we use to identify such person-objects are personality terms like 'extrovert' and 'neurotic'. Having identified social 'objects', people as observers characteristically then attribute causal powers to those objects. For example in explaining the self-serving behaviour of an individual, we may say the individual is a psychopath – hence the behaviour is due to his psychopathic disposition. However, it is a well established tenet of attribution theory that there are two main causal explanations – 'internal' and 'external'. 'Internal' explanations refer to some disposition of the person, including attributes such as personality traits, ability, motivation etc., while 'external' refers to stimuli in the environment. There is a normal tendency for people to attribute behavioural events to dispositions in the case of others, but to situational causes in the case of oneself, though this is more the case with regard to bad behaviours, and the reverse may happen with regard to good behaviours, for example 'he's an asshole, I'm a victim of circumstances.' There are other important classes of attributions, in particular (1) the degree of stability of the behaviour across time and (2) its globality across situations.

Secondly, evaluations. Ordinary, everyday language is concerned not only with explanations but also gives a central focus to human *value*. A very important part of language use is 'gossip', preoccupied as it is with moral judgments about self and others – of right and wrong, indignation and scorn, shame and guilt. Name-calling and bad language are the richest vocabularies of moral judgment – people use four-letter words to describe others and themselves when moral condemnation is strongest. The study of this phenomenon is what Harré calls 'ethogenics' (Harré, 1979). It is about people, as agents, making choices, and through their choices trying to conduct their lives in ways which largely conform to rules of moral behaviour, and within such constraints, to seek their personal goals and those close to them.

People follow, or fail to follow rules, meet or fail to meet standards, and the performers or others can judge whether they performed correctly or not, or deviated from a norm or standard. The failure to conform to, or follow a rule, which specifies a norm or standard or exemplary practice, may be judged as substandard, a failure, deviant etc, ie it can be judged *evaluatively*. Such judgments are made against a background of tacit moral rules and assumptions for 'proper' conduct, such as responsibility, self-control, other-serving, and a host of social, cultural and family rights and duties (Goffman, 1963). It is vital to distinguish this as a uniquely human and social activity. While people and other objects in nature exhibit regularities, it is only people who can follow rules, while natural bodies are bound by, or determined by laws, and it makes no sense to evaluate whether they behave 'correctly' or not.

Failure to conform, breaking the rules or failing to meet required standards, invites actions of social censure, the form of which is also governed by meta-rules (Scheflen and Scheflen, 1972). Furthermore, individuals each have self-standards (more accurately, have internalized social/cultural/family standards) to which each aspires, and by which each monitors, evaluates and adjusts his or her performances (Carver and Scheier, 1984) in the process of self-presentation. Indeed Harré and others have argued that self-presentation is synonymous with the pursuit of a moral career, that is the continuing construction of a morally worthy person.

EXPLAINING AND EVALUATING COMBINED

If we put together the processes of explaining and evaluating, we can see more clearly the picture of ordinary accounts of psychological problems. Individuals observe behavioural events, decide on the most likely direction of cause (the person or the situation), and the type of cause. They then also evaluate the behaviour by comparison to a desired norm. For example, if someone shoplifts, a neighbour may attribute this, say, to a row at home (situational cause), judge it to be a one-off (unstable rather than stable) and specific to one situation (rather than global across situtations). They may then evaluate the act as bad (breaking a norm) but excusable (given further meta-rules for accountability) and not serious (because not stable and global). Of course a quite different account could be given, underlying the fact that people vary and often 'negotiate' by way of such mechanisms as gossip, the explanation and evaluation of actions.

HEALTHY AND UNHEALTHY ACCOUNTS

There are 'healthy' and 'unhealthy' ways of explaining and evaluating one's own and others' actions. One of the unhealthiest combinations is as follows: Have perfectionistic standards which you cannot reach, judge your action inevitably as a failure, attribute the cause to some major negative defect in your personality to create low self-esteem, make the attribution stable (namely a *permanent* characteristic) and global (namely it will affect *all* situations) to generate feelings of worthlessness, helplessness and hopelessness, or what Peterson *et al.* (1982) call, the depressive attributional style.

Alternatively, one of the 'healthiest' accounting styles is to have realistic standards for your ability level, accept responsibility for a failure, but refuse to make internal, stable and global attributions for it, ie refuse to generalize from a failed action to a *total* failure of self and thereby of worthlessness and uselessness (Ellis, 1962).

In summary, people not only make attributional inferences about events, but also make moral evaluations of them – that is make judgments about actions and the perceived initiators of the actions, as good or bad. Invariably these judgments are also turned upon the self as well as others.

'SCIENTIFIC' EXPLANATIONS OF PROBLEMS

At times people 'break down' in that their anxieties about probable failure or depression about actual failure (as perceived) lead them to judge themselves as morally worthless persons. Alternatively, esteem-threatening events lead them to self-protective aggression, which in turn leads to moral condemnation by self and others (Ellis, 1962). In both cases they are switching to the 'unhealthy' ways of accounting for events. What happens when such clients come in contact with the helping professions? Effective therapies should work against the 'unhealthy' set of assumptions and foster the second, 'healthy' set. However, behaviour therapy, as an applied science, may do the reverse to the extent that the therapist follows the paradigms of 'science'. Firstly, in so far as behaviour therapy is objective and value-free, they will persuade their clients that the entire language of values is inappropriate and unscientific. They are indoctrinated into giving up their ordinary understanding of what has happened and offered alternative 'scientific', objective accounts, which are the 'real' accounts of what happened and much more 'authoritative' than the ones the clients had hitherto believed. Part of this indoctrination process has been well described by Scheff (1975) and others. This is, in essence, a powerful process which would be hard to resist by the psychologically strongest individuals, whereas those already 'demoralised' are likely to succumb quickly.

What does this imply? In terms of SST, it can mean that clients must give up thinking of themselves as intentional agents with standards who pursue goals, whose actions can fail but who can make new attempts and improve their performances. Instead they are to think of themselves as organisms who through conditioning and other external causal processes are now deficient in social cognitive skills. Clients need to 'buy' the behaviourist philosophy before they will even take part in therapy (as pointed out to me by clinical psychologist Paul Gilbert). Therefore you have to sell them a philosophy of themselves before you can even start. This is demonstrated in one SST approach to depression which *tells* clients that low emission of positively reinforceable behaviour causes depression (Lewinsohn, 1974), and in the approach to agoraphobia which tells clients that the disorder is due to avoidance behaviour. What is the depressive and the agoraphobic to conclude about him or herself when they correct their behaviour but still do not recover?

In so far as this logic is consistently followed – and it is fortunately not consistently followed – the client cannot, as a passive recipient of malignant forces, be *blamed* in any way, but, on the other hand, cannot *do* anything (short of simple avoidance) but has to be acted upon by the 'helping' professionals. Here we have an example surely of the 'unhealthy' accounting referred to earlier, an example close to the depressive attributional style – internal (deficient organism), stable (permanent without external intervention) and global (general). Admittedly a behavioural account would appear to be an external attribution – to external contingencies – but this is a two-edged sword in that faulty conditioning *produces* a deficient organism, and it is the latter attribution people tend to make when distressed (Metalsky and Abramson, 1981).

THE INSIDIOUS SWITCH FROM AMORAL TO IMMORAL

I would argue (and this can be empirically tested) that there can be little true difference in the minds of clients between such terms as mentally ill, psychologically disturbed, behaviourally maladaptive, socially inadequate, socially deficient, socially phobic, psychotic, neurotic, or even simply mental or psychiatric patient. The arguments made so far would not have too much force, however, if such terms were truly amoral – as scientific behaviour therapy and psychiatry would have it. However, the evidence is overwhelming that such terms carry the worst of all social stigmas, and it is clear that the client pays an enormous price in becoming a patient – becoming a social reject, suffering a loss of normal rights and having a sense of worthlessness confirmed (eg Miles, 1981).

The literature on the stigma of metal illness is now extensive, particularly in America. Farina (1982) concludes at the end of his review that contemporary attitudes continue to be extremely unfavourable, just as they were in the past. The mentally disordered are held in very low regard by all segments of society and even mild problems in adjustment bring social rejection. They are refused jobs, they are not wanted as neighbours, and under some conditions are treated more harshly because of thier problems. Raimy (1975) surveyed a number of student samples and found that about 20 per cent of men and 30 per cent of women described experiencing fear of insanity. It is also one of the most prominent fears among psychiatric patients, such as agoraphobics (Last and Blanchard, 1982).

THE POWER OF THE ORGANISM APPROACH

The power of the organism approach can be described at the social level and at the individual level. Ingleby (1981) has made a challenging case that psychiatry, armed with the medical model, provides an alternative means of control of 'dissidents' in the population outside the police and criminal law system. Psychiatry, which has served the purpose so well by turning protest into pathology, by *de*moralizing the victims of *im*moral circumstances, is extending rather than retreating, by what Ingleby calls the 'psychiatrization' of the whole population. What this means is that mental 'illness', like physical 'illness', 'can occupy segments of everbody's minds.' This means everyone is vulnerable to having their rights limited and their *validity* as citizens suspended by a simple diagnosis.

CONCLUSION

In this chapter I have argued that scientific behaviour therapy shares the same paradigms and is in danger of serving the same purposes as medical psychiatry, operating as it does from largely the same institutional set-up. If this is true, then it has more sinister implications about the purposes of 'therapy'.

I have emphasized the power of the organism approach at the individual level. I have argued that scientific behaviour therapy seeks to persuade clients that they are deficient organisms rather than fallible agents, and therefore in addition to implying helplessness and hopelessness, also implies valuelessness or badness. Negative self-evaluation and passivity characterize many, if not the majority of mental health clients. In other words, clients think and behave like passive organisms – and this is precisely the problem. The solution lies in the direction of helping people recover or discover their agency. The criticism of scientific behaviour therapy is that along with medical psychiatry, it tends to work against this objective, by encouraging clients, relatives, friends and the helping professionals alike, to think of clients in terms of passive, deficient, helpless organisms.

I have described fully a conception of an alternative agency approach elsewhere (Trower, 1984). The approach outlined there views man as a rational (and sometimes irrational) agent who chooses means to try to satisfy personal ends, is active rather than passive in seeking out and processing information, and generates, monitors and controls his actions. Therapy is aimed at helping a person restore his agency, particularly through changing self-defeating cognitions. In this chapter I have tried to make the case for a commitment from behaviour therapy practitioners to reject the organism approach and endorse the agency approach, together with its underlying assumptions. The agency approach is the cornerstone of a truly cognitive 'revolution'. Self-efficacy (Bandura, 1977), self-acceptance (Ellis, 1962) and similar core constructs in cognitive therapy, are *dependent* on helping clients to recover or discover their agency.

REFERENCES

Agras, W.S., Kazdin, A.E. and Wilson, G.T. (1979), *Behaviour therapy: Toward an applied clinical science*, San Francisco, W.H. Freeman.

Antaki, C. (1981), *The psychology of ordinary explanations of social behaviour*, London, Academic Press.

Baer, D.M. (1982), 'Applied behaviour analysis', in G.T. Wilson and C.M. Franks (eds), *Contemporary behaviour therapy*, New York, Guilford.

Bandura, A. (1977), *Social learning theory*, Englewood Cliffs, New Jersey, Prentice Hall.

Bellack, A.S. Hersen, M. and Kazdin, A.E. (1982), *International handbook of behaviour modification and therapy*, New York, Plenum.

Carver, C.S. and Scheier, M.F. (1984), 'A control-theory approach to behaviour, and some implications for social skills training', in P. Trower (ed.), *Radical approaches to social skills training*, London, Croom Helm.

Coyne, J.C. (1982), 'A critique of cognitions as causal entities with particular reference to depression', *Cognitive Therapy and Research*, 6, pp.3–14.

Douglas, J.D. (1977), 'Existential sociology', in J.D. Douglas and J.M. Johnson (eds), *Existential sociology*, Cambridge, Cambridge University Press.

Ellis, A. (1962), *Reason and emotion in psychotherapy*, New York, Lyle Stuart.

Farina, A. (1982), 'The stigma of mental disorders', in A.G. Miller (ed.), *In the eye of the beholder*, New York, Praeger.

Franks, C.M. Wilson, G.T., Kendall, P.C. and Brownell, K.D. (1982), *Annual review of behaviour therapy*, vol.8, New York, Guilford.

Goffman, E. (1963), *Behaviour in public places*, Glencoe, Illinois, Free Press.

Harré, R. and Secord, P.F. (1972), *The explanation of social behaviour*, Oxford, Blackwell.

Harré, R. (1979), *Social being*, Oxford, Blackwell.

Ingleby, D. (1981), 'Understanding "mental illness" ', in D. Ingleby (ed.), *Critical psychiatry: The politics of mental health*, Harmondsworth, Penguin.

Last, C.G. and Blanchard, E.B. (1982), 'Classification of phobics versus fearful non-phobics: Procedural and theroretical issues', *Behavioural Assessment,* 4, pp.195–210.

Latimer, P.R. and Sweet, A.A., (1984), 'Cognitive versus behavioural procedures in cognitive-behaviour therapy: A critical review of the evidence', *Journal of Behaviour Therapy and Experimental Psychiatry,* 15, pp.9–22.

Levis, D.J. (1982), 'Experimental and theoretical foundations of behaviour modification', in A.S. Bellack, M. Hersen and A.E. Kazdin (eds), *International handbook of behaviour modification*, New York, Plenum.

Lewinsohn, P.M. (1974), 'A behavioural approach to depression', in R.M. Friedman and M.M. Katz (eds). *The psychology of depression: Contemporary theory and research*, Washington, DC, Winston-Wiley.

Liotti, G. and Reda, M. (1981), 'Some epistemological remarks on behaviour therapy, cognitive therapy and psychoanalysis', *Cognitive Therapy and Research,* 5, pp.231–6.

McCulloch, G., Personal communication.

Mahoney, M.J. (1974), *Cognition and behaviour modification*, Cambridge, Massachusetts, Ballinger.

Mahoney, M.J. (1984), 'Behaviourism, cognitivism, and human change processes', in M.A. Reda and M.J. Mahoney (eds), *Cognitive psychotherapies: Recent developments in theory, research and practice*, Cambridge, Massachussetts, Ballinger.

Metalsky, G.I. and Abramson, L.Y. (1981), 'Attributional styles: 'Towards a framework for conceptualisation and assessment', in P.C. Kendall and S.D. Hollon (eds), *Assessment strategies for cognitive-behavioural interventions*, New York, Academic Press.

Miles, A. (1981), *The mentally ill in contemporary society*, Oxford, Martin Robertson.

Mischel, W. (1973), 'Toward a cognitive social learning reconceptualization of personality', *Psychological Review,* 80, pp.252–83.

Peterson, C. Semmel, A., von Bayer, C., Abramson, L.Y., Metalsky, G.I., and Seligman, M.E.P. (1982), 'The attributional style questionaire', *Cognitive Therapy and Research,* 6, pp.287–300.

Raimy, V. (1975), *Misunderstandings of the self*, San Francisco, Jossey-Bass.

Scheff, T.J. (1975), *Labeling madness*, Englewood Cliffs, New Jersey, Prentice Hall.

Scheflen, A.E. and Scheflen, A. (1972), *Body language and the social order*, Englewood Cliffs, New Jersey, Prentice Hall.

Schwartz, R.M. (1982), 'Cognitive behaviour modification: A conceptual review', *Clinical Psychology Review,* 2, pp.267–94.

Searle, J. (1983), *Intentionality: An Essay in the Philosophy of Mind*, Cambridge, Cambridge University Press.

Smail, D.J. (1978), *Psychotherapy: A personal approach*, London, Dent.
Szasz, T.S. (1961), *The myth of mental illness*, New York, Hoeber-Harper.
Trower, P. (ed.) (1984), *Radical approaches to social skills training*, London, Croom Helm.
Wilson, G.T. (1978), 'Cognitive behavior therapy: Paradigm shift or passing phase?', in J. Foreyt and D. Rathjen (eds), *Cognitive behaviour therapy: Research and application*, New York, Plenum.

Radical Behaviourism and the Ethics of Clinical Psychology

Glynn Owens

INTRODUCTION

It is unfortunate that for many people behaviourism is still equated with the rather crude statements of intent made by J.B. Watson shortly before World War I (see eg Watson, 1913). Watson's original concept of behaviourism may be seen as largely consisting of a methodological strategy for the conduct of psychological investigations. Only those phenomena which could be independently observed were to be acceptable as subject matter for psychology. Unobservable entities such as dreams, thoughts, feelings and so forth were not in themselves observable and could not therefore be accepted into the domain of psychology.

Whilst Watson's own research contribution was rather limited, his manifesto gave rise to a number of schools of psychology, with the research of Clark Hull (eg Hull, 1943) in particular gaining considerable influence around the middle of the century. Eventually however it became clear that stimulus-response (S-R) psychologies such as Hull's were unworkable and such approaches fell into disfavour. From this it is possible to discern two particular consequences. One was the wholehearted rejection of behaviourism in any form: behaviourism was seen to have failed and a return to the old cognitive approach seen as unavoidable.

An alternative conclusion held that S-R psychology had failed not because it was too behavioural but because it was not behavioural *enough*. Rather than accept defeat with respect to such unobservable phenomena as thoughts, emotions etc., why not approach the study in the light of the lessons learned in the behavioural laboratory? Whilst Hull had been developing his S-R psychology, B.F. Skinner at Harvard had been systematically working at the foundations of a new, radical form of behaviourism, which aimed to apply the conclusions of the behavioural research to the whole of human experience. The demise of S-R psychology left the way open for Skinner's aggressive new approach, and over a relatively short period many psychologists adopted the new paradigm, variously known as Skinnerian psychology, operant psychology, the Experimental Analysis of Behaviour or radical behaviourism.

METHODOLOGICAL AND RADICAL BEHAVIOURISM

To many people the impact of radical behaviourism in psychology is nothing short of revolution. Platt (1973) for example has compared the impact of Skinner in psychology with that of Einstein in physics or Darwin in biology. To attempt an exhaustive list of the differences between radical and methodological behaviourism would thus be futile. It is, however, instructive to consider some of the major distinguishing features.

Perhaps the most obvious difference between methodological and radical behaviourists concerns what the latter have referred to as 'private events'. Events which take place within the skin of the individual, and to which only that individual has access, were deemed unacceptable as subjects for methodological behaviourism's consideration. No matter how interesting such topics might be, they were unfortunately incapable of being scientifically investigated. By contrast the radical behaviourist may regard such phenomena as 'the heart of a science of behaviour' (Skinner, 1969). In consequence a good deal of theorising within radical behaviourism has been concerned with the status of such unobservables. Skinner (1969) for example has provided accounts of such activities as perceiving, problem solving, and so on in terms of processes which can themselves be easily demonstrated in the laboratory. At an empirical level, too, researchers have demonstrated directly the processes involved in such phenomena as 'attending' (Terrace, 1966), dark adaptation (Blough, 1958) and self-control (Redd *et al.*, 1974). Each of these (and similar demonstrations in the literature) has been conducted with non-human subjects, illustrating clearly the way in which such phenomena can be investigated without recourse to the use of hypothetical internal constructs as attempts at explanation. That is to say, radical behaviourism provides accounts of private events, but in terms of phenomena and processes which are themselves directly observable.

A less obvious, but nevertheless crucial feature of radical behaviourism is its emphasis on a functional, rather than a topographical or operational approach. In practice this means that the role of particular variables in an analysis is specified by their effects, not by their form or by an investigator's preconceptions. Thus an event may function as a reinforcer even though it would, by its form, appear unpleasant; similarly an event may not reinforce some particular behaviour despite an investigator's preconception that such an event would have reinforcing properties. In practice it has been found that seemingly aversive events may have reinforcing properties, and that events which one may expect to have reinforcing effects (eg interpersonal attention) may not always do so. In this sense a radical behavioural approach may be seen as paralleling a phenomenological approach, with variables being defined in terms of their effect on the individual (or, putting it another way, their 'meaning' for that individual).

Perhaps the most distinctive feature of radical behaviourism, however, is its explicit recognition of the role of the environment in the determination of behaviour. In particular it is recognised that quite different environmental factors may be implicated in the origins and later in the subsequent maintenance of a problem. In this it differs from many traditional approaches to psychotherapy which emphasise the role of the past in the development of problems but neglect the maintaining role of the present environment, or certain behavioural approaches which do the opposite.

The emphasis on the concept of reinforcement leads to a distinction between radical and methodological behaviourism which is of crucial importance in the consideration of ethical issues. The break with S-R psychology has led to a marked change in the perspective of the radical behaviourist. In particular the notion of operant behaviour, behaviour primarily under reinforcement control, is almost if not totally equivalent to a traditional notion of voluntary behaviour. Watching an operant conditioning experiment will typically reveal nothing which could be seen as coercive.

The pigeon which pecks at a disc on the wall 'chooses' to do so. If it so wished it could spend its time preening itself, cooing or simply doing nothing. Instead, out of all the options open to it, it decides to peck at the key on the wall. Yet although this is voluntary behaviour on the part of the pigeon, its choosing to do so can be predicted with considerable accuracy. No stimulus may be presented to prompt the subject, and even when such a stimulus is present its role will typically be markedly different from that in Pavlovian or S-R paradigms. At all times it is possible to claim that the experimental subject is acting under free choice; yet the outcome of the free choice can be reliably predicted.

A consequence of such demonstrations has been that the radical behaviourist typically has no equivalent to the concept of 'free will'. In common with many other approaches in psychology (eg the strict Freudian), the radical behaviourist adopts a position of strict determinism. Going further than traditional approaches, however, explicit consideration is given to the fact that people typically experience the feeling of acting freely. Skinner (1971) has equated the feeling of making a free choice with behaving under the control of positive reinforcers, that is to say events whose presentation is reinforcing. By contrast the feeling of acting under coercion is associated with behaviour under the control of negative reinforcers, that is to say events whose removal is reinforcing. Thus the person who hands over money in order to purchase an object will typically feel that a free choice has been made; the same person handing over money in order to remove the threat of being shot by an armed robber will typically feel coerced. The behaviour is the same in both circumstances; the change in experience is a direct function of the differing contingencies.

It is appropriate to consider at this stage why the individual should experience different sensations as a function of the different contingencies of reinforcement. It is taken as axiomatic that the different sensations people report reflect different bodily states. From an evolutionary viewpoint it is clearly advantageous to react differently to each type of contingency. In particular it is characteristic of negative reinforcers that reinforcement will occur either if the specified behaviour occurs *or* if the individual can escape from the contingencies. Positive reinforcers, by contrast, require the occurrence of the behaviour; leaving the contingencies has quite different consequences and leads to non-reinforcement. Thus under conditions of negative reinforcement it is clearly advantageous for the body to react in such a way as to facilitate escape, whilst under conditions of positive reinforcement there is no need for such a reaction. These differences in bodily state are identified by the individual and associated with particular feelings, including feelings of freedom and coercion. From the viewpoint of an observer, however, behaviour under either condition can be seen to be a function of the relevant contingencies.

For a number of reasons such issues come to be of particular importance with the extension of radical behaviourism to the solution of applied problems in such settings as clinical psychology. Early applications of radical behaviourism consisted of little more than demonstrations that the same principles could be applied to clinical subjects. Thus Fuller (1949) demonstrated that the process of operant conditioning could produce learning of a simple response in a patient previously assumed to be incapable of learning. The technology soon spread to other problems, however, proving to be of considerable value where other procedures were inapplicable. With the severely mentally handicapped, for example, a number of self-care skills could be taught despite such problems as language difficulties which precluded traditional teaching methods.

More recently the use of these simple techniques has evolved into a more general strategy for the analysis and solution of clinical problems. In particular the procedures of functional analysis (including the identification of relevant variables and their relationship to each other and the problem) have been applied to problems presented by those who would normally fall within the province of traditional psychotherapy (Owens and Ashcroft, 1982; Foster, Owens and Newton, 1985).

The particular effectiveness of radical behaviourism has led, paradoxically, to a high degree of concern with ethical issues. The realisation that not only is the control of human behaviour possible, but that it is possible without disturbing the individual's feeling of acting freely has given rise to considerable concern. Peck (1979) in a rough comparison of clinical psychology textbooks found a significantly greater discussion of ethical issues in those written from a radical behaviourist perspective. As with any discussion of ethical problems, the result has often been the production of as many questions as answers. Radical behaviourism's distinct paradigm has led, as Kuhn (1962) would predict, to a marked shift in emphasis, with questions raised by traditional analyses seen often to be meaningless, and with new, quite distinct questions arising from a change of viewpoint.

ETHICAL ISSUES I: SPECIFIC TECHNIQUES

Ethical issues concerning the use of radical behaviourism in clinical psychology involve both specific issues relating to individual procedures and more general issues concerning the wider problems involved in most psychotherapeutic procedures but highlighted from a behavioural viewpoint. There is an increasing extension of a radical behaviourist approach from the application of simple techniques to its more general use in a full functional analysis of clinical problems, ie an analysis of the interrelationships between clinical problems and the various factors of which they are a function. However, there is no doubt that specific techniques will continue to be used for a considerable time. Before discussing the broader issues, therefore, it is appropriate to take a brief look at some of the ethical problems of the specific techniques, usually considered under the problems of punishment and deprivation.

PUNISHMENT

The detailed study of the effects of punishment by workers within the Experimental Analysis of Behaviour has, in general, led to a rather critical view of its value. Most workers regard punishment as being at best a technique whose effectiveness is of limited value and highly sensitive to the detailed parameters of the programme. Some regard the whole use of punishment as questionable on both ethical and practical grounds (eg Skinner, 1953). Punishment may be considered ethically unjustifiable, for example, on the grounds that there are other non-punitive and more humane ways to control behaviour.

From a practical viewpoint punishment is seen by many to be of limited effectiveness. In particular, laboratory studies have suggested that punishment may have only a temporary suppressive effect, that it may be of limited value if intermittent, and that it may be associated by the subject more with the conditions under which it occurs (setting, presence of others, etc.) than with the behaviour (Estes, 1944; Skinner, 1938). Nevertheless there have been a number of reports which suggest a value for punishment in certain extreme cases. Lovaas, Shaeffer and Simmonds (1965) for example reported the use of electric shock to eliminate severe self-injurious behaviour. One client had bitten her fingers so badly that amputation was necessary; another had chewed the flesh from the shoulder exposing the bone. The use of shock permitted the elimination of such self-injurious behaviour with no recurrence at three-year follow-up.

Few people are particularly critical of the use of punishment when such extreme benefit can be shown and where the cost of failing to punish is so high. When, however, punishment is used with less severe problems, there is inevitably some disquiet. A major problem seems to result from the fact that the use of punishment generally provides considerable reinforcement to the user. The risk therefore is that punishment will be used when not essential, simply because it produces a quick, cheap and easy alternative to more humane procedures.

In an attempt to regulate such procedures various authors have produced ethical guidelines. Such attempts however have generally been naive and unsatisfactory. One such set of guidelines, later to become known as the *Minnesota Guidelines* was published in 1968 following a workshop involving concerned professionals (Lucero, Vail and Scherber, 1968). Like many similar attempts these contain many errors of fact, inconsistencies and impracticalities. With respect to punishment, which the authors describe erroneously as 'aversive reinforcement', it was suggested that it should never be used in a general programme, and only in individual programmes involving physical abuse of the self or others. The use of such a programme, it was decided, should be cleared with the medical director of the Medical Services Division. Yet such guidelines are clearly unworkable. Punishment is a part of everyday activity, from the punishment implicit in society's explicit rules (eg the punishment of crime) to the punishment which is part of our everyday interactions (eg complaining if someone does something which annoys us). Even to attempt to eliminate these aspects from programmes could mean the client being inadequately prepared for the world at large. The situation is further confounded by the fact that events may have both reinforcing and punishing effects simultaneously. The presentation of food on a fixed interval schedule, for example, appears both to reinforce and punish the behaviour on which it is contingent. Finally of course it is clear that in evaluating such programmes the medical profession has no special status. Most members of the medical profession receive little if any specific training regarding the psychological effects of punishment. Nor, moreover, do they usually receive any substantial training in ethical issues generally.

Rather more productive forms of control have been proposed by those actually involved in the administration of relevant programmes. Miron (1968) for example notes the use of a rule whereby therapists, using electric shock procedures, must first try the shock on themselves. It is easy to envisage this being established in such a way that the administrator of the shock was 'yoked' to the client in such a way that each shock was delivered to both client and therapist. Such a procedure constitutes an example of the 'countercontrol', discussed later in this chapter, which radical behaviourists have proposed as a safeguard against exploitation. Whilst the provision of similar countercontrol for other forms of punishment may be administratively difficult, it is likely that in many cases some similar form of countercontrol could be devised.

DEPRIVATION

In the design of operant conditioning programmes it is clear that the use of certain reinforcers requires the occurrence of a period of deprivation. Thus food will normally have little reinforcing effect on an individual who has just eaten a hearty meal. The use of deprivation procedures as part of a therapeutic programme, with the intent of enhancing the value of a reinforcer like food, has been condemned in various ethical statements; in the *Minnesota Guidelines*, for example, the authors stated simply that 'Deprivation is never to be used'. Such a rule appears to have been introduced with the aim of ensuring that patients were not deprived of their ordinary rights. Yet this again raises problems. Not only is it difficult to decide what constitutes the 'ordinary rights' of which a person is not to be deprived (is access to a TV set an 'ordinary right'?), but the issue misses the point of operant conditioning programmes. As Cahoon (1968) points out, for operant conditioning to be effective, the individual involved must receive the reinforcers; if reinforcement is not delivered, it cannot have an effect. In a well designed operant conditioning programme, the client concerned will receive a high level of reinforcement, often higher than that which applied prior to the programme. All that has changed has been the scheduling and the contingency. In many cases it is indeed possible to monitor the client's access to specific reinforcers before and during a programme, and to adjust the programme in such a way as to ensure no overall loss.

A conceptual problem with the notion of deprivation has been raised by Miron (1968) to the effect that to ban certain treatments, because they involve deprivation, may itself deprive the client of effective rehabilitation. If the deprivation system is the only way to produce effective reinforcement and a successful return to society, how much is the client deprived if the technique is banned?

Finally it should be noted that, as with the punishment guidelines, such recommendations on deprivation will often be impractical. Social reinforcement, for example, is often powerful on a hospital ward. If I sit in my office writing a report, I may well be depriving a client of the social reinforcement provided by my attention. If later I go to see this client, my attention may be all the more reinforcing. Whether or not my 'depriving' of the client is an act of deliberate policy (eg when I feel it would be better for the client to manage alone) or whether it simply reflects the fact that there are other demands on my time, it could still be seen as deprivation. Yet few would suggest that all professionals involved with clients should be available to them at all times.

ETHICAL ISSUES 2: GENERAL ISSUES

The therapeutic application of radical behaviourism, however, involves ethical issues which extend way beyond those of simple techniques. The whole perspective raises more general issues involved not only in the use of radical behaviourism as part of the functional analysis of behaviour but also in the application of other forms of psychotherapy. Two major issues in particular are involved in most ethical discussions in this area. These are the problems of free will and reinforcement. Each of these gives rise to difficulties at what may be termed micro and macro levels, the former referring to the specific problems of individual consultations and the latter to the larger societal context of such work.

FREE WILL

The problem of 'free will' is, as mentioned earlier, not specific to radical behaviourism but is shared by other deterministic approaches in psychology such as the classical Freudian model. The problem is, however, intensified in the context of radical behaviourism's analysis of the feeling of freedom and its recognition of the role of reinforcement in determining 'voluntary' behaviour. The notion that people's behaviour may be subject to manipulation without their feeling controlled conjures up images of brainwashing and dictatorial control against which most individuals will intuitively react. As a result a radical behaviourist approach has been subject to considerable criticism as providing a possible technology by which a society of obedient, acquiescent citizens would be produced. Suggestions that a better, happier society could be produced through the systematic application of radical behaviourist principles have been greeted with horror and the fear that this involves placing trust in the hands of unknown controllers. At the heart of the fear is the feeling that human freedom is under threat, and that unless humanity resists such an approach all human freedom will be lost.

Perhaps the first point to note about such objections is that they implicitly accept the reality of a radical behaviourist analysis; any suggestion that the approach was impractical would also imply that the threat was merely illusory. At times critics appear a trifle confused in this respect. Chomsky (1972), for example, exhorts his readers to resist the behavioural approach, whilst at the same time arguing that it provides only a hopelessly inadequate account of human functioning. Such an argument is either inconsistent or presupposes a remarkably disparaging view of humanity, such that the human race would be capable of sinking to a level where a hopelessly inadequate account eventually became sufficient.

In most cases, however, the fear is real that a radical behaviourist account does adequately represent human functioning, and that a number of ethical issues are thus critical; for those who believe that the account is inadequate the whole affair can be seen as misguided and the ethical issues are no greater than those of any other spurious science like phrenology or astrology. The following discussion of ethical issues will therefore assume the veracity of the account, and confine itself to the problems which arise from such an assumption. As mentioned earlier, these problems can be seen at both micro and macro levels.

PROBLEMS AT THE MICRO LEVEL

Perhaps the most obvious problem at the level of individual consultations stems from the loss of the concept of free will. Traditional therapies can often avoid confronting many ethical problems by resorting to the notion of free will. If a client 'freely' chooses therapy then the client can take responsibility for any ethical problems. Of course in traditional therapies such an approach is often accepted as having limitations. Numerous occasions arise where a decision may appear to be free but where even from a traditional viewpoint the notion of free will is questionable. Such problems usually revolve around the client's inability to make a choice either because of limitations in knowledge or from the operation of covert constraints or hidden pressures.

The former problem has been long recognised in law where it is accepted that certain groups of idividuals are not capable of making important decisions for themselves. The most obvious examples are those of children, the psychotic and the mentally handicapped who, it is argued, are not at the time sufficiently well informed to take decisions in their own best long-term interests. More recently it has been recognised that such procedures as signing consent forms for potentially dangerous operations may raise similar problems, the patient not having adequate knowledge to judge the wisdom of a decision. As a result the notion of informed consent has become popular, with professionals carrying a responsibility not only to request consent but also to provide information on which to base the decision.

The problem of hidden pressures has also proved particularly acute in a forensic setting, where a convicted sex offender may, for example, 'choose' to undergo potentially dangerous medical treatment (eg the use of hormone implants) in order to improve the chances of obtaining a light or non-custodial sentence. Civil libertarians have been quick to point out that this is tantamount to saying 'if you don't agree you will be put in prison', an arrangement which many would see as clearly coercive, although even here not all people are willing to reject the notion that the individual is making a free choice.

From a radical behaviourist perspective, however, such problems represent only the tip of the iceberg in discussing problems of free choice and consent. When all choice is seen to be a function of particular determinants, the notion of free choice becomes problematic. To discuss such issues without specifying the reinforcement contingencies involved may, it is argued, be totally meaningless. At its simplest level, if I know an individual's preferences, then I can predict that individual's behaviour when confronted with a choice between these preferences. If, in addition, I can control the preferences with which the individual is confronted, then I can control the individual's behaviour. Thus to require that a client consent to a procedure may be meaningless; if I am presenting the client with alternatives I should be able to arrange them in such a way that I can obtain the necessary consent. The control of human behaviour also permits the control of signing consent forms.

The problem cannot be solved by simply deciding not to be a radical behaviourist, as the problem is not exclusive to radical behaviourism, only its recognition. To decide to opt out is simply to return control of the client's behaviour to the existing contingencies; whether we like it or not, the behaviour is already controlled.

The problem is also involved in such issues as the maintenance of therapy. Where the traditional therapist may see a client's withdrawal as an expression of free choice, and purely the client's responsibility, the radical behaviourist is forced to accept at least a part of the responsibility. If, for example, participation in therapy was inadequately reinforced it would be unsurprising that the client dropped out. Yet undoubtedly a major reinforcer in much therapy is the making of progress. If insufficient progress is made, is not the therapist at least partly responsible? It is no excuse to claim that progress is the client's responsibility. The client approaches the therapist for help in changing, and for change to occur the therapist has to be skilled in matching the help given to the nature of the problem. If the client chooses prematurely to drop out of therapy, therefore, this can be seen as a failing of the therapist rather than an expression of free choice, since participation in therapy, whilst not an end in itself, is at least a precondition of the therapist being of value.

None of this of course should be taken as implying that there is no need for traditional consent procedures. Rather it implies that such procedures are at least minimally required. Additionally it is clear that therapists cannot afford to be smug in this respect; whilst such procedures may be essential, this does not necessarily mean they are adequate. For the client to make a meaningful choice it is necessary that only those factors relevant to the choice be allowed to operate. Of particular importance here is the functional significance of relevant variables. Whether or not, for example, a therapist explicitly offers total confidentiality may be less important than whether such confidentiality is assumed by the client. A similar problem may arise regarding a client's assumptions regarding the therapist's expertise. If the client believes that the therapist must know best, it may be necessary to correct this impression before giving any recommendation to the client. At a more detailed level a therapeutic consultation may need to allocate a considerable amount of time to the indicating of possible functional links between different factors and the client's behaviour. If these variables do in fact exert some control over the client, the problem is not solved by ignoring the relationships; rather a meaningful concept of freedom will involve the client's recognition of these relationships in order that a reciprocal control be established. That is to say the client does not deny the influence of the variables on behaviour but rather by appreciating their influence is able to obtain a meaningful self control by taking control of the variables themselves in such a way as to produce the desired result.

The outcome of such an enterprise is the conduct of therapy as a collaborative enterprise between client and therapist. For such collaboration to be effective each must share similar goals; when (as often happens) it becomes necessary to change these, such changes must result from negotiation by both parties. The task then becomes a joint problem-solving task between the therapist and the client. Each will have particular areas of expertise and typically each will rely on the other's expertise in specific areas. For example the therapist will normally have a great deal of expertise regarding the psychological processes involved in a problem, the practicality of different interventions, and the viability of different forms of evaluation (both of the problem and of the outcome of therapy). The client on the other hand will have considerable expertise regarding the context of the problem (in terms of both aetiology and maintenance), will be the final arbiter of the desirability of possible outcomes of therapy and will usually be a competent judge of whether hypothesised relationships between different factors and the problem are in fact plausible. Therapy can then be seen as a pooling of resources on the part of the client and therapist concerned. The client provides information about the problem, with the therapist often providing a guide as to what may be most relevant. Typically a therapist will attempt to identify the important relationships between relevant variables and the problems presented. The sum total of such interrelationships constitutes a model of the problem, usually designated a tentative formulation. Such a tentative formulation will often have a number of loose ends or uncertainties which can be clarified by obtaining further information (eg by additional discussion with the client). The aim at this stage is to provide a formulation which is at the same time consistent both with the therapist's knowledge of behavioural principles and the client's personal experience. In practice such a formulation is usually easy (too easy) to obtain, and there will be a number of similarly plausible accounts capable of providing an adequate explanation. The adequacy of any one account can, however, be assessed directly by designing an appropriate intervention. Hypotheses regarding the influence of different factors on the problem also constitute hypotheses regarding the outcome of manipulation of these factors. Thus if a spouse's behaviour is hypothesised to have a reinforcing effect on a problem behaviour, it is a straightforward matter to predict the outcome of a change in this contingency. If the outcome turns out as predicted all is well; if not this provides further information which helps the client-therapist team choose between different formulations.

In general the aims of therapy in this context will include providing clients with sufficient understanding of their own behaviour to permit them to take control of the necessary variables and thus obtain a real freedom, rather than the illusory freedom implicit in pretending that the control is not there. If certain variables are controlling behaviour but the client fails to recognise them, the control will continue without the client being part of that control. If, however, the role of such variables is acknowledged and recognised, the client is able to directly influence them so that a system of reciprocal control is established between the individual and the variables which control behaviour. By the conclusion of therapy the client should have at least a knowledge of what variables affect the problem and how they do so. Often some knowledge of the general psychological principles involved will also have been acquired. A successful client will thus take on the expertise of the therapist regarding the problem in question; as a result the therapist becomes redundant and clients are able to conduct their own therapy. Usually such learning will be gradual. In the treatment of a dental patient for a problematic gagging reflex, for example, the early stages of therapy were dictated almost entirely by the therapist. Towards the end of therapy, however, a consultation consisted of little more than the client calling in for five or ten minutes every few weeks to outline his plans for the coming few weeks, to ask the therapist's opinion and obtain reassurance (Foster, Owens and Newton, 1985). Such teaching of clients to become therapists not only has the advantage of their learning useful and lasting skills; the involvement of the client at all stages of therapy in the decision-making increases the chances of an effective formulation. A functional analysis of a clinical problem can usually be explained without recourse to highly technical language, and once such an explanation has been given the client will usually be able to provide critical feedback, correcting and amending the therapist's formulation. On the occasions where therapist and client disagree on the relevance or role of some particular variable this will either have implications for therapeutic outcome, in which case the disagreement will be decided by the effectiveness or otherwise of the intervention, or there will be no therapeutic implications in which case the disagreement is of little practical importance.

If therapy is conceived of, and organised as a joint problem-solving venture between therapist and client such issues as 'free choice' may be of less obvious relevance. Such an approach does, however, place stringent demands on the integrity of the therapist. It is not, in practice, possible for the objectives of both therapist and client to be exactly identical. In particular most therapists will have objectives of their own which may be of minimal concern to the client. These may include maintaining a good reputation amongst professional colleagues, adequate career development, earning a living, allocating time fairly to various clients and so forth. However, whilst these objectives will not usually be shared by the client, they will rarely conflict with the shared objectives. Much more problematic is the situation where therapist objectives and client objectives are in conflict. For example, in a survey of the sexual exploitation of clients by US clinical psychologists, Holroyd and Brodsky (1977) found that 5.2 per cent of male clinicians had experienced sexual intercourse with a client; such contact was often at a time when the emotional needs of the therapist, rather than the client, were unusually great, suggesting that such interactions were often largely for the therapist's, rather then the client's benefit. From a radical behaviourist viewpoint it is hard to see such interaction as anything but exploitative. Because of the way therapy operates there is inevitably a period during the pooling of expertise when the client entrusts to the therapist a considerable amount of personal information. In such a situation a therapist is in a highly powerful position, possessing both the general knowledge and the specific information necessary for behavioural control with that particular client. Moreover the therapist is likely to be seen by the client as a potentially powerful source of reinforcement, again placing the therapist in a potentially powerful position. Similar problems will of course arise in a number of other contexts, for example between students and teachers. Such abuse of power obviously needs to be guarded against, with existing precautions apparently failing to provide total protection. From a traditional viewpoint the solution might be seen in purely elitist terms. If such abuse is possible, it could be argued, only those of the highest personal integrity should be admitted to such positions. Such an approach is clearly impractical, since even if integrity were an intrinsic characteristic of certain individuals, we should have no means of assessing this. More importantly, however, from a radical behaviourist perspective, such an analysis begs the question of why certain individuals should be of high integrity and others not. By contrast radical behaviourism, like Marxism, looks outside the individual to the societal context of the behaviour, asking what kinds of environment produce behaviour seen as exemplifying integrity. That is to say, if certain individuals are of 'high integrity' or 'extremely trustworthy' we still need to explain why they are so.

From a radical behaviourist perspective the answers are to be sought in the present and past environments of such individuals.

In considering this issue a central concept has been that which Skinner (1971) has termed 'countercontrol'. Exploitation and abuse, Skinner points out, are most common when the victims of the control are not in a position to exert similar control over their exploiters. Thus victims of abuse and exploitation include the elderly, children, prisoners, the psychotic and other groups whose control over their exploiters is minimal or non-existent. To such a list might be added those whose countercontrol is weak; the poor, the unemployed and so forth. Abuse here is rarely as extreme as in the cases first mentioned, since some degree of countercontrol is apparent, yet the countercontrol is so weak that much abuse of a lesser degree can go unchecked. In this context it can be seen that the issue of reinforcement is central to a behavioural analysis of exploitation. According to the analysis, those who control the reinforcers will be likely, unless countercontrol is established, to exploit those who do not. The analysis of course directly parallels that of Marx, except that where Marx spoke of access to the means of production resulting in exploitation, a radical behaviourist extends this to all forms of reinforcement.

In terms of therapy such an analysis carries a number of implications. Firtly therapy should be conducted in such a way as to minimise the imbalance of power between therapist and client; professional bodies should be willing to investigate claims of abuse by clients and be in a position to control the actions of their members. Implicit in this is that those in such positions should be required to subscribe to an explicit and public code of conduct. Therapists should be subject to strict external control of their activities.

At present within the United Kingdom the central professional body of clinical psychologists exerts strict control over standards of qualification permitting employment in the National Health Service, such control having the backing of the relevant Government body (the Whitley councils). However, no specific legal control can as yet be applied to clinical psychologists once qualified except where such criminal offences as misrepresentation or criminal negligence are apparent. Possibly the attempts to establish a charter or legal register of psychologists will go some way towards providing such countercontrol.

A second implication is that, as far as possible, therapists and clients should be subject to similar contingencies, at least as far as the presenting problems are concerned. At its simplest level this implies that each should stand to gain from the successful outcome of therapy. In most cases this will apply automatically, since seeing a client improve will itself serve to reinforce a therapist's behaviour. In some circumstances, however, the contingencies may be significantly different. At various times it has been suggested that groups like dentists, surgeons and others who are paid for specific procedures rather than by results may tend to opt for more expensive, but not necessarily better treatments, simply to inflate the final bill. Thus in the UK there have been suggestions of dentists treating healthy teeth, and in the US of Caesarian deliveries being more common than necessary.

Within the framework of radical behaviourism a number of problems have arisen with powerful procedures like token economies, with examples of target behaviours (eg helping to clean the hospital ward) being selected which operate more for the benefit of staff than clients. A radical behaviourist analysis emphasises the need not only to consider the reinforcement contingencies operating on clients, but also those operating on therapists. In particular it is necessary to give close consideration to the provision of countercontrol to those who are vulnerable to exploitation. In considering this issue, however, we are inevitably confronted with the broader societal context of the problems, and in conclusion it is perhaps appropriate to discuss briefly radical behaviourism's ethical problems at the macro, as well as the micro level.

PROBLEMS AT THE MACRO LEVEL

The point has often been made that psychotherapy is inherently repressive since it serves to adjust people to society rather than adjusting society to people. In this sense a radical behaviourist approach to psychotherapy can be seen to be at least slightly redeemed by the emphasis placed on the environment and the explicit recognition that the cause of problems is to be sought outside, rather than inside, the individual. In practice much of what goes on in a radical behaviourist attempt at psychotherapy can have an effect only on local variables, leaving the larger social problems untouched. Nevertheless the emphasis on the role of environmental factors inevitably directs the attention of the therapist to the need for social and political change. O'Leary (1975), for example, has commented on the way that recognition of the relationship between socio-economic factors and the problems of clients forces the therapist into an explicitly political role.

Some particular problems of the technological application of behavioural principles have been highlighted by Holland (1974). The availability of an effective behavioural technology inevitably presents the possibility that certain individuals or groups in possession of the technology will use it for ends which might be considered inappropriate. Examples quoted by Holland include the use of contingency management procedures to encourage conformity in schoolchildren and the use of a token economy procedure in the basic training of the US Army. What is highlighted by the examples given is that irrespective of the availability of the technology, those in possession of the power to reinforce the behaviour of others will have the control. The point of a well-designed behavioural culture is that such control is recognised and made explicit, in order that precautions can be built into the system to prevent inequitable access to control of reinforcement. Amongst the illustrations given by Holland of attempts to circumvent traditional elitism are the handing over of major elements of teaching courses to the consumer (Keller, 1968), the use of money to reinforce participation in welfare rights campaigns and the organisation of therapeutic procedures in a State hospital in such a way that the clientele became not 'patients' but 'students', learning the behavioural principles necessary for dealing with their problems (Rozynko *et al.*, 1971). The critical issue in a behavioural technology is that recognition of controlling variables highlights the need to prevent gross inequalities of power. Whilst traditional approaches deny the controllability of behaviour, the need to extend access to the relevant factors is minimised, and exploitation can continue because the victim denies the control, unconsciously colluding in the process.

Even within the limited area of clinical psychology, broader societal implications cannot be avoided. At the very least the need for clinical services highlights the need for societal change. One of the problems of providing a clinical service is that it may constitute a societal palliative, patching up the failings of the society and relieving the pressure for more fundamental changes. Thus, providing treatment for groups whose problems are, at least in part, determined by social problems and inequalities may reduce the motivation to demand resolution of such problems.

Unlike traditional approaches to therapy which place the causes of behaviour within the individual, radical behaviourism cannot avail itself of the excuse that the clients are themselves to blame for their problems. Traditional psychotherapies have often been seen as saying, in effect, that if a person has problems it is in some way that person's fault. Rowe's (1983) discussion of the construct systems of depressed individuals, for example, has been seen by some workers as saying that depressed people have no one to blame but themselves. Depressed people, Rowe says, build themselves a prison and put themselves in solitary confinement. Depressed people are accused of using cunning ploys 'to put the therapist in the wrong'. The depressed person is accused of fending off the therapist's 'skilful approaches' (Rowe, 1983). The tone of such a description contrasts markedly with that of radical behaviourist analyses which concentrate on the role of particular environmental contingencies in producing depression (eg Ferster, 1973). The radical behaviourist approach, placing the controlling variables squarely in the environment, must also place the blame for clinical problems in the broader society. In a similar way radical behaviourism cannot use the excuse that since some people survive difficult environments, personal qualities must be partly to blame. Firstly a radical behaviourist analysis still demands to know the origins of these personal qualities, seen as themselves traceable to present and past environments, and secondly the radical behaviourist is sceptical of the assumption that any two people have similar environments. The latter point is highlighted by radical behaviourism's emphasis on functional rather than physical concepts. In this respect even two people in the same place at the same time may still be in totally different environments, since the functional significance of aspects of that environment is likely to be different for the two individuals. What one individual finds reinforcing, another may find punishing; a stimulus which controls one behaviour in the first individual, may control quite a different behaviour in a second. Seen from this point of view, it becomes obviously meaningless to talk of any two people 'coming from the same environment'.

Of course it is possible to argue that variations in behaviour *are* due to intrinsic differences, certain individuals being genetically predisposed to certain kinds of behaviour; from an ethical viewpoint, however, it is obviously no more reasonable to blame people for their genetic structure than it is for their environments. From a practical viewpoint it can in any case be argued that discussions on topics like the heritability of 'intelligence', or 'personality' are seen as at best premature, since any conclusions drawn will themselves depend on the existence of certain types of environment. Since no one pretends to know exactly what are the essential environmental parameters of such concepts it is not possible to say whether the same results would be obtained tomorrow, since in a constantly changing environment there may well be changes in crucial variables. It is rather as if a creature from outer space attempted an analysis of a person's behaviour by seeing them go to work every day. By simply observing that this was what the person regularly did, a spurious impression of knowledge could be given; yet if the significance of the environmental event (the workplace) was not appreciated, the whole analysis could be overturned when the person observed changed jobs.

CONCLUSION

Clearly radical behaviourism has developed considerably (some would say unrecognisably) from its crude beginnings in the early part of the century. It must, moreover, be recognised that a chapter like the present one represents the views of *a* radical behaviourist, not *the* radical behaviourist. Nevertheless there are certain aspects of radical behaviourism which are likely to remain central even as the paradigm develops further. Perhaps most important here are the emphasis on the interaction between behaviour and the environment and the acceptance of a complete determinism. In a clinical context such a perspective has a number of implications, particularly that both the client and the therapist are subject to the same laws of behaviour. It is assumed (as it must be in all therapies) that the client's behaviour will at least in part be a function of the therapist's behaviour (otherwise it would make no difference what the therapist did). Correspondingly it is accepted that the therapist's behaviour will also be determined, in part, by the behaviour of the client.

Considering such a system in terms of its ethical implications, it is perhaps obvious that early attempts at producing ethical guidelines (eg the *Minnesota Guidelines*), though well intentioned, were far too simplistic to be practical. Nevertheless the guidelines implicitly indicate both the potential for exploitation against which clients need protection and the value of countercontrol as a means of providing such protection. What is needed is a system of countercontrol which will be flexible enough to cope with the widely varying contingencies which may arise in practice but which will also provide protection for all concerned. In the context of psychotherapy this implies a need to make therapists subject to explicit countercontrol in order to compensate for the gross power imbalances implicit in most therapeutic relationships. Simply appealing to the personal characteristics of the therapist is not enough, neither is assuming that as long as consent is obtained the problem disappears; both viewpoints neglect the possibility that consent or the activities characteristic of integrity are themselves behaviours with their own determinants. Recognition of such determinants places the onus on those involved in therapy to ensure that conditions are propitious for therapists to behave with integrity and for clients to give a meaningful consent without being influenced by power imbalance.

In the broader context of society at large, the radical behaviourist as therapist is confronted with a number of problems. Of particular importance is the recognition that the environment has a causal role in the development of the clinical problems with which therapists are confronted. Such recognition may indicate the need for greater or lesser degrees of social change; as Skinner has put it, the 'aim is to change not people, but the world in which they live'. The radical behaviourist may thus be confronted directly with the need to take political action, in order that social practices causing clinical problems be eliminated. Radical behaviourists may thus find themselves campaigning for the rights of women or minority groups whose clinical problems result from prejudice or discrimination in the larger society. Issues like inequality, unemployment, the threat of nuclear warfare and other political problems may be seen as major determinants of clinical problems, requiring political rather than clinical solutions.

Finally it should be noted that therapists themselves may be confronted with a conflict between the ethical demands of therapy and those of the wider societal context. To treat the problems produced by an inadequate and inequitable society may be seen as providing a palliative, patching up the more obvious failings of the system without providing any fundamental change. In this sense the therapist may be seen as colluding with the existing system. Traditional therapies may not encounter such difficulties, since the root cause of clinical problems is placed within the individual, without any necessary indictment of society. By contrast, radical behaviourism, with its explicit recognition of the role of the environment, is forced into the acknowledgment that the clinical problem is also a political one.

REFERENCES

Blough, D.S. (1958), 'A method for obtaining psychophysical thresholds from the pigeon', *Journal of the Experimental Analysis of Behaviour,* 1, pp.31–43.

Cahoon, D.D. (1968), 'Issues and implications of operant conditioning: balancing procedures against outcomes', *Hospital and Community Psychiatry,* 19, pp.228–9.

Chomsky, N. (1972), 'Psychology and ideology', *Cognition,* 1, pp.11–46.

Estes, W.K. (1944), 'An experimental study of punishment', *Psychological Monographs,* 57, pp.1–40.

Ferster, C.B. (1973), 'A functional analysis of depression', *American Psychologist,* 28, pp.857–70.

Foster, M. Owens, R.G. and Newton, A.V. (1985), 'Functional analysis of the gag reflex', *British Dental Journal,* 158, pp.369–70.

Fuller, P.R. (1949), 'Operant conditioning of a vegetative human organism', *American Journal of Psychology,* 62, pp.587–90.

Holland, J.G. (1974), 'Political implications of applying behavioural psychology' in L.R. Ulrich, J. Stachnik and J. Mabry (eds), *Control of Human Behaviour* vol.3, Scott Foresman & Co, Illinois.

Holroyd, J.C. and Brodsky, A.M. (1977), 'Psychologists attitudes and practices regarding erotic and nonerotic physical contact with patients', *American Psychologist,* 32, pp.843–9.

Hull, C.L. (1943), *Principles of Behaviour*, New York, Appleton Century Crofts.

Keller, F.S. (1968), 'Goodbye teacher . . .', *Journal of Applied Behaviour Analysis, 1*, pp.78–9.

Kuhn, T.S. (1962), *The Structure of Scientific Revolutions*, Chicago, University of Chicago Press.

Lovaas, O.I., Schaeffer, B. and Simmonds, J.Q. (1965), 'Building social behaviour in autistic children by the use of electric shock', *Journal of Experimental Research in Personality,* 1, pp.99–109.

Lucero, R.J., Vail, D.J. and Scherber, J. (1968), 'Regulating operant conditioning programs', *Hospital and Community Psychiatry,* 19, pp.53–4.

Miron, N. (1968), 'Issues and implications of operant conditioning; the primary ethical consideration', *Hospital and Community Psychiatry,* 19, pp.226–8.

O'Leary, K.D. (1975), 'The entrée of the paraprofessional into the classroom' in L.S.W. Bijou and E. Ribes-Inesta (eds), *Behaviour Modification; Issues and Extensions*, New York, Academic Press, pp.93–108.

Owens, R.G. and Ashcroft, J.B. (1982), 'Functional analysis in applied psychology', *British Journal of Clinical Psychology,* 21, pp.181–9.

Peck, D.F. (1979), 'The ethics of behaviour modification: an empirical note', *Behaviour Analysis, 1*, pp.60–1.

Platt, J.R. (1973), 'The Skinnerian revolution' in E. Wheeler (ed.), *Beyond the Punitive Society*, London, Wildwood House, pp.22–56.

Redd, W.H., Sidman, M. and Fletcher, F.G. (1974), 'Time out as a reinforcer for errors in a serial position task', *Journal of the Experimental Analysis of Behaviour, 21*, pp.3–18.

Rowe, D. (1983), 'Resistance to change' in E. Karas (ed.), *Current Issues in Clinical Psychology* vol.1, New York, Plenum, pp.171–7.

Rozynko, V.V., Flint, G.A., Hammer, C.E., Swift, K.D., Kline, J.A. and King, R.M. (1971), 'An operant behaviour modification program', presented at meeting of the Western Psychological Association; cited in Holland (1974).

Skinner, B.F. (1938), *The Behaviour of Organisms*, New York, Appleton Century Crofts.

Skinner, B.F. (1953), *Science and Human Behaviour*, New York, Macmillan.

Skinner, B.F. (1969), *Contingencies of Reinforcement: a theoretical analysis*, New York, Appleton Century Crofts.

Skinner, B.F. (1971), *Beyond Freedom and Dignity*, New York, Knopf.

Terrace, H.S. (1966), 'Stimulus Control' in W.K. Honig (ed.), *Operant Behaviour: Areas of Research and Application*, New York, Appleton Century Crofts.

Watson, J.B. (1913), 'Psychology as the behaviourist views it', *Psychological Review, 20*, pp.158–77.

Ethical Issues in Psychotherapy for Women

Sue Llewelyn

INTRODUCTION

When does care for a client become indulgence of the carer's need for admiration, and when does the warm and intimate bond between a therapist and client, which could be seen as a restorative, emotional experience, become lustful exploitation? When does the reintegration of a distressed client back into her family become the imposition of the values of an oppressive society onto a woman who is struggling to free herself from a stereotyped sex role? What is the difference between the experience of men and women that leads more women than men to experience mental health problems, and what should clinicians be doing about it? These are some of the questions raised by this chapter, which will examine some of the special problems that must be faced by mental health professionals who are working psychotherapeutically with women.

During the chapter, it will be argued that these problems exist partly because of the rather exceptional nature of the therapeutic relationship which permits two people to behave towards each other in a way which is most unusual in our society; and partly because of the particular status of women in our society. This status, as will be seen later, has a number of consequences for women's mental health. The focus of concern is on women both because the issues are thrown most clearly into relief when the dependent partner in the therapeutic relationship is a woman, and the therapist is a man; and also because of the predominance of women in the mental health statistics. This does not, of course, preclude the existence of ethical questions when the client in psychotherapy is male; such questions obviously exist. However, it is important to point out that in therapeutic situations where the client is a woman and the therapist is a man, the client has less social power and status not simply because she is a client, but also because she is a woman. This therefore means that questions involving ethical issues are particularly pertinent. The experience of women as clients will be central in this chapter, and it should be noted from the outset that the points of view to be expressed reflect some of my own concerns as a woman and as a woman therapist. However, some of the conclusions drawn clearly apply to any individuals involved in psychotherapy.

In 1897, the American short story writer, Charlotte Perkins Gilman, published a fictional account of the mental breakdown of a woman which was at least in part caused by the nature of the so-called treatment prescribed for her. The story, *The Yellow Wallpaper*, which was based on Gilman's own experience, is an eloquent description of the 'rest' cure; the distressed woman was supposed to do absolutely nothing, least of all engage in any creative work, until she recovered her 'normal' disposition, which again would involve not doing anything particularly useful apart from domestic duties. This story has since been taken by many feminists as an exemplar of the approach taken by much of the psychiatric system to women's psychological distress; that is, that the mental health problem is seen as something that results from a basic female inadequacy, and is best treated by inducing her to conform to a caricature of feminine behaviour. It also reflects the experience of many women, as typified by the famous example of Freud's patient Dora, that at least the initial (and sometimes continuing) response to their problems is that they are imagining, over-emphasising, or over-dramatising things.

In this sense, then, the interventions of clinicians can be seen as serving more to protect the notion of what is feminine, than to act in the interests of the individual woman, who may have different ideas about what she wants to be, or who may have experiences which do not correspond to the clinician's view of reality. If this is indeed the case, it might well be said that clinicians are not acting ethically in that they are not acting in the interests of the client.

In the subsequent discussion, therefore, it will be proposed that a clinician is acting in an ethically questionable way not only in fairly obvious cases, when he or she uses the psychotherapeutic relationship for purposes which are not directly connected with the welfare of the client, but also in less obvious cases, when he or she imposes onto a client a personal opinion about appropriate behaviour, rather than encouraging the individual to consider options from a wide range of potential life-styles. It will also be argued that a therapist is acting unethically if he or she chooses to ignore certain aspects of the social context, which seem likely to influence that woman's free choice.

So what evidence is there for unethical behaviour, of either the 'obvious' or less 'obvious' kind, in the actions of psychiatrists and psychotherapists in the present day? There are a number of ways in which it would be possible to examine this question, ranging from analyses of individual cases, through to an examination of the social system within which women experience, and are treated for, their mental distress. In the next part of this chapter, I shall consider the most overt and clear-cut examples of non-ethical behaviour carried out by therapists, and following this, I shall look at the wider question of the pervasiveness of an attitude towards women which may not be directly in their best interest. In order to do this, the incidence of mental distress in men and women will be examined, together with an analysis of the usual treatment approaches offered to clients suffering from mental distress. Related to this I also look at some particularly influential theories that have been advanced to explain women's psychological problems. The last part of the chapter will consist of a discussion of some implications for clinical practice.

NON-ETHICAL BEHAVIOUR IN THERAPY

This section will consider the behaviour of some therapists in therapy with their clients. As will be shown later, individual psychotherapy is not a frequent mode of treatment in the UK, although it is more common in the USA. When it does take place, in both the National Health Service and in private practice, the most likely dyad will be a female client with a male therapist. This is partly because of the predominance of female clients and partly because of the predominance of men amongst those sections of the mental health professions who carry out psychotherapy. Of course there is a wide array of procedures which claim to be psychotherapy, and no one definition is likely to do full justice to all of the different approaches which fall under this label. In fact, Prochaska and Norcross (1982) estimate that in 1975, there were over 150 different therapies; this now seems likely to be an underestimation as 250 is the figure often quoted. However, most psychotherapies involve a reasonably prolonged relationship between two individuals, one of whom is a socially sanctioned healer who uses a number of psychological techniques, in the context of a confiding relationship, to persuade the other to change (Frank, 1973). In most cases the client has approached the therapist and asked for help, and consequently the therapist is in a position to wield a considerable amount of power over the client. When we talk about psychotherapy, therefore, we are most commonly talking about a persuasive encounter in which a professional (and hence higher status and more powerful) male attempts to change certain aspects of the personality and life-style of a non-professional (lower status and less powerful) female.

Put as starkly as that, the process of psychotherapy can be clearly seen as one in which ethical issues are likely to be salient. Of course, similar issues are also present in other professional relationships, such as between doctors and patients; lawyers and their clients; and teachers and students. But what makes it so important to consider the ethical issues involved in the therapist/client relationship is the extremely personal nature of the relationship that develops between therapist and client, which in many ways mimics the social context in which it is set.

In most therapies, this personal relationship is central. Although Freud originally thought of the transference in therapy as an impediment to therapeutic progress, it soon become recognised that important aspects of the client's pathology could be understood by interpreting the way that he or she re-lived, through the relationship with the therapist, certain conflicts and preoccupations. Hence the relationship between the two became a focus of the treatment. Subsequent developments of the theories of therapy, many of which can be seen as modifications of Freud's ideas, have de-emphasised the importance of the transference, but have continued to place importance on the therapist/client relationship. Research on therapeutic outcome (for example Strupp and Hadley, 1979; Orlinsky and Howard, 1977) has suggested that relationship factors are central in the achievement of therapeutic change. The content of the relationship obviously varies with the type of therapy; nevertheless a constant feature is likely to be the warm, intimate interchange in which the client is encouraged to reveal feelings, doubts and desires to the therapist, and to place a high degree of trust in the therapist, without requiring very much information in return, on which to base that trust.

What all of this suggests therefore is that the therapist is potentially in a position of considerable personal power, complicated by the fact that the two individuals concerned are usually of opposite sex, and that, in the social world, the two sexes have an unequal access to power and status. A number of feminist writers such as Chesler (1974) and Tennov (1973) have suggested that the institution of therapy parallels that of marriage: in both cases the woman is expected to be subservient to the man and not to question his authority to know what is best for her. Chesler's views are as follows:

> For most women (the middle-class-oriented) psychotherapeutic encounter is just one more instance of an unequal relationship, just one more opportunity to be 'helped' by being (expertly) dominated . . . Each woman, as each patient, thinks (her) symptoms are unique and are her own fault: she is 'neurotic'. She wants from a psychotherapist what she wants – and often cannot get – from a husband: attention, understanding, merciful relief, a personal solution – in the arms of the right husband, on the couch of the right therapist (pp.108–9).

In a similar vein, Tennov wrote that:

> Psychotherapy is an unproven and expensive tyranny of one individual over another . . . it is an intransitive and hierarchical relationship in which the therapist is defined as a person able to understand the patient, but not the reverse . . . it is always disrespectful (p.107).

Although the reaction to the above passages, from most therapists and indeed from most clients, would probably at least initially be either of amusement or outraged dismissal, there are some points which seem to be worthy of consideration. What about the parallel between marriage and therapy? Do therapists behave disrespectfully towards their female clients? And do they behave tyrannically? As a partial answer to this question, I shall concentrate on the issue of the sexual relationship between therapist and client, as this most clearly points to the ethical issues present in a relationship which is indeed supposed to be intimate and personal, at the same time as being professional and formal.

Although there is a limited amount of data in the UK, in North America there is a considerable amount of evidence suggesting that the incidence of sexual relations between therapists and clients is surprisingly widespread, despite the fact that such behaviour is clearly proscribed by the ethical codes of all professional groups. The British Psychological Society, for example, in its *Guidelines for the Professional Practice of Clinical Psychology* published in 1983, points out that: 'Psychologists shall not exploit the special relationship of trust and confidence that can exist in professional practice to further the gratification of their personal desires.'

Indeed, most professionals in most professions would have little hesitation in questioning the morality of engaging in a social or sexual relationship with a client, when the normally accepted purpose of the professional relationship is the delivery of a professional service to a client; which in this case is the amelioration of the client's psychological distress, through the techniques of the therapist based on his training. Yet the evidence is that sexual relationships do occur, and that they tend to be between male therapists and female clients far more frequently than between male clients and female therapists.

Only a small proportion of the evidence will be presented here. Holroyd and Brodsky (1977), for example, carried out a randomly sampled, anonymous postal survey of 1,000 licensed psychologists in the USA from which they obtained a 70 per cent response rate. The results revealed that 8.1 per cent of male therapists, and 1 per cent of female therapists, stated that they had had intercourse with one or more clients, either during or within three months of termination of therapy. In another example, Kardener, Fuller and Mensch (1973) reported a study of psychiatrists in which they found that 10.5 per cent had engaged in some form of erotic behaviour with clients (5 per cent having had intercourse). Furrow (1980) has documented a number of cases in which therapists were sued by clients for malpractice, following prolonged sexual intimacy or promises of marriage; and Hall and Hare-Mustin (1983) have also noted details of cases where sexual relationships have led to legal action. Of course, in all of the above reports, only the instances which are known, or admitted, are included in the figure; it is probably safe to conclude that there is a considerable under-reporting of the incidence of sexual contact between therapists and clients. It seems reasonable to assume, for example, that individuals who did not respond to the surveys were more likely to have engaged in sexual behaviour with clients, than those who did respond to the surveys. The fact that there are not more complaints from clients is not surprising; a similar problem exists in the under-reporting of rape (see Brownmiller, 1975).

When erotic contact between therapists and clients does take place, a number of justifications are usually put forward, many of which centre on the notion that it is done in the interests of the client. The therapist for instance contends that he is putting the client in touch with her sexuality, allowing her to experience a truly satisfying erotic relationship, and so on. But as one therapist quoted by Furrow (1980) remarked:

> most erotic breaches of the therapist-patient relationship occur with women who are physically attractive; almost never with the aged, the infirm or the ugly; thus giving the lie to the oft-heard rationalization on the part of such therapists that they were acting in the interests of the patient (p.34).

One of the other justifications provided by therapists who behave erotically with clients is that the client herself initiated the activity. This is of course related to the justification that is sometimes presented by men who assault children, or by fathers who commit incest. Of course it may well be that the children in question acted seductively; nevertheless the law holds the adult to be responsible in such cases. It also seems likely that, in some cases, some female clients do behave seductively towards their male therapists. But here again, all professional ethical codes proscribe such activities, and hold the therapist responsible for such actions.

There will be few clients who go through an effective therapeutic relationship, untouched by a number of complicated emotional reactions, including feelings of attraction towards the therapist, as well as anger and resentment towards him. In addition, feelings of confusion are likely, especially at the start of therapy. The therapeutic situation is socially ambiguous, that is, it is an interpersonal relationship which is conducted in a socially most 'abnormal' way. Most of the 'rules' of ordinary conversation are broken; for example it is appropriate for the client to say whatever comes into her mind without censorship, and the therapist is not expected to talk about himself for any length of time. Besides this 'abnormality', the client is also likely to be distressed by the task that she is facing in therapy. Indeed, one of the normal concomitants of the therapeutic process is the vulnerability that the client usually experiences as she disassembles the defensive structures that have allowed her to cope in the past, and yet which may be the cause of her difficulties in the present. This vulnerability occurs at a particularly crucial time; she is likely to be feeling low in self-confidence and is needing the acceptance and care of her therapist. At the same time, as has already been suggested, the therapist is probably behaving in a way which is quite unlike most of the other people that the client encounters in her daily life. That is, he is being reassuring, attentive, accepting and gentle. It is highly likely that the interaction is going on in a room that is quiet and private. As Frankland (1981) has pointed out, such a combination of features is one which is presumably familiar to the therapist, but not to the client.

If these two factors (the vulnerability of the client and the intimate nature of the therapeutic encounter) are occurring simultaneously, it may not be surprising if the client mistakes the situation for an erotic one; the other times when she has given personal and intimate confidences to another person, who has been giving her total and undivided attention, have probably been during courtship. It is possible, therefore, that she may start to behave erotically towards the therapist.

In some situations, of course, it may be the therapist who initiates the sexual interaction, which the client is not in a particularly strong position to refuse. For all she knows this may be what normally goes on in therapy. (See the discussion by Burgess, 1981, of some of the confusion experienced by patients of gynaecologists who abuse their patients.) Whether the therapist responds to seductive behaviour, or whether he initiates it, the client is from henceforth in a very difficult situation.

So what happens to a woman who has a sexual relationship with her therapist? Although it is possible that such a relationship could be warm and loving, it is hardly equal, and nor is it conducive to the resolution of the conflicts which the woman probably brought to therapy. Instead of being able to rely on the therapist's concern for her as a person, she becomes reliant on his acceptance of and need for her as a lover. Kardener (1974) and Stone (1983) suggest that the consequences are as problematic for the client in this situation, as for the victim of incest. In an incestuous relationship the child is expected to bear responsibility for an adult relationship, for which she is not ready, and in addition, loses the support of a parent who should be able to protect her from trauma. The incest victim, like the seduced client, has lost the support of someone who should be caring for her in an unambiguous way; as Kardener (1974) says: 'In an exactly parallel way the physician, as a source of healing, support, and succour, becomes lost to his patient when he changes roles and becomes a lover. It is psychologically a frighteningly high price the patient must pay . . .' (p.1135).

In addition, she will be unable to use the therapeutic relationship to examine her ways of relating to others, because the prime task will become the disentangling of her relationship with the therapist. If a psychoanalytic model is being employed, it might be argued that the case would be even more serious: the little girl has succeeded in seducing her father; hence she will have little hope of gaining insight into and renouncing her infantile wishes, which have now been so effectively gratified. Apfel and Simon (1985) suggest that female clients, who have had sexual contact with their therapists, tend to present a number of difficulties specifically connected with their therapeutic experience, including constricted intimacy with other men; an excess of guilt and shame; ambivalence toward therapists and therapies; and rage and desire for revenge towards men in general.

A very clear example of the way in which the therapeutic relationship can be abused has been noted in a study by Temerlin and Temerlin (1982) of 'psychotherapy cults'. The Temerlins describe the growing phenomena of therapists who gather around themselves a number of clients, ex-clients and students, all of whom are encouraged to remain with the therapist and may simultaneously function as lovers, as sources of finance, and as clients. In almost every single case, the individuals at the centre of such groups are men. In such a situation, it is difficult for the observer to disentangle what is supposed to be therapeutic from what is clearly exploitation; it must be even more difficult for the client to do so. As in the case of the individual psychotherapy patient, the psychotherapy cult member is actively discouraged from seeking outside advice about her experience, as this is seen as betrayal of the trust which is supposed to exist between therapist and patient.

Similar points have been made by Hochman (1984) in his study of ex-members of the 'Feeling Centre', a therapy cult which demanded commitment to and involvement with to the group while actively discouraging contact with the world outside.

Of course, there are a variety of ways in which the therapist may misuse his power in the therapeutic relationship, which also apply to male clients. Examples here include the keeping of 'pet' clients, who can be used as a means of inflating the therapists' sense of importance, or who are simply attractive people to have around. The power imbalance inherent in the therapeutic relationship already referred to above, is clearly an issue in all types of therapy, no matter what the sex or sexual orientation of therapist or client. The example of the sexual relationship between therapist and client is simply a particularly pertinent one because of the key link between sex and power described by many men, which is particularly evident in cases of sexual assault and abuse. This does not mean, of course, that issues of power and abuse of that power, do not exist for female therapists and male clients.

The question that follows from the discussion above concerning sexual abuse is whether this is an aberration of standards of behaviour which are normally high, or whether it is merely a particularly striking reflection of an approach to women in psychiatry and psychotherapy which is profoundly disrespectful. In other words, is unethical behaviour, in the sense of abuse by sexist assumptions and practices of psychotherapy and psychiatry, actually very widespread? Although each case of sexual abuse of a woman client is one too many, it is of course true that in the vast majority of therapies, the therapist would not dream of treating his client in this way. Nevertheless, is it the case that this specific type of abuse merely reflects an underlying contempt for women clients, and a disregard for the importance of their own experiences, which is actually another form of abuse? Is this latter form of less obvious, or covert abuse, pervasive? The question that then needs to be answered becomes whether psychiatry and psychotherapy are, by nature and practice, sexist, as some feminists have suggested, or whether they are normally free from bias against women and their aspirations.

WOMENS' MENTAL HEALTH PROBLEMS – INCIDENCE AND THEORIES

In order to suggest an answer to the question raised above concerning the pervasiveness or otherwise of abuse, it is necessary firstly to consider both the overall incidence of women's mental health problems, and the nature of the treatment which is normally offered to them. Recent estimates concerning the mental health of men and women suggest that women are far more likely than men to spend some portion of their lives in psychiatric hospitals (DHSS, 1977), such that women have a one in six chance of entering psychiatric hospital at some point in their lives, compared with a one in nine chance for men (DHSS, 1975). The incidence of depression is generally accepted to be twice as high for women than for men (Weissman and Klerman, 1977); and diagnoses such as histrionic personality disorder and dependent personality disorder are given far more frequently to women than to men (Kaplan, 1983).

Many researchers have tried to account for these differences in incidence between the sexes, using a wide variety of possible explanations and causes. These range from the biochemical theories (that women are pre-disposed to psychiatric difficulties because of hormonal imbalance or faulty dopamine receptors); to the sociological (that it is a part of women's stereotyped role to complain about psychological problems); and to the psychodynamic (that women have a weaker super-ego structure than men). Of course, these theories vary in their impact on the type of treatment that is available to most women, but the one that has the most impact is probably the biochemical/biological. The implications of this will be discussed below.

The problem with many of the theories, and especially with the biological/biochemical approach, is that they fail to take account of the very different social structures within which men and women co-exist. That is, such theories tend to ignore the social reality in which men and women have to live and which has an enormous impact on the sense which men and women, as individuals, are able to make out of their lives, and which also structures the assumptions and expectations that others may hold about them.

It is important to note here that I am not arguing that social factors alone lead to the increased likelihood that women experience psychological distress, although there is little doubt that they do have some effect. I merely want to point out that social factors form the context within which an individual has to create his or her own ways of coping with the world. Thus I am suggesting that we must recognise a number of aspects about the lives of most women which are likely to predispose them to express their distress in a particular way. For example, women almost always have responsibility for the emotional expression of the family (Eichenbaum and Orbach, 1982), as well as having the major responsibility for child care. Further, they tend to be less in control than men of what happens to them, for instance because of the expectation that women will move home to fit in with male employment requirements, and because of their poorer economic position. It may of course be easier, and more convenient for clinicians not to acknowledge the importance of such social and personal factors in the genesis of psychological distress; convenience or ease for the clinician do not, however, seem to be adequate grounds on which to ignore factors that are highly likely to have an impact on a woman's mental health. For instance, Brown and Harris (1978) have shown that depression in women is highly likely to follow a disturbing life event if more than two of the following four predisposing factors are true: the woman is unemployed, has more than two young children under the age of fourteen, lost her mother during childhood, or has no confiding relationship with her husband. Yet most theories of the mental health problems of women ignore factors such as these, tending to locate the problem within the biochemistry or head of the individual woman. The implications of this lack of attention to social factors is that the treatment, which is based upon ignoring such issues, runs the risk of encouraging women to fit back into existing structures which limit and restrict them. It is in this sense in which it could be said that the psychiatric system abuses women, although the nature of this type of abuse is covert, rather than overt. A brief examination of the approaches to treatment which are normally experienced by women with mental health problems will now follow, in order to consider whether such covert abuse is in fact pervasive.

The care that is received by the vast majority of women admitted to mental hospital is primarily medical, in that the treatment on the whole consists of medication and nursing and/or custodial care, with relatively little attention being paid to psychological or social concerns. In some parts of the country, some patients do have limited access to psychotherapeutic help while in hospital, although that is usually only available to patients on the admission wards, and even here the amount of time devoted to the therapy is minimal in comparison with amount of time spent on medical procedures or time-filling occupational therapy tasks. The same is true for those who simply present their mental health problems to their family practitioners as out-patients, where the treatment of first resort is usually medication; hence over twenty million prescriptions for the minor tranquillisers are issued each year in the UK. In a review of research mainly carried out in North America, Cooperstock (1979) showed that between 67 per cent and 72 per cent of prescribed psychotropic drugs go to women, who tend to be both more frequent and steadier users of such drugs than men. Such medical treatment is of course quintessentially mechanistic and individualistic; it is of apparently very little relevance for a clinician, who is employing a medical approach, to consider *why* a particular problem should have developed within one particular woman within our particular social structure, and why it should be women, more often than men, who suffer from such problems.

This points immediately to an issue which must be faced when talking about the ethical implications of psychotherapy: most patients never actually get the chance of looking at personal questions, which is offered by psychotherapy. The treatment available for most women is based on the pseudo-medical notion of symptom relief leading to re-adjustment, without provision of any opportunity to examine the issues which may have led to the mental distress in the first place. In this sense, then, the treatment available does not respect the subjective experience of individual women. (The same point of course also applies to men.) Although there are problems with it, as has already been shown, at least psychotherapy can provide some opportunity for the client to reconsider her life and values. It might be fair to say, therefore, that the predominance of the medical approach to psychological distress, which seems to offer re-adjustment without examination, itself raises considerable ethical issues, especially as there is considerable evidence that it is the situation in which women find themselves which is conducive to emotional distress.

Some of the other, non-medical theories that have been advanced to account for the mental distress experienced by women will now be examined, in order to consider the degree to which they may have implications for women which are covertly abusive. Of course, probably the most important single influence on the psychotherapeutic treatment of women in the past century has been that of Freud. Considerable debate rages concerning the degree to which Freud's approach to women is misogynist, and merely reflects the assumption which would have been current in his time that women were weaker and poorer specimens than men; or to what extent Freud was in fact sympathetically describing the existing state of affairs as seen in the women he treated. Examples of these two viewpoints are Van Herik (1984) and Mitchell (1974). Without entering into this debate, an extremely oversimplified account of Freud's views is to see women as morally rather deficient creatures, whose main task in life is to resolve their anguish over the loss of a penis. According to this view, any attempt to become active and achieving in the external world tends to be seen as compensatory. Although it seems likely that these ideas are misunderstandings of Freud, and that they have been taken prescriptively rather than descriptively, there is no doubt that psychiatry has taken and used Freudian concepts to persuade women to accept their status in the family and in society, with little regard for the contrary wishes or characteristics of individual women. It is probably also true to say that on the whole Freudian theory and its developments have tended to ignore the very real problems which women have faced in being able to assert themselves in a social and political world which is male-dominated. As an example of some of the assumptions made by at least some post-Freudians, Chesler (1974) quotes Jung as follows:

> But no-one can evade the fact that, in taking up a masculine calling, studying and working in a man's way, woman is doing something not wholly in agreement with, if not directly injurious to, her feminine nature. (p.77).

Such a view of 'feminine nature' is clearly going to have restricting and limiting consequences for individual women.

Recently, however, a number of feminist writers and feminist therapists have tried to use the insights of Freud to develop an understanding of women's mental health problems in a way which does not deny the validity of women's striving for autonomy and achievement, and which also recognises the problems faced by women in a society in which they are more or less subordinate citizens. In particular the work of Eichenbaum and Orbach (1982); Chodorow (1978); Dinnerstein (1978); and Mitchell (1974), have been very central to this endeavour. It remains to be seen whether these theoretical developments will have any impact on the activities of most practising therapists.

Other theorists who have tried to develop an understanding of the mental health problems of women, include those who have looked at the psychological consequences for both the sexes of certain types of sex-typed behaviour. An example of this type of approach has been to examine the sex-role stereotypes to which both men and women tend to conform. It has been shown, for example, that the stereotype, which most people hold about women's behaviour compared with men's behaviour, is that women are much more passive, emotional, dependent and unassertive than men (eg Spence and Helmreich, 1978; Bem, 1974; Block, 1973). It has also been shown that this has consequences for the mental health of men and women. For example, Bem (1974) has shown that individuals who are psychologically androgynous, that is, who possess characteristics that are both stereotypically male and stereotypically female (both leadership and tenderness, for instance), are likely to be able to behave more adaptively in a variety of circumstances, than those whose behaviour is not androgynous. This has clear implications for mental health, since individuals who act according to a stereotyped role are far less likely to be able to cope when circumstances become difficult, than those whose behavioural repertoire is more varied.

Yet these findings appear to have little impact on the assumptions held by many clinicians about their clients. This can be seen in the evidence which currently exists concerning the behaviour of clinicians towards their female clients, as demonstrated both by the ways in which clinicians diagnose their women clients; and also by the ways that therapists react towards their female clients in therapy.

In recent years, a number of studies have examined the question of the degree to which clinicians hold biased views about the mental health of men and women. One of the first studies was that of Broverman and colleagues, carried out in 1970. Broverman *et al.* showed that when clinicians were asked to make judgments about personal attributes that were characteristic of normal mentally healthy adults, and of men and women; those attributes which were seen as *unhealthy* in adults (such as 'cries easily', or 'excitable in minor crises') were seen as *healthy* in women. Equally, those characteristics, seen as unhealthy in women (such as 'independent' or 'assertive'), were seen as characteristic of healthy adults.

Since this work was first reported over a decade ago, a number of studies have tried to replicate the results, with mixed findings. For example the studies by Whitley (1979) and Lee Smith (1980) have failed to replicate these findings, whereas Swenson and Ragucci (1984) confirmed the results. It may of course be that this study has not always been replicated because the views of clinicians have changed over recent years; however Swenson and Ragucci's recent modification of Broverman's work suggests that the 'double standard' for mental health is still operating, in that while mentally healthy men and women may well now show personal attributes which are characteristic of the other sex, women should not show the 'male' characteristics too strongly. Hence if women are *too* assertive or independent, they are still not seen as healthy.

Certainly there is plenty of observational evidence for sex-role stereotyping in the behaviour of many clinicians towards their clients. In a case study published elsewhere, I and my colleagues have described the emotional problems of a female client who presented extremely 'feminine' behaviour, which clearly led to intrapersonal dificulties (Parry, Llewelyn and Davis, 1984); yet the clinicians responsible for her care were only too willing to encourage her 'femininity'. Similarly, evidence from many sources (eg Kaplan, 1983, Voss and Gannon, 1978) indicates that most professionals do not see the reinforcement of 'sex-appropriate' behaviour as problematic; despite the evidence that androgynous individuals are more likely to be mentally healthy than sex-typed ones, we do not often see psychotherapists encouraging their female clients to become more dominant in their marriages or to reconsider whether marriage and motherhood is what they should aim for in life. In fact, the American Psychological Association's 'Task Force on Sex-Bias and Sex-Role Stereotyping in Psychotherapeutic Practice' (reported in Voss and Gannon, 1978) noted three areas of concern in the behaviour of clinicians:

First, the high frequency of sexist values and standards of behaviour held by therapists and imposed on clients.

Second, the dependence of many psychotherapeutic theories on male personality development and behaviour.

Third, the incidence of sexual relations between therapists and clients (as noted above).

Such findings do not encourage confidence in the capacity of clinicians to act in the interest of women. They also strongly support the evidence presented so far in this chapter.

IMPLICATIONS

It seems to me that the implications of this discussion for clinicians who are attempting to work with their clients in a way which frees, rather than constrains them, are threefold. The first, obviously, is to be aware of the dangers of the overt abuse of clients in the therapeutic situation, which in the case of women, is especially evident through sexual involvement. The second is to become aware of the dangers of reinforcing existing power structures in the therapeutic relationship, and the third is to become aware of the ease with which sex stereotyped behaviours are adopted by both therapists and clients, in ways which may not be productive for personal development or happiness. Too often, the psychiatric system, within which both clinician and client are operating, serves to reinforce the existence of stereotyped behaviour, against the interests of a particular client. Hence it becomes incumbent upon the clinician to try to understand the social structure of the world which his clients inhabit. If this is not done, the consequences of the interventions of the practitioner may well be covertly abusive.

Smail (1984) clearly demonstrates how the prevailing assumptions about appropriate behaviour for women have implications both for the ways in which clients are treated, and for the ways in which clients see themselves. For example, he describes the way in which women can become 'ill' when the circumstances in which they live, which are perceived as 'normal' by the rest of society, become in practice unbearable:

> It is certainly no accident that so many people who are overcome by 'symptoms' of anxiety acute enough for them to seek professional help are relatively young women with small children, cut off from close contact with their own families, and dependent for survival of their identity on

> husbands who have changed from being attentive lovers to near-strangers who come home late, tired from work, and unwilling to talk about anything . . . trapped in a form of drudgery which is these days no longer socially valued, such women find themselves additionally drained by the demands of their own children who call upon resources for love and attention which seem rapidly to be running dry . . . our cultural mythology has it that this kind of situation is utterly 'normal' and desirable, so that women who find themselves in it have . . . no critical purchase on it: if they feel unhappy, anxious or unreal, it must be because they are either 'ill' or 'inadequate' (Smail, pp.28–9).

To treat such women as if their problem is their personal inability to cope with the feminine role is to ignore the personal needs of the woman, as well as to ignore the social context in which her mental health problems develop. The suggestion of this chapter is that it is actually covertly abusive behaviour on the part of the psychiatric services to locate the problem within the individual woman and to ignore the sexist assumptions being made by assuming that a woman's distress is unrelated to her role in society. This of course also raises the question of whether the clinician is really acting in the interests of the woman if he ignores these other questions, either through ignorance or choice.

This does not mean, of course, that to act ethically, a therapist has to insist that a woman should totally reject the view held by the wider society about appropriate behaviour for men and women; rather it means that a clinician should be sensitive to the experience and strivings of individual women in their attempts to cope with their lives. Lerner (1978), for example, suggests that an individual's mental health is likely to depend on the extent to which he or she has consolidated a comfortable and stable gender identity, and that to prescribe, or proscribe certain behaviours on the basis of sex is clearly unhelpful. Kaplan (1979) on the other hand points out that this too is problematic: certain characteristics, such as dependency, are more likely to be accepted in women so will be less likely to be worked upon in therapy.

Kaswan (1981) has pointed out that psychological or psychotherapeutic services have both latent and manifest functions. That is, they exist both to care for the individual, and to ensure the apparently smooth running of society. The psychiatric care of women demonstrates very clearly the problems that can occur when these two functions conflict. There are no easy answers for the mental health professional who wants to act in the best interests of the client. It goes almost without saying that sexual abuse of female clients is not going to help them in their search for mental health. Beyond this, however, an important first step is perhaps that the clinician should become aware of the issues that have been raised in this chapter, so that, as a minimum, the latent function of the psychiatric and psychotherapeutic service (the maintenance of the sexual status quo) does not intervene in the manifest function of caring for a client. This can happen simply because of the unwillingness of a clinician to think about the implications of the way that he is behaving in therapy, or because of the value judgments that he is making. But as a second step, perhaps the clinician should also contemplate acting to promote changes in the way therapy is conducted, and in the objectives that are held out for their clients. Only in these ways can clinicians really be seen to be acting according to high ethical standards in the interests of their clients, both men and women.

REFERENCES

Apfel, R.J. and Simon, B. (1985), 'Patient-therapist sexual contact', *Psychotherapy and Psychosomatics, 43*, pp.57–62.

Bem, S.L. (1974), 'The Measurement of Psychological Androgyny', *Journal of Consulting and Clinical Psychology, 42*, pp.155–62.

Block, J.H. (1973), 'Conceptions of Sex Roles: Some Cross-Cultural and Longitudinal Perspectives', *American Psychologist, 28*, pp.512–27.

BPS (1983), *Guidelines for the Professional Practice of Clinical Psychology*, Leicester.

British Psychological Society (1985), 'A Code of Conduct for Psychologists', *Bulletin of the British Psychological Society, 38*, pp.41–3.

Broverman, I.K., Broverman, D.M., Clarkson, F.E., Rosenkrantz, P.R. and Vogt, S.R. (1970), 'Sex Role Stereotypes and Clinical Judgements of Mental Health', *Journal of Consulting and Clinical Psychology, 34*, pp.1–7.

Brown, G.W. and Harris, T. (1978), *Social Origins of Depression*, London, Tavistock.

Brownmiller, S. (1975), *Against Our Will: Men, Women and Rape*, New York, Simon and Schuster.

Burgess, A.W. (1981), 'Physician Sexual Misconduct and Patients'

Responses', *American Journal of Psychiatry, 138*, pp.1335–42.

Chesler, P. (1974), *Women and Madness*, London, Allan Lane.

Chodorow, N. (1978), *The Reproduction of Mothering*, Berkeley, California, University of California Press.

Cooperstock, R. (1979), 'A Review of Women's Psychotropic Drug Use', *Canadian Journal of Psychiatry, 24*, pp.29–34.

DHSS (1975), *Better Services for the Mentally Ill*, London, HMSO.

DHSS (1977), *Inpatient Statistics for the Mental Health Enquiry for England 1975*, London, HMSO.

Dinnerstein, D. (1978), *The Rocking of the Cradle*, London, Souvenir Press.

Eichenbaum, L. and Orbach, S. (1982), *Outside In, Inside Out*, Harmondsworth, Penguin.

Frank, J.D. (1973), *Persuasion and Healing*, Baltimore, Maryland, John Hopkins University Press.

Frankland, A. (1981), 'Mistaken seduction', *New Forum, 7*, pp.79–81.

Furrow, B.R. (1980), *Malpractice in Psychotherapy*, Lexington, Lexington Books.

Gilman, C.P. (1981), 'The Yellow Wallpaper', in *The Charlotte Perkins Gilman Reader*, London, The Women's Press.

Hall, J.E. and Hare-Mustin, R.T. (1983), 'Sanctions and the Diversity of Ethical Complaints Against Psychologists', *American Psychologist, 38*, pp.714–29.

Hochman, J. (1984), 'Iatrogenic symptoms associated with a therapy cult: examination of an extinct "new psychotherapy" with respect to psychiatric deterioration and "brainwashing" ', *Psychiatry, 47*, pp.366–77.

Holroyd, J.C. and Brodsky, A.M. (1977), 'Psychologists' Attitudes and Practices Regarding Erotic and Nonerotic Physical Contact with Patients', *American Psychologist, 32*, pp.843–9.

Kaplan, A. (1979), 'Toward an Analysis of Sex-role Related Issues in the Therapeutic Relationship', *Psychiatry, 43*, pp.112–20.

Kaplan, M. (1983) 'A Woman's View of DSM–III', *American Psychologist, 38*, pp.786–92.

Kardener, S.H., Fuller, M. and Mensch, I.N. (1973), 'A Survey of Physicians' Attitudes and Practices Regarding Erotic and Nonerotic Contact with Patients', *American Journal of Psychiatry, 130*, pp.1077–81.

Kardener, S.H. (1974), 'Sex and the Physician-Patient Relationship', *American Journal of Psychiatry, 131*, pp.1134–6.

Kaswan, J. (1981), 'Manifest and Latent Functions of Psychological Services', *American Psychologist, 36*, pp.290–9.

Lee Smith, M. (1980), 'Sex Bias in Counselling and Psychotherapy',

Psychological Bulletin, 87, pp.392–407.
Lerner, H.E. (1978), 'Adaptive and Pathogenic Aspects of Sex-Role Stereotypes: Implications for Parenting and Psychotherapy', *American Journal of Psychiatry, 135*, pp.48–52.
Mitchell, J. (1974), *Psychoanalysis and Women*, London, Allan Lane.
Orlinsky, D.E. and Howard, K.I. (1977), 'The Therapists' Experience of Psychotherapy', in A.S. Gurman and A.M. Razin (eds), *Effective Psychotherapy: A Handbook of Research*, Oxford, Pergamon Press.
Parry, G., Llewelyn, S.P. and Davis, A. (1984), 'Women and Mental Health: Towards an Understanding', in A. Davis (ed.), *Women and Social Work*, London, Tavistock.
Prochaska, J.O. and Norcross, J.C. (1982), 'The Future of Psychotherapy: A Delphi Poll', *Professional Psychotherapy, 13*.
Smail, D.J. (1984), *Illusion and Reality*, London, Dent.
Spence, J.T. and Helmreich, R.L. (1978), *Masculinity and Femininity: Their Psychological Dimensions, Correlates and Antecendents*, Austin, University of Texas Press.
Stone, A.A. (1983), 'Sexual Misconduct by Psychiatrists: The Ethical and Clinical Dilemma of Confidentiality', *American Journal of Psychiatry, 140*, pp.195–7.
Strupp, H.H. and Hadley, S.W. (1979), 'Specific Versus Nonspecific Factors in Psychotherapy: A Controlled Study of Outcome', *Archives of General Psychiatry, 36*, pp.1125–36.
Swenson, E.V. and Ragucci, R. (1984), 'Effects of Sex-role Stereotypes and Androgynous Alternatives on Mental Health Judgments of Psychotherapists', *Psychological Reports, 54*, pp.475–81.
Temerlin, M.K. and Temerlin, J.W. (1982) 'Psychotherapy Cults: An Iatrogenic Perversion', *Psychotherapy: Theory, Research and Practice, 19*, pp.131–41.
Tennov, D. (1973), 'Feminism, Psychotherapy and Professionalism', *Journal of Contemporary Psychotherapy, 5*, pp.107–11.
Van Herik, J. (1984), *Freud on Femininity and Faith*, London, University of California Press.
Voss, J. and Gannon, L. (1978), 'Sexism in the Theory and Practice of Clinical Psychology', *Professional Psychology*, pp.623–33.
Weissman, M.M. and Klerman, G. (1977), 'Sex Differences and the Epidemiology of Depression', *Archives of General Psychiatry, 34*, pp.98–101.
Whitley, B.E. (1979), 'Sex Roles and Psychotherapy: a Current Appraisal', *Psychological Bulletin, 86*, pp.1309–21.

Ethics and Family Therapy

Rudi Dallos

Prior to their second session the mother in one family phoned to cancel the session. She explained that they could not attend 'because they were having family problems'. This apparent absurdity exposes a fundamental dilemma in the practice of family therapy in that few families attend intending to have 'family therapy'. Instead, almost invariably, one person is designated as the root or cause of their problems. In many cases this understanding may be the exclusive area of agreement in the family. This represents a fundamental difference between the understandings of the therapist and the family. For example, the parents in a family may complain about their child being disobedient and uncontrollable but be quite unaware that they show conflict, confusion and disagreement in their dealings with the child and that they have failed consequently to develop or implement any consistent ways of dealing with him. At times one or more of the parents may even be covertly encouraging a child to engage in the very types of actions that they are complaining about. In one family the father, completely unaware, smiled tenderly at his son, while the ten-year-old boy recounted tales of his mischief and misdemeanours at the psychiatric unit that he was attending.

INDIVIDUAL PROBLEMS AND FAMILY DYNAMICS

There are various schools of family therapy (strategic, structural, existential, psychodynamic, behavioural) with important differences in approach and theory. Yet a major point of agreement between them is the need to consider the problems displayed, usually by one person identified as the patient, within the total family situation. They share the belief that it is necessary to convene as many 'significant' family members as possible in order to observe and facilitate change within the family. It is worth noting that this position contrasts not only to the practice of individual therapies, but to attitudes about the involvement of relatives in the therapeutic endeavour. Freud (1963), for example, was quite explicit in his views and likened the relative's involvement to an undesirable intrusion in a surgical procedure: 'Ask yourselves now how many of those operations would turn out successfully if they had to take place in the presence of all the members of the family, who would stick their noses into the field of the operation and exclaim aloud at every incision.'

The term 'family' is used loosely here to refer to any nexus of intimately involved people. So any variant of family life: single parent, lesbian or gay couples, unmarried parents, friends and even people physically distant but psychologically 'close' may be included in family therapy. Perhaps a more accurate term would be interactional or brief therapy. Even the term therapy with the 'community of intimates' has been suggested but, not surprisingly perhaps, has not caught on.

The arguments in this chapter will focus on work within a strategic family therapy approach. This employs systems theory as its basic theoretical model. One simple but fundamental fact behind this type of therapy is that it attempts to be 'brief'. The guiding principle is that of 'neutrality' wherein the therapist's task is to enable the family to regain the ability to solve their own difficulties, rather than to offer prescriptions or mould them into socially acceptable configurations. This is a stark contrast to psychodynamic approaches for example, which attempt to 'delve deeply' in order to 'root out' the causes of the difficulties. Jay Haley (1980) in contrast has argued that one of the most positive interventions that a family therapist can make is to discharge the family!

The approach taken in this chapter derives from the idea that problems emerge from and are maintained by the ongoing patterns of interactions. More precisely Don Jackson (1957) first articulated the idea that the repetitive patterns and apparent resistance to change demonstrated by families was analogous to the behaviour of self-regulative systems, for example the regulation of heart-rate, blood-sugar levels or a central heating system. Families likewise can be seen as having a capacity for self-regulation, whereby change can be kept within certain limits. Such a model appeared to fit many families displaying pathologies as exemplified by cases where the identified patient improved after being removed from the family only to relapse on rejoining it. Such families appeared to display 'resistance' to change in therapy by engaging in various sorts of 'sabotage' or manoeuvre such as 'forgetting' to turn up for a session or to carry out a task. Families appeared to maintain a pathological state despite the high cost in terms of emotional and practical discomfort. Jackson suggested that a family in this state acts 'as if' it 'requires' a sick member and cannot 'manage' without one.

Superficially such a view of family life sounds extremely reductionist and mechanistic. Some therapists like Minuchin (1974) have warned of a new dogma emerging in family therapy whereby there is a danger of losing sight of individual responsibility and choice of action. Yet this need not be the case. Paul Watzlawick and his colleagues (1967, 1974) and Harry Procter (1980) have suggested instead that each person in a family is potentially free to make his or her own decisions. However since these impinge on the others in the family their views must be taken into consideration. Over time each person forms a web of anticipations, based on their shared experiences, about how the others will react. This is, of course, necessary for them to be able to organise their lives and to manage the task of living together. Out of this shared experience can be seen to develop a shared construct system which structures, but also constrains, what each person believes to be possible or permissible. This can give a sense of unity and security to everyone in the family. However problems can arise when a family undergoing difficulties holds desperately to limited ways of construing the situation. This can result in them becoming stuck in a cycle of failed solutions. For example, the parents in a family, in which the adolescent daughter is acting delinquently, may construe their alternatives when she is at the leaving-home stage in a very limited way. They may see the alternatives as being between 'keeping an eye on her' at home, with the consequent tension and distress that this involves, or allowing her to leave with the risk that she will 'ruin her life' and possibly 'end up a criminal'. For her part the girl may make repeated attempts to assert her independence by acting in deliquent ways. Yet by so doing she may merely reaffirm to her parents her immaturity, in turn leading them to tighten their grip and delay her transition to adult status. Though everyone may be appearing to be making their own decisions, the choices are constrained by the others. In some cases the outcome can be that a knot is tightened whereby the choices in the family become extremely limited.

A view of families as composed of people who necessarily constrain not only each other's actions but their understandings poses some important ethical issues for the therapist. Most importantly it raises questions about whether the therapist should attempt to disabuse the family of their 'misconceptions' and whether this should only be attempted with the family's permission. A common assumption in many schools of therapy was that people could be assisted by simply encouraging them to communicate in order to gain insight into their difficulties. However Jay Haley (1976) has emphasised that the task of the therapist must be much more active, since the processes of communication and the content can become extremely predictable and constrained. For example, a wife's continuous attempts to talk to her husband in order to 'sort things out' may be construed by him as a punishing 'nagging'. When he subsequently withdraws, her attempts to pin him down may merely validate his view that she is in fact 'nagging'. As a consequence the issues remain unresolved and their communicational difficulties become worse with each attempt to rectify them (Watzlawick *et al.*, 1974). A fundamental task for the family therapist in this situation is to intervene, perhaps by offering a new way for the couple to see each other's actions. For example, it can be suggested that the wife is trying to keep close to him and that her husband is protecting her from his anxieties at work. The important point is that the therapist is 'active' and makes an input into the situation.

Haley (1976) suggests that a central task of the therapist is to manage the flow of information in a family. In the example above we can see that there is virtually no new information being exchanged between the couple. Neither of them is doing or saying anything which is new; it has all become very predictable. In order to facilitate any change the therapist must intervene in some way, no matter how low-key, in order to enable information to flow again. But, it is highly unlikely that it is sufficient to merely 'share' understandings with the family. Telling the couple above that they have a communication problem is unlikely to help. As Haley suggests they are almost certain to know this already. What they don't know is what to do about it and they require a 'diplomatic' procedure to overcome their problems. In some instances this may involve interventions, the purposes of which are outside the family's awareness.

To summarise so far, it is being suggested that it is helpful to regard each person's actions in a family as based upon a set of constructs or premises which are not merely individual but have evolved out of the family dynamics. Since these premises are also seen to be shared, no one individual is regarded as holding unilateral responsibility for the circumstances that have developed, including the current problems. Such an approach offers a potentially neutral way of regarding problems. The identified person in the family is not blamed nor are the others. Rather the problem is seen as a consequence of their dynamics. We should remember that this view is likely to contrast strongly with the view of the family. Even the identified patient has usually accepted that they are 'the problem'. Since they have usually already done something 'strange' in order to gain their patient role, this view is very compelling for all concerned.

THERAPISTS' AND FAMILY'S CONSTRUCTS

Putting the issue very baldly, it could be said that the therapist regards the family's understandings as misconceived in being framed in individual terms. Bateson (1972) in fact argued more broadly that the perception of problems in personal or individual terms was part of a cultural misconception particularly prevalent in Western societies. Others (Laing, 1971 and Szasz, 1961) have expressed great concern about the political processes involved in attributing a 'sick' label to individuals without paying attention to the prevailing social factors. Likewise Selvini Palazzoli and her colleagues (1978) proposed that our language predisposes us to think and explain problems in a linear, individual manner. As an example she argues that adjectives such as honest, neurotic, extrovert, intelligent lead us to think in terms of invariant individual characteristics. Instead, it is possible to think of different types of actions emerging out of different interpersonal contexts. In a confused, contradictory family situation, for example, it may be difficult to act honestly or intelligently.

A similar set of arguments surround the issue of whether the entire family is ascribed 'blame' either explicitly or implicitly. The latter is reflected in the uncritical use and acceptance of typologies of family functioning and structure, such as 'disorganised', 'rigid', 'enmeshed-disengaged' which clearly have judgmental overtones. Many families have likewise felt compelled to accept that there is something 'wrong' with them and feelings of guilt and inadequacy may function to prevent them from uniting to confront injustices, for example at work and with bureaucracy, which place unbearable strains upon them. Alternatively it is possible to see the family structure, in an analogous way to the behaviour of individuals within it, as 'emerging' out of the immediate and wider social contexts within which it is located (Laing, 1971; Keeney, 1979).

An important question that faces the family therapist then is what to do about these differences in understanding between himself and the family. It could be argued that the ethically justifiable course is to attempt to change the family's understandings only with their consent. Unfortunately this raises major problems, not least of these being that many families are reluctant to participate at all, if 'family' therapy if proposed. On the other hand they may attend, if the focus is, initially at least, on the identified patient. Obviously our wish as therapists is to assist people and relieve their distress. But we cannot do very much if they won't participate. This forces us to face the ethical dilemma of which is less ethically justifiable, to 'trick' a family into attending for therapy or to leave them in distress out of a principle of 'honesty'? Furthermore the issue becomes extremely serious when there is a need to act quickly, for example in cases of suicidal threats, self-starvation, severe psychosis and violence.

This obvious need to establish contact in order to allow the possibility of any therapeutic work to proceed is not simply a justification for acting in potentially unethical ways. Rather, this initial contact between the family and the therapist can be seen to be complex and as requiring diplomacy. The presentation of one person as the problem is a powerful communication by the family about how they wish to approach the situation. It has usually taken them some time to arrive at this as the best solution to their circumstances and an early confrontation of it may be seen as unsympathetic and threatening.

This issue of the definition of the problem can be seen as part of a wider 'power struggle' between the therapist and the family to do with gaining control of the situation. Much of this may be communicated without either side's awareness of it. For example a family that quibbles about the times and dates that they can attend, may indirectly be expressing that they wish to have control or to be treated respectfully. Similarly, a therapist's insistence that all members attend may in part be an unintentional communication that she wants her services to be valued and due appreciation shown by all the family taking the time to attend. However this may not be the most useful strategy as regards engaging the family or maintaining manoeuverability in the future. One implication here is that the therapist needs to be aware of these possibilities and to deal with them in a strategic way.

THE PRACTICE OF FAMILY THERAPY

As a prerequisite for further discussions of ethical issues it is necessary to describe briefly what is involved in the practice of family therapy.

WORKING AS A TEAM

Family therapy is usually carried out in a team situation. Normally this consists of one or more therapists working directly with the family. This work is supervised 'live' by the others who act as consultants. This may be by means of video and an observation screen. Such equipment is an aid but it is possible to work in a similar way without it. The consultants can sit in the same room or merely be available for discussion without actually viewing the session. Whatever the variety of working, it is always carried out with the family's consent.

This arrangement can involve a reasonably honest declaration that the team will attempt to manipulate the family in order to facilitate changes for their benefit. There is nevertheless a danger that some families may experience an element of coercion, for example if they are unhappy with such an arrangement but are afraid to object.

One of the potential advantages of working as a team is that it offers some safeguards against forms of unconscious manipulation by the therapist (and by the family). On the other hand it is also possible that the team can exert greater and more subtle coercions than an individual therapist. Many teams attempt to offset such coercive effects by ensuring that a team consists of a variety of professionals: social workers, psychologists, psychiatrists, nurses. In this way a range of perspectives and hopefully greater critical awareness (challenging of their own assumptions about a family and appraisal of the relationships between the family and other institutions) is encouraged.

Despite the potential dangers of working as a team, it is important to contemplate the even greater ones involved with a therapist working alone. However well-meant, unintentional manipulation may inevitably occur and is likely to go unrecognised. Alternatively, a therapist may be drawn into the family dynamics and end up taking sides or becoming emotionally over-involved to the point of becoming therapeutically impotent. An indication of this can be when one member of the family becomes excessively friendly or hostile towards the therapist. At the family level there may also be a danger of the therapist becoming the family's 'champion' and 'fighting' a variety of other institutions and professionals. Of course this may at times be appropriate but there may also be great risks, both for the therapist and the family, if this becomes an emotive position and goes unrecognised. For example a family may subsequently be seen as 'difficult' or 'uncooperative' with consequent sanctions and 'punishing' tactics employed against them.

ENGAGEMENT

However obvious and dramatically painful the problems and difficulties they face, it is often difficult to persuade a family to enagage in therapy. As was indicated earlier, more often than not the members of the family including the patient, will hold the belief that one of them is 'ill' as opposed to the others who are 'well'. Frequently this leads to the position that the other members are reluctant to attend for therapy, especially if they feel that they may in some way be blamed or accused of contributing to the problem. Obviously this is a vital issue. If we cannot persuade a family to attend for therapy or even to permit home visits, then therapy cannot proceed. Consequently the problems may persist or become worse. If direct appeals are unsuccessful or felt to be inappropriate the therapist may request a family to attend in order to 'gather information and opinions about the patient's difficulties', or alternatively, to discuss, 'how the others can help to monitor or administer the treatment programme'. In some cases a key person is presented by the family as the one who is resistant to attending. In many cases this is the father which perhaps has to do with conventions regarding sex roles, in that the emotional life of the family is seen as the wife's domain. One approach that can be taken here is to praise father by letter: . . . 'for being mature enough to allow the other members some space, and trusting them to talk freely and frankly about the difficulties: this despite knowing that they may be saying many intimate things about his own behaviour and thoughts.'

Such an indirect approach can often succeed not only because it puts the man in a positive light and stimulates his curiosity, but also because it can serve to break up an important family game. For example, the other members may be colluding against dad, perhaps blaming him for the problems that, for example, the daughter is experiencing. This manoeuvre, however, can be utilised positively in therapy since it indicates that the family has already made an important step towards a view of the problem as involving more than one person in the family. This can provide a powerful therapeutic bridge towards looking at family rather than individual issues, and thereby helps to move the focus from the sole indentified patient – the girl in this instance.

The nature of the understandings in the team must also be taken into account. In a case such as the one above, some members of the team may be drawn into seeing the father in a bad light; as obstructive, difficult, and resistant. The therapy team will usually meet to discuss a case before the session so that such perceptions may surface and alternative and more positive ways of seeing the situation can be suggested. Through discussion the team can move towards a more neutral position; seeing how each person's actions fit into the total pattern of the family.

INTERVENTIONS

One of the fundamental aims of family therapy is to break up patterns of repetitive behaviour or circularities incorporating the problem. Typically, family therapists adopt a number of approaches in order to do this. In some rare instances merely the chance to talk about the difficulties in the form of a friendly discussion with the therapist may be enough to produce important changes. More often though, it is necessary to use some strategic and less direct approaches.

Reframing

The therapist might try to suggest a new and positive way of seeing aspects of the situation in the family. For example, the situation in a family with a child who is 'misbehaving' may be reframed as parents having provided the opportunity for the child to learn to express herself and to test the rules and limits in the family. The parents may be praised for their openness and courage in allowing this. At the same time they may be encouraged to negotiate and articulate clear guidelines to allow the child to develop further, and to be able to act in ways which are acceptable outside the family.

Paradoxical techniques

The intention behind paradoxical techniques is to produce a relief in the problems indirectly by prescribing the opposite of what is intended. For example, a family may be asked to maintain or even increase their symptoms. Frequently this is done when a family appears 'resistant' to the therapist's suggestions. Hence when the therapist prescribes the symptoms, in order to continue resisting, the family must act to reduce the symptoms. Alternatively they may start to be co-operative which also represents a change and a positive step. As an example, a young woman who obsessively fidgeted with her hair, resulting in a bald patch, was directed to make frequent measurements of the lengths of her hair on different parts of her head. She was to do this with the help of her mother in order to provide a detailed picture for the team, and her mother, of her condition. Mother soon became tired of this task and one consequence of this was that she allowed a little more space for her daughter and her husband (who were living with them) to develop their marrriage.

This intervention did not question the basic premises of the family, namely that there was something 'wrong' with this young woman. Instead, by acting consistently upon them and in fact by encouraging the symptomatic behaviour, of fidgeting with (measuring) her hair, the effect was to unbalance the situation enough to allow some change.

It is possible to consider such techniques in terms of how they match the communicational modes or strategies that the family is employing. After all it is a paradoxical position and communication for a family to attend for therapy, to seek help but then not to comply with at least some of the suggestions of the therapist. In some families, especially those with schizophrenic symptoms, contradictory ways of communicating may be quite fundamental (Haley, 1980; Selvini Palazzoli *et al.*, 1978). Distress may be communicated in such families in an indirect way through the symptoms. As in the case above, the young woman was clearly unable to express openly that her marriage was in difficulty and that her mother's interference was not helping matters. As Haley (1976) suggests, if such issues could be openly expressed the family wouldn't be coming for therapy: They wouldn't need the symptom. Therefore, at times, it can be argued that the therapist has little choice but to engage in paradoxical forms of communication in order to make any progress.

Directives and tasks

In a similar way, directives and tasks may address problematic issues in an indirect and implicit way. For example, it may be suggested to a couple that they change roles as an experiment in order to observe how their problematic child's behaviour will change as a result. This may in some instances produce important changes in the family dynamics, for example when the father wakes to change a child's wet bed instead of mother, he may become much more sympathetic to his wife's previous role and come to actively co-operate with her to solve the problem.

Again, however, the family may not be fully in the picture about the therapist's intentions. In fact, were the therapist to openly declare what her intentions were, almost certainly the strategy would not work. There is a story of a trainee therapist who had a tendency to announce paradoxical interventions to a family by starting off: 'This may sound paradoxical to you. . . .' Needless to say, the family was left confused and the 'paradoxes' weren't as effective as they could have been!

Circular questioning

This is both a way of gathering information about what happens in a family, especially regarding the events surrounding the problem or symptoms, and also a way of producing change. Considerable new information is made available by the use of questions such as; 'Who gets most upset when mother is crying . . .?', plus detailed questioning about the sequence of events surrounding the problem, and also by asking each member of the family to comment on the relationship between the others. Most importantly the family members are encouraged, in an indirect way, to see the problems in 'interpersonal' terms.

We can see from the description of some of the techniques in the practice of family therapy that there are important ethical concerns. Not only is the family therapist often in disagreement with the family about the definition of the problem as interpersonal as opposed to personal, but also some of the techniques, especially paradoxical interventions, at first sight appear quite dishonest and manipulative. A great danger both for the practice of family therapy and for the discussion of the ethics of these techniques is to see them in isolation. Trainee therapists sometimes ponder what paradox they could try on a family. But this is a serious mistake. Family therapy, like other therapies, is founded on a relationship of trust. It is in this context only that, for example, a paradoxical intervention can work. In other words the family must know that the therapist is genuinely concerned and wants them to overcome their problems. Otherwise being told, for example, to increase one's symptoms might just appear insulting or even sadistic.

Before exploring some of the issues that the practice of family therapy raises, it is also necesary to outline some basic ideas from communications theory on which the practice of family therapy rests. Above all else any therapy requires communication between the therapist and the client/s. But in this truism hides a deceptively simple but remarkably ignored fact: communication requires a sender and a receiver of the message. As Watzlawick *et al.* (1967) point out the message intended may not be the same as the one that is received. Consequently if we try to talk to a family that is used to talking in an ambiguous or even paradoxical way we may, at least initially, need to talk in the same way. For example, the following extract is from a family in which the son aged 24 was displaying schizophrenic symptoms:

Therapist	'Could you tell me a little bit about what sort of problems Steven has been having.'
Father	'Oh he's just not fit, he's had 'flu. Anyway he tries to put things out of his mind'.
Steven	'That's right I can't remember . . .'
Therapist	'Well I can see that's a good thing to do at the moment. Perhaps we can come back to it at another time . . .'
Father	'I think Steven got very upset when a friend died . . . it kept playing on his mind . . .'

Repeated attempts to encourage the family to talk about their son Steven's schizophrenic symptoms met with little success. However, by simply going along with the denial, which of course makes a nonsense of coming for therapy, the effect was quite immediate and father gave out some more information about the problems.

One vital point here is to do with how the therapist gets through to the family. As we have already seen often they have quite different ideas to that of the therapist about the causes of the difficulties. Consequently the therapist has to be aware of the potential interpretations that a family may ascribe to what he says to them. As in the case above the therapist could have reassured the family that it was safe to talk about the problems. But for a distressed family such assurances may not work. On the other hand the slightly crazy message that it is all right to come for therapy but not talk about the problems may indirectly have communicated more acceptance and fostered a sense of trust.

Such ideas are based largely on the model of communication developed by Gregory Bateson (1972) which proposes that any communication inevitably contains two parts. One part, usually the verbal, contains the content of the message or specific information, whereas the other, usually the non-verbal, carries a definition of the relationship between the sender and the receiver. Much of the time the two levels confirm and complement each other. However at times of uncertainty and distress in families there may be considerable incongruity, such as when a husband at the end of his tether may make comforting remarks in an angry tone to his distressed wife.

From the discussion so far a number of ethical themes have started to emerge which must now be taken up in more detail. Paramount is the question of whether the practice of family therapy involves unethical manipulation of the family by the therapist as opposed to a process of mutually negotiated influence and change. This and other issues will be discussed within the framework of the aims and intentions of family therapy and the ends and means employed for achieving them.

Manipulation

A communicational analysis shows that like the members of a family the therapist will also non-verbally, and at times unconsciously, communicate her feelings. This throws doubt on the claims of some schools of therapy which advocate a non-directive approach. For example films of the work of 'non-directive' therapists such as Carl Rogers and Fritz Perls reveal patterns of selective encouragement and discouragement of which they appear to be unaware. (Fisch (1967) likewise makes this point.) More broadly Watzlawick (1967) points out that it is impossible in any social situation not to communicate and hence to influence. It has been forcibly argued by a number of family therapists (Haley, 1976; Minuchin, 1974; Watzlawick *et al.* 1974), that all forms of therapy must of necessity involve an element of manipulation in order to effect change.

Milton Erickson (1980), for example, openly declares to a family that he will direct them but that they should only comply if they wish. Yet this apparently straightforward approach raises some fundamental questions. At one level such an open declaration is ethically sound in being open and honest. At another it functions as a therapeutic paradox. By inviting resistance in this way some families are often much less likely to remain defensive and resistant.

The important point here is that the family can choose to agree to participate in a relationship in which they will be manipulated. However, by the therapist making this overt they have more freedom to withdraw from the situation if they wish. On the other hand, claims to avoid manipulation may be self-deceptive and in a sense dishonest because they offer an impossibility. Erickson has drawn out, in this respect, the fundamental differences between therapeutic and pernicious forms of manipulation involved in paradoxical (double-bind) communications in table 1.

In the therapeutic situation the requests or injunctions are typically positive such as suggesting the client do more of something they are already doing. However, what is more important, as Haley (1976) points out, is that the therapist's intentions are regarded as being genuinely on the family's behalf. In other words, that he is acting for their own good and not simply for his own interests or those of agencies or institutions. This is particularly an issue with cases where the penal system is involved. In probation work, for example, an officer may suggest to a family that they don't reveal any more information to him, since he would be forced to reveal it to their detriment. This may declare indirectly to the family more powerfully than any assurances of confidentiality that the therapist has their well being at heart and is trying to remain neutral. It is only within such a firm basis of trust that paradoxical/double-bind procedures can function therapeutically.

A vital point is to distinguish between types and degrees of manipulation. In the extreme we can consider the unlikely case of a therapist who acts in ways which are for his benefit primarily rather than the family's. Alternatively we have been considering a 'benevolent' form of manipulation which is primarily for the family's benefit. Of course the therapist must check with the family that this is in fact the case and he has not got it all wrong. There are analogies here with the practice of medicine; with some treatments the patient will experience discomfort and resist, nevertheless being manipulated, physically and psychologically 'for one's own good' is accepted as part of the treatment.

Table 1

The Bateson schizogenic bind	The Erickson therapeutic bind
1 *Two or more persons* The child 'victim' is usually ensnared by mother or a combination of parents and siblings.	1 *Two or more persons* Usually patient and therapist are ensconced in a positive relationship.
2 *Repeated experience* Double bind is repeated occurrence rather than one simple traumatic event.	2 *A single or series of experiences* If one is not enough, a series of double binds will be *offered* until one works.
3 *A primary negative injunction* 'Do not do so-and-so or I will punish you.'	3 *A primary positive injunction* 'I agree that you should continue doing such and such.'
4 *A secondary negative injunction* Conflicting with the first at a more abstract (meta) level and like the first enforced by punishments or signals which threaten survival.	4 *A secondary positive suggestion* At the meta level that facilitates a creative interaction between the primary (conscious) and meta level (unconscious). Responses at both levels are permitted to resolve stalemated conflicts.
5 *A tertiary negative injunction* Prohibiting the victim from escaping the field.	5 *A tertiary positive injunction* (Rapport, transference) that binds the patient to his therapeutic task but leaves him free to leave if he chooses.
6 Finally the complete set of ingredients is no longer necessary when the victim has learned to perceive his universe in double-bind patterns.	6 The patient leaves therapy when his behaviour change frees him from transference and the evoked double binds.

While I put patients into a double-bind, they also sense, unconsciously, that I will never, never hold them to it. They know I will yield anytime. I will then put them in another double-bind in some other situation to see if they put it to constructive use because it meets their needs more adequately. *From* Rossi (1980).

Negotiation

It is possible to see family therapy as a process of negotiation rather than manipulation between the therapist and the family. Both inevitably influence each other to arrive at new understandings which are mutually acceptable. George Kelly (1955) argues more broadly for such a position. In his view psychological theories should be reflexive. So, in therapy the activity of the therapist is seen as identical to that of the family's. In the process of family therapy we can see the family and the therapist offering each other a range of hypotheses or understandings about the problems. It is necessary for these to become mutually acceptable in order for therapy to proceed. Difficulties, for example, are often to do with the therapy team becoming unable to construe a family in a new way or to see the changes that have already occurred. As an example with one couple, our attempts to encourage them to communicate about their relationship in order to stop the man's episodes of indecent exposing made little progress. It was realised eventually that for the husband talking was construed as undesirable and he preferred to communicate in physical ways. He had told us that his father had used to say 'Some things are best left unsaid.' When the team came to realise this vital difference between their hypotheses and the couple's about what would work, it became possible to proceed more effectively. It is important to understand a family's construing not only for avoiding inappropriate paths but also because when a family feels that the therapist understands and accepts their construing of the problem they are more likely to co-operate and attempt changes.

ENDS AND MEANS

Alan Watts (1961) elegantly describes therapy as involving benevolent trickery. This is illustrated not only in recent paradoxical techniques but in many ancient approaches:

A Japanese coastal village was once threatened by a tidal wave, but the wave was sighted in advance, far out on the horizon, by a lone farmer in the rice fields on the hillside above the village. At once he set fire to the fields, and the villagers who came swarming up to save their crops were saved from the flood. His crime of arson is like the trickery of the guru, the doctor, or the psychotherapist in persuading people to try to solve a false problem by acting consistently upon its premises.

Similar techniques are recounted in stories used by the Sufis to teach and illuminate their philosophy, such as that of the sterile woman:

> A man went to a doctor and told him that his wife was not bearing children. The physician saw the woman, took her pulse, and said: 'I cannot treat you for sterility because I have discovered that you will in any case die within forty days'. But she did not die at the time predicted.
>
> The husband took the matter up with the doctor, who said: 'Yes, I knew that. Now she will be fertile'.
>
> The husband asked how this had come about. The doctor told him: 'Your wife was too fat, and this was interfering with her fertility. I knew that the only thing which would put her off her food would be fear of dying. She is now, therefore, cured'
>
> The question of knowledge is a very dangerous one (Shah, 1968).

Alan Watts (1961) goes on to justify this use of trickery by suggesting that there is no way of disabusing the sufferer directly. Telling someone that their 'cherished disease is a disease' is unlikely to help. Instead if people are to be helped they must be tricked into changing their actions which may consequently lead them to changed insights:

> If I am to help someone else to see that a false problem is false, I must pretend that I am taking his problem seriously. What I am actually taking seriously is his suffering, but he must be led to believe that it is what he considers as his problem.

In some ways the position suggested by Watts may appear slightly arrogant -- as if the therapist 'knows' better than the patient what is best. The excuse for this is that his intention is a virtuous one, namely to get the sufferer better. However in the practice of family therapy this issue is even more complex. The truth of the matter is that usually the therapist does not know what is the best course of action. This is an extremely important point. Goffman (1961) has warned of the dangers of coercing people into socially acceptable roles. Paradoxically, however, in family therapy there is no clearly defined model of what a 'normal' family is and consequently this may be less of a danger than in individual therapies. What is perhaps a more crucial problem concerns the construings of the therapist and the team. Often a first step is for the therapist to disabuse himself of his negative conceptions about the family. Initially this can be a kind of a 'head game' wherein the therapist and the team try to look for the 'silver lining' under the dark clouds of the family's problems. To novice therapists this can seem a crazy exercise: for example to think about the positive aspects of how an anorexic girl is keeping her family together. Yet the experience of engaging in this kind of double-think is very profound. Once new ways of seeing things have been attempted, no matter how crazy they may sound at first, it becomes almost impossible to see the family in exactly the same way as before. This suggests that the therapist is initially engaged in an attempt to change the construings or premises underlying the problem but not in any specific direction. In other words, if manipulation is involved it must be a very non-specific form, at least initially. Subsequently the family responds to these new suggestions and may reject or accept them.

As an example in one family, Sarah, a young girl of seven was described as disruptive and uncontrollable. After several sessions with the girl and the family it emerged that a key issue was the way that her father 'teased' her mercilessly. The girl was upset by this and didn't know what to do about it. Initially this negative view of father's teasing was very compelling but it was possible to view it in a different light. The family had been reconvened after individual work with Sarah, during which she had been playing with a doll's house with the therapist. On the previous occasion her father had made a severely sarcastic remark about the 'stupid' way that she had arranged some of the furniture:

Therapist (to Sarah)	'I wonder what mummy and daddy will say to you this time when you show them how you have arranged the doll's house. I bet daddy will tease you. What do you think he will say?'
Sarah and parents	No reply.
Therapist	'Teasing is an important game, you can learn to read people's faces and develop a sense of humour. But it's a bit hard for you, isn't it, Sarah? Perhaps daddy could teach you how to do it. You could play games like cards and he could tell you when he's teasing or bluffing so that you can learn to do it back to him.'

Father 'I could always keep a deadpan face. I used to play a lot of poker when I was younger'.
Therapist 'Yes it must be very useful for card games . . .'

In some ways the test of an intervention is not only whether it produces an effect on the family but also whether it produces changes in the therapist, especially in how the family is seen. In the case above, the father was now seen as a man who was not necessarily punishing his daughter for not being that son that he had wanted, but was trying to have fun with her, though unfortunately, his attempts were not working. Ultimately the paradoxical reinterpretation of the father's behaviour altered not only the family system but also the family-therapist system.

It is possible in this way for the therapist and the family to make a joint journey whereby they arrive at some mutually satisfactory understandings of the situation that permit growth and development to be resumed. In some cases a new perspective can be arrived at almost as a by-product of the therapy. In other families though this becomes a central issue. For example in some highly educated families there may be considerable pressure exerted on the therapist to provide explanations. In one family which contained a girl suffering from anorexia, there was great interest shown in understanding the problems. Both parents were teachers and the children were either at, or heading for, Oxbridge education. The parents had read widely on the subject of anorexia and held interesting psychological theories. In the therapy sessions the parents made frequent requests for explanations and each offering from the therapist would be politely rejected, just as the family rejected each other's. Even the strategy of offering surrender, by saying that perhaps psychological knowledge had not yet advanced far enough, was dismissed by yet another explanation by the family. Finally the family was asked whether they would be content with an improvement in the girl's condition without knowledge of how it had occurred. The family accepted this and agreed that they would be content for change to occur without, as the team joked, a thesis having to be published.

This tactic helped to confront the issue of excessive theorising in this family. It also made it possible for people to state clearly what was more important – relieving the condition of their daughter or proving their theories. Indirectly an expression of feeling for each other, rather than intellectualisations, was facilitated without ever directly pushing the family to attempt this difficult action. It is also important to recognise that a change in the therapist's approach was also involved and that this was contingent on how the family responded to the suggestion. In some cases a family may continue to insist that they do want theories and it may be necessary to utilise this in some positive ways such as asking them to take detailed notes, similar to a scientific observation. No matter what approach is taken it necessarily involves changes in the therapist's understandings and the devising of strategies, many of which were not foreseeable at the onset of the therapy. It is possible in this way to see the therapeutic process as involving mutual rather than unilateral manipulations.

AIMS AND INTENTIONS

It might seem that the arguments here are pointing towards a utilitarian or pragmatic approach – the ends justify the therapeutic means. This in itself would be a dangerous position if we don't consider what the aims and intentions of the therapist are. Clearly a fundamental aim is to produce relief of the problems and symptoms that are being presented. Since these are usually displayed principally by one person the first step is to ease their situation. At times this raises the difficult issue of whether the identified patient's needs should be given priority over that of other members of the family or the family as a whole. This issue is particularly acute in cases of child and other forms of abuse where there may be a strong case to separate the abused person from the family. However the experience of work with such cases suggests strongly that it is important to consider both the short and long-term needs of the people involved. Furniss (1983) has shown that in the long-term a satisfactory outcome must be reciprocal so that both the 'abused' and the 'abuser's' needs are dealt with. Failure to do this may result, for example, in the abusing parent becoming suicidal which in turn can have disastrous consequences of shame and guilt for the abused child. Grosser and Paul (1971) further support this view that the needs of all the members of the family must, and can, be met by a family therapy approach. Furthermore, they add that individual approaches may in fact be more likely to miss the possible negative effects on the other family members that improvement in the identified patient may have.

This relates to a more general and vital point. It is not the job of the family therapist to alter the dynamics of the family because she does not like them or disagrees with what is going on. For example the sex-role divisions in a family may contrast strongly with a therapist's own views. It is essential here to be able to separate personal views from those of the family. Haley (1980) makes clear that the family therapist should make a minimal input and leave people to manage their own affairs. Likewise Watzlawick (1974) warns of the 'utopian syndrome', that is, the aim for perfection. Instead it can be argued that life, especially family life, is problematic and will necessarily involve tensions and conflicts, both within the family and between the family and the outside world. The central aim of family therapy is to provide some assistance so that the family can resume sorting out its own problems. An obvious implication of this is that often when a family leaves therapy there may still be many problems visible. Also at times, the therapy team may have to resist pressure from other institutions to alter the family to a socially acceptable mould. It is important therefore to insist that the greatest indication of change is that the family feel capable of working on further problems by themselves.

Of course it would be naive to suggest that therapists don't impose their own ideas on a family. A particular family, for example, may activate many unresolved conflicts for the therapist. A danger can be that the therapist becomes drawn in and perhaps unconsciously uses the family to work out some of his own problems. It can on the other hand be a powerful experience for a therapist to realise that he, like the family, will have to endure some pain and that there may not be a simple 'cure'.

CONCLUSION

The chapter has attempted to consider some ethical issues that are raised in the practice of family therapy. A prime cause for concern is the possibility that some of the techniques are unethical in that they are dishonest and manipulative. One important distinction that has been made is that the practice of family therapy is 'manipulative' but not necessarily dishonest. Family therapists as well as some individually oriented therapists such as George Kelly (1955) have stated that the job of the therapist is to produce change and that it is a pretence to assume that this does not involve some manipulation. Elaborating on this point it has been argued that in the process of family therapy this is a joint influence. The family also attempts in many powerful ways to affect the therapist. Furthermore communication theory has been examined in this context to suggest that all communication necessarily involves manipulation and that much of this occurs outside of our conscious awareness.

It has also been argued that the techniques of family therapy must be seen within the overall therapeutic context, including, especially, the intentions of the therapist. For the type of strategic family therapy described here the intentions are to provide a minimal input which is sufficient to enable the family to become autonomous so that people can work together to solve their own problems and difficulties. This contains a recognition that therapy is 'non-utopian' and that stresses and crises are an inevitable part of family life. In many ways this position can be seen as a safeguard against excessive 'meddling' by the therapist with the family.

Finally there are some broader political dangers involved with the practice of family therapy. One of these is that the 'family' may become the scapegoat for inadequacies in various aspects of social welfare provision. For example the place of women in society, lack of work opportunities and inadequate nursery provision may have much to contribute to a case of depression in a young mother. Specific family dynamics may also be involved but it can be a great mistake to ignore the wider social factors. Similar issues may arise with families containing elderly and physically or mentally handicapped members. From an ecological perspective a family can always be seen as part of a wider network and involved with other systems. It is helpful to remember that focusing on the family unit is a convenience. To focus on it exclusively may merely spread the stigma frequently attached to individuals, to a set of individuals.

A therapist cannot be removed from the wider political context. This must necessarily intrude into and colour what is done with a family. On the other hand it is suggested here that an ethically defensible, though perhaps imperfect position is to accept that therapy will involve a process of negotiation and mutual manipulation. To some extent the therapist has the upper hand in this. It is suggested though that the power and resilience of families should not be underestimated. We see many extreme problems which require strategies as sophisticated and powerful as those employed by the family members themselves if any benefit is to result. To shy away from the task of inducing some change, by default, leaves us in the ethically unjustifiable position of abandoning people to their distress.

REFERENCES

Bateson, G. (1972), *Steps to an Ecology of Mind*, New York, Ballantine Books.

Erickson, M.H. (1980), *The Collective Papers of Milton H. Erickson*, vol.1, (ed. E.L. Ross), Irvington.

Fisch, R. (1967), 'Resistance to Change in the Psychiatric Community', in P. Watzlawick and J.H. Weakland (eds), *The Interactional View*, New York, Norton.

Freud, S. (1963), 'Analytic Therapy', in J. Strachey, (ed.), *The Complete Psychological Works of Sigmund Freud*, vol. 16, London, Hogarth Press, p.460.

Furniss, T. (1983), 'Family Process in the Treatment of Intrafamilial Child Sexual Abuse', *Journal of Family Therapy*, vol.5, no.4. pp.263–79.

Goffman, E. (1961), *Asylums:Essays on the Social Situation of Mental Patients and Other Inmates*, Harmondsworth, Pelican.

Grosser, G.H. and Paul, N.L. (1971), 'Ethical Issues in Family Therapy', in J. Haley (ed.), *Changing Families*, New York, Grune and Stratton.

Haley, J. (1976), *Problem Solving Therapy*, San Francisco, Jossey-Bass.

Haley, J. (1980), *Leaving Home*, New York, McGraw Hill.

Jackson, D.D. (1957), 'The Question of Family Homeostasis', *Psychiatry, Quarterly Supplement, 31*, pp.79–90.

Keeney, B. (1979), 'Ecosystemic Epistemology: An Alternative Paradigm for Diagnosis', *Family Process, 18*, pp.117–29.

Kelly, G.A. (1955), *The Psychology of Personal Constructs*, vols.1 and 2, New York, Norton.

Laing, R.D. (1971), *The Politics of the Family*, Harmondsworth, Pelican.

Minuchin, S. (1974), *Families and Family Therapy*, London, Tavistock.

Procter, H.G. (1980), 'Family construct psychology: an approach to understanding and treating the family', in S. Walrond-Skinner (ed.), *Developments in Family Therapy*, London, Routledge & Kegan Paul.

Selvini Palazzoli, M. *et al.* (1980), *Paradox and Counterparadox*, New York, Jason Aronson.

Shah, I. (1968), *The Way of the Sufi*, Harmondsworth, Penguin.
Szasz, T. (1961), *The Myth of Mental Illness*, New York, Harper.
Watts, A. (1961), *Psychotherapy: East and West*, Harmondsworth, Penguin.
Watzlawick, P., Beavin, J.H. and Jackson, D. (1967), *Pragmatics of Human Communication*, New York, Norton.
Watzlawick, P., Weakland, J.H. and Fisch, R. (1974), *Change*, New York, Norton.

The Moral Context of Therapy

Ron McKechnie

I became explicitly interested in the ethical and moral dimensions of therapy on becoming puzzled by what I saw going on in relation to two strands of clinical work in which I was involved. This paper represents some thoughts I have indulged around these issues over the subsequent few years.

To begin I shall consider the puzzles and look at what they have in common and then go on to analyse the sources of moral or ethical influences impinging upon therapy and present a generalised conclusion.

The first puzzle concerned the definition or nature of problem drinking and the second concerned the nature of group work. These will be used as examples from my own experience but you could probably generate examples from your own experience which would illustrate the point just as well.

PROBLEM DRINKING

When first involved in the area of problem drinking it seemed clear that there was a fairly well-defined disease/disorder called 'alcoholism'. More recently the term alcoholism has been replaced by terms like 'alcohol abuse' and 'alcohol dependence syndrome'. Despite these changes in labelling the concepts still rest upon value judgments made by others about someone else's drinking, as had 'alcoholism'. There is an attempt to define 'abuse' without reference to 'use' thus largely considering it out of its proper context. Almost all the literature on drinking problems is influenced by a pervasive belief that drinking alcohol is a bad thing *per se*. A review of the literature on the effects of alcohol will reveal hundreds of papers on bad consequences and very few on benefits (see Turner *et al.*, 1981 for review). Even when benefits are discovered as a by-product of a study, the benefits are not emphasised unless this was the object of the study. Such a bias allows society and alcohololologists to pretend that they don't know that drinking is predominantly beneficial to most drinkers. This anti-alcohol attitude is not simply a thing of the past. Such a view was being expressed in a recent journal (Madden, 1984). The writer was discussing possible pharmacological approaches to the prevention of alcohol problems and argues:

> Here a caveat must be entered if the prevention of physical dependence could also inhibit tolerance. A drug that allows repeated alcohol consumption without the acquirement of tolerance would favour repetitive intoxication from relatively small amounts of alcohol. The preparation might then be taken deliberately to permit cheap and easy drunkenness (Madden, 1984).

Dr Madden obviously does not think that would be a good thing even if it were harm free.

Similarly at a recent conference on prevention of alcohol problems, the delegates were asked to choose between increasing or decreasing the congener content (congeners are by-products of the manufacturing process and are usually thought to be responsible for hangovers) of alcohol deliberately in order to make hangovers worse or less severe respectively. Most delegates voted for making hangovers worse because that would stop people drinking so much. In the absence of any evidence the delegates can only decide on the basis of a value judgment again demonstrating the same bias as above.

Another example of the 'Let's pretend we don't know' phenomenon arose last year when I was invited to address a conference on the 'Problems of Normal Drinking'. Such an invitation can only be issued by pretending that the audience, all workers in the field of alcohol problems and mostly drinkers themselves, do not know from their own experience. There may be technical biochemical consequences of the effects of alcohol that people are unaware of, but that wasn't what was being asked. The organisers were pretending that they and the audience did not know the consequences of their own drinking.

GROUP WORK

A similar mystery or puzzle arose in relation to group work which is shrouded in mystery as to the techniques and processes that go on. The most common question asked is 'What's it like in a group?'. Again such a question can only be asked by pretending that you do not know. Whilst preparing such a talk on group therapy a few years ago I realised that we ignore our own experience in asking such questions since we live, move and have our being in groups. We are born into a group, are raised by it, are influenced by its example, and go on to create new ones. There is one group that we all have some experience of and this is the family. So why pretend we do not know? One answer is to say that the answers to the questions raised are technical or scientific. Such a stance is not difficult to take since most therapists claim some scientific basis for their work and its efficiency. By declaring these questions to be 'scientific' we require scientific answers to be judged by the effectiveness of our manipulations or otherwise. In adopting such a position, our own experience and understanding of groups is not considered to be relevant since it is ordinary and not scientific. And since science is considered to be value free there is no need to consider the morality of its answers. Such a perspective allows us to avoid facing up to the moral dimensions of what we are engaged in (see Smail, 1982). The implications of accepting that drinking is predominantly beneficial, or that group work might be judged by the same standards we expect of family life are so demanding and far reaching that we persist in a predominantly anti-alcohol theme and are satisfied with fairly perfunctory routine caring practices which we would think appalling if demonstrated within a family.

SOURCES OF MORAL INFLUENCE

I now wish to consider what ethical/moral pressures and influences impinge upon therapeutic intervention or activity. In using the word 'moral' I shall be referring to that aspect of any issue, situation or decision involving value judgment rather than scientific judgment.

In attempting to construct a general framework, I will identify five distinct sources of moral influence and illustrate these with examples from my involvement with a drinking problems team working from a base within a mental hospital.

The five sources are:
1 Cultural beliefs and expectations
2 Institutional beliefs and practices
3 Specialities' (or disciplines') beliefs and practices
4 Therapists' beliefs and practices
5 Clients' beliefs and expectations

These are not isolated or separate but overlap and interact with each other giving rise to the moral context of therapy. I will outline each briefly and offer illustrations from my own work place.

CULTURAL BELIEFS AND EXPECTATIONS

Each culture or society develops its own particular system by which those in trouble or in need of care are dealt with. In our society there is a strong emphasis on well trained, professional services, staffed by fairly well paid people whose livelihood depends essentially on the misfortune of others. The expectation is that these well trained professionals will have knowledge and expertise relevant to these problems such that the sufferer can bring their problem along and receive appropriate advice or help. Such knowledge is not expected to be available from people at large. This knowledge therefore bestows power and authority on the helper and the client is generally expected to follow the advice given. Such a model of caring has implications for the self-determination, self-reliance and autonomy of the client. Because the helper has power and authority it is necessary to make explicit that clients should not be exploited materially or physically. The content of ethical codes of conduct for therapists usually reflects this above all else.

INSTITUTIONAL BELIEFS AND PRACTICES

Whereas the cultural beliefs set a broad setting within which therapy is conducted the base or location within which it occurs also has its own set of beliefs and practices which do more than reflect those of society. It was Goffman (1961) who made us aware of the fact that most institutions are run for the benefit and convenience of staff primarily, even if they have a manifest function of providing a service to the public. This can be clearly seen in hospitals with each level of staff protecting the staff in the level above from contact with the clients and a general tendency of staff to ensure that clients do not get too much out of the system.

A particular example of institutional beliefs arose early in my experience of working with problem drinkers within an acute admission ward for psychiatric cases. The team working with problem drinkers had discussed and agreed upon a philosophy for our practice which would emphasise client responsibility and autonomy. Such a philosophy ran counter to the prevailing philosophy within the ward where the majority of patients had other psychiatric problems and it was assumed that encouraging client responsibility and autonomy were inappropriate for them. The clash in philosophy resulted in two groups of staff working within the same ward handling patients in very different ways. In such ways, the institution can hold a general view of its clients and the nature of their disorders which is at odds with that which might apply to specific groupings with resulting confusion for both staff and clients. It is the prevailing dominant philosophy which determines the environment within which the client and staff have to work, yet it is often not made explicit.

In its wisdom our institution allowed us to have a separate unit for our problem drinkers. It would be comforting to think that the institution was convinced by the power of our argument for running a comprehensive service for problem drinkers of both sexes. In fact we were given our own premises because the institution believed that 'alcoholics' are violent, trouble making and unworthy customers and no one else wished to work with them anyway. Thus the negative beliefs of the institution actually worked in favour of the problem drinkers in this case in terms of service provision, but highlight the moral setting within which our unit exists and the standard by which it will be judged. The success of the unit is frequently reported by others in terms of how little trouble there has been.

SPECIALITIES' (OR DISCIPLINES') BELIEFS AND PRACTICES

Specialities and disciplines exist as a kind of institution in the sense that they are organised systems with established ways of doing things. If we consider the alcohol field as a speciality and pay attention to some of its established beliefs and ways of doing things it illustrates the moral influence fairly clearly.

When I began working with problem drinkers the first piece of advice I received from a much respected mentor was the 'alcoholics are no different from other patients except you must never believe anything they tell you.' Such advice reflects the belief that alcoholics are liars and untrustworthy. When treated as such they certainly do become devious but in my experience they are no less trustworthy than any other category of patients.

As indicated above, there is within the speciality an assumption that drinking *per se* is bad. Unfortunately this attitude generalises beyond the activity to the drinkers themselves and thus the problem drinker is shunned, avoided or singled out for special treatment. The history of the treatment of problem drinkers reads like a catalogue of imprisonment and torture second only in horror to the treatment of homosexuals. If such methods were effective they would/should have been used for other disorders also. In this instance so called scientific based treatment reflects the every day bias and prejudice of society.

Some writers (eg Glatt, 1976) extol the virtue of the medical model of 'alcoholism' because it stopped problem drinkers being labelled as bad. In fact this may have been part of the strategy of those who wished 'alcoholism' to be recognised as a disease (see Jaffe, 1978; Strauss, 1976; Lovell, 1951). As you will see from the comments above, concerning the problem drinker's patient status, it was at best only partially successful. What the medical model did allow was for the problem drinker to excuse himself from responsibility for his condition, although he was still told only he could do anything about his recovery. Whilst it was true that doctors could treat the complications or consequences of excessive consumption, only the alcoholic himself could remain abstinent ie stay away from alcohol. (See Siegler, Osmond and Newall, 1968; and Cameron, 1983.)

The team in which I work is frequently accused of having a moral model of drinking problems. To such an accusation we plead guilty. What seems to be forgotten is the distinction between having a moral model and being moralistic. It is possible to have a moral model which emphasises the importance of choice and responsibility without being judgmental, blaming and derisory. Such a model can be empathic, understanding of people's predicaments, and the circumstances within which they experience a limitation or restriction of choices. As a team we have spent some time developing a consensus philosophy about the nature of people, drinking problems and the service we offer. It has obvious moral dimensions which we attempt to make explicit both to ourselves and our clients.

THERAPISTS' BELIEFS AND PRACTICES

The therapist is influenced by the culture within which he lives, the institution from which he practises and the speciality within which he works and also has his own set of beliefs as a result of his individual experience.

Within our psychology department at Crichton Royal, each therapist is asked from time to time to give an account of him/herself as a therapist, to say what has influenced them and what they think they are doing in therapy. One thing which is fairly clear from such accounts is that for many of the therapists their concept of the nature of man is fairly firmly fixed before being exposed to academic psychology, and their prevailing concept of man is not greatly influenced by academic psychology. It is therefore a product of their earlier life experience at home and school. The family especially is important in this respect, especially when it is large, since this exposes one to intimate knowledge of a variety of different individuals. The concept of human nature is also greatly influenced by spiritual, in its broadest sense, experiences.

Counsellors in general tend to be an optimistic bunch and have an optimistic view of human nature (Halmos, 1965). They are thus a group with a particular view of human nature and not representative of the range of views held within our society in this respect. They, therefore, do not simply reflect the beliefs of their culture or necessarily of their institution. (See also Roman, Charles and Karasu, 1978.)

CLIENTS' BELIEFS AND EXPECTATIONS

Like the therapist the client is influenced by cultural beliefs and expectations, but he will have modified these in the light of his own experiences. He will thus have his own view of the nature of man and of the predicament in which he finds himself. This is one aspect of the client's assumptive world and without acquiring knowledge of this world it is difficult to speak to him where he is. It may be, and frequently is, his assumptions, being contradictory, limiting or wrong, that give rise to problems. Though it is not essential that the client believes what the therapist believes in order to be helped, it is probably essential that the client is helped to make his/her beliefs explicit.

THE MORAL CONTEXT

At each of these five levels there are influences which derive from essentially moral decisions about the nature of man and his predicament. In attempting to elaborate the moral context of therapy it is important that these influences are made explicit in such a manner that one can answer 'What system of values encompasses the activity of therapy?'

Within our culture most people are referred to the therapist in the same manner as someone is referred to a specialist by one's general practitioner. In such circumstances it is difficult to refuse such a referral. The specialist is a kind of expert, albeit in a limited domain, but the patient expects to be told what to do and is expected to do it. Such a system, with its imbalance of power and authority, may be inappropriate for problems with living. Some therapists who depart from such a system feel obliged to make explicit how they work because it does not conform to the usual pattern and therefore might contradict or clash with the client's expectations. Another reason for making their system explicit is because it is good practice to do so.

Other questions about the interaction and intervention might also be asked and are relevant to answering the question about the system of values. These include 'What model of man is used?'; 'What model of relationship is involved – is it health manager, advisor, friend, or guide?'; 'What implications do these models have for the rights, duties and responsibilities of each of the participants?'; and 'What kinds of equality/inequality exist in the relationship?'

Except where a strictly medical/technical model is adopted the answers to these questions are essentially moral. Even in the strictly medical case there are moral dimensions to the answers. (See Siegler, Osmond and Newall, 1968 for fuller discussion.)

We cannot avoid moral decisions, even if we had infinite knowledge. What is essential is that we make our moral decisions explicit and ensure that they are consistent. In some of the examples given above, difficulties arise when activities and practices rest on different moral bases, yet the morality of caring is rarely talked about in caring institutions.

We have seen that a myriad of value sources give rise to the moral context within which therapy is conducted. This is not a static context, it changes with different staff, with different clients, with different perspectives. What is clear to me, however, is that it is the moral/ethical context of therapy which is the effective ingredient in therapy rather than the techniques. It is the example of treating/dealing with/caring for people in a particular manner which makes the difference and not the particular brand or school of therapy adhered to by the therapists. Such a conclusion allows us to make sense of treatment. Outcome studies suggest there are 'good' therapists and 'psycho-noxious' therapists practising the same techniques (see Truax and Mitchell, 1968) and variation in the application of the same techniques in different settings (Moos, 1974).

With so many influences going into the creation of the context is there anything that can be said in general? Here it is worth considering the work of Moos in the development of the 'Ward Atmosphere Scale' (Moos, 1974). A brief look at the 'Relationship and Personal Development' dimensions of the scale reveals that they can readily be interpreted as, or translated into, ethical/moral dimensions to do with 'Responsibility', 'Caring for others',

'Equality', 'Freedom of Expression', 'Independence', 'Sharing of Experience', and 'Openness to Emotions'. As you can imagine wards vary from each other with there being better ward atmosphere where patient numbers are small and where there are good staff/patient ratios. This influence, however, does not just create a nice place to be, but appears to affect the level of violent and disruptive behaviour on the ward and decrease the length of admissions (Moos, 1974; Ng, Tam and Luk, 1982). Such experiments lead us to ask what might be an ideal environment or context within which to be cared for or treated.

LOVING ENVIRONMENTS

The answer of course is a *loving* environment. To explore such a concept it is essential to talk about love. Love may make the world go round but it has largely escaped the attention of psychologists. The kind of love to be considered here is what is referred to as agape. This kind of love is not the prerogative of those with religious faith – it can be manifest by anyone. This kind of love is referred to in many ways, as neighbour love, concern for all human kind; it embodies 'respect for persons', it is love which restores full value to every individual, 'an active concern for the life and growth of that which we love' (Fromm, 1972).

Or as Campbell (1984) says, 'Agape requires that no help, however well intentioned, should stamp out one's own or another's individuality.'

The importance of value in this love is stressed by Campbell:

> We can regard love as in a sense both 'creating' and 'discovering' value. Neither word, however, is quite accurate enough. Scheler quotes Carl Jaspers in this regard: 'In love we do not discover values, we discover that everything is more valuable'. In other words, love achieves the enhancement of values already inherent in that which is the object of love (Campbell, p.77).

It is important to notice that discovery and/or enhancement is not just by one person about another but is also about the person themselves. Thus agape is very closely related to warmth (Rogers) and 'unconditional positive regard' (Truax and Carkhuff) which are believed to be vital ingredients of therapeutic change (see Rogers, 1951 and Truax and Carkhuff, 1967). Unfortunately many writers on this topic talk as though love were a technique to be manipulated, to have more or less of. What I wish to suggest is that love is the context within which therapy is conducted or techniques practised. In this sense love is a context within which we act, care. A place to be at home in, to be ourselves in.

But love is not like a pink painted room – it is also relational. As Fromm says 'it is an attitude, an orientation of character, which determines the relatedness of a person to the world as a whole'. In practice 'loving' will mean many things; my argument is that to create a loving environment it is necessary to make explicit the values and moral principles around which the practices of therapy will be woven and these must value the person. And it is my belief that it is not the techniques of therapy which are effective but the pervasive influence of examples of loving – the background as it were rather than the foreground. Thus not all caring is loving – but caring that is carried out within the context of love or done lovingly will be more beneficial than that which is carried out in some other context. The challenge of this is that it is not just the prerogative of those with religious faith to be loving – it is a challenge to us all in all of our lives. If that happened paid therapists might be redundant.

REFERENCES

Cameron, I. (1983), 'Moralising in the Fifties', paper presented at New Directions in Study of Alcohol Group Conference, North Berwick.

Campbell, A,V. (1984), *Moderated Love: A Theology of Professional Care*, London, SPCK.

Fromm, E. (1972), *The Art of Loving*, London, Allen and Unwin.

Glatt, M.M. (1976), 'Alcoholism Disease Concept and Loss of Control Revisited', *British Journal of Addiction, 71*, pp.135–44.

Goffman, E. (1961), *Asylums*, New York, Doubleday & Co.

Halmos, P. (1965), *The Faith of the Counsellors*, London, Constable.

Jaffe, A. (1978), 'Reform in American Medical Science: The inebriety movement and the origins of the psychological disease theory of addition', *British Journal of Addiction, 73*, pp.139–47.

Lovell, H.W. (1951), *Hope and Help for the Alcoholic*, New York, Doubleday & Co.

Madden, S. (1984), 'Whether Alcoholism?', *Alcohol and Alcoholism, 19*, pp.91–5.

Moos, R.H. (1974), *Evaluating Treatment Environments: A Social Ecological Approach*, New York, Wiley.
Ng, M.L., Tam, Y.K. and Luk, S.L. (1982), 'Evaluation of Different Forms of Community Meeting in a Psychiatric Unit in Hong Kong', *British Journal of Psychiatry, 140*, pp.491–7.
Rogers, C.R. (1951), *Client-Centred Therapy*, Boston, Houghton-Mifflin.
Roman, M., Charles, E. and Karasu, T.B. (1978), 'The Value System of Psychotherapists and Changing Moves', *Psychotherapy: Theory, Research and Practice, 15*, pp.409–15.
Siegler, M., Osmond, H. and Newall, S. (1968), 'Models of Alcoholism', *Quarterly Journal of Studies in Alcoholism, 29*, pp.571–91.
Smail, D. (1982), 'Psychotherapy Deliverance or Disablement?', paper presented at Ethical Issues in Caring Conference, Manchester.
Strauss, R. (1976), 'Problem Drinking in the Perspective of Social Change, 1940–1973', in W.J. Filstead, J.J. Rossi and M. Keller (eds), *Alcohol and Alcohol Problems*, Massachusetts, Ballinger.
Truax, C.B. and Carkhuff, R.R. (1967), *Towards Effective Counselling and Psychotherapy: Training and Practice*, Chicago, Aldine.
Truax, C.B. and Mitchell, K.M. (1968), 'The Psychotherapeutic and the Psychonoxious: Human Encounters that Change Behaviour' in M.S. Feldman (ed.), *Studies in Psychotherapy and Behavioural Change, vol. 1 Research in Individual Psychology*, New York, University of New York.
Turner, T.B., Bennett, V.L. and Hermandez, H. (1981), 'The Beneficial Side of Moderate Alcohol Use', *John Hopkins Medical Journal*, 148, pp.53–63.

Psychology in Medical Settings

Annabel Broome

INTRODUCTION

The author considers that there have been two major and rather different aspects of psychological approaches in medicine of importance to this volume. These are the service-based and patient-based approaches. It is clear that psychologists attempting to innovate in medical settings have, of necessity, to collaborate with the power holders who work mainly in a service-based, biochemical framework, although a psychologist would more naturally adopt a client-based view, which seems more promising in dealing with health problems.

This chapter will be concerned with the feasibility of promoting person-based approaches which require patient partnership and responsibility, while working within a medical service. This approach is considered important for respecting the individual's perspective, for giving them choices for action and in allowing them some responsibility for outcome. Unless knowledge is shared on the problem, and choices of action discussed, the patient remains controlled by the experts of the system. It is considered ethically more desirable to create an informed atmosphere for consent and there is some evidence that improving information transfer, self-efficacy and a sense of control will improve health outcomes (O'Leary, 1985; Janis and Rodin, 1979).

Developments in behavioural medicine will be briefly catalogued in order to understand the context of today's work in applying psychology in medicine, and the difficulty of working within a system based on a biomedical model of care, which appears incompatible with psychosocial models.

The subject of health promotion will be explored, not only

because the problems of modern living in the developing world are forcing health carers and clinical psychologists to take different views to people's health choices and health behaviours, but because it provides a useful example of how current psychological theory can be used to seek explanatory mechanisms and thereby provide appropriate interventions for health problems. Health promotion is also an area undeniably concerned with personal beliefs, motivation and decision making and therefore highlights important areas of concern – particularly in deciding where control and responsibility lie.

DEVELOPMENTS IN BEHAVIOURAL MEDICINE

Leventhal and Hirschman (1982) suggest that major developments in behavioural medicine have been fostered by, and responded to, the needs of medical practice. The contingencies for medical practice are clearly different for different health care systems, and although we are very much dependent on transferring information from the US, where major developments have been made in behavioural medicine, the American fee-for-service and the British pre-paid health system clearly offer us quite different organisational power bases and contingencies. So we must be cautious in transferring information from the US to other types of health care systems.

However, it is instructive to identify the catalysts to the fostering of behavioural medicine (particularly in the US) as suggested by Agras (1982) and Weiss (1981). They suggest the following influences:

1 A growth in one-to-one work in behaviour therapy and biofeedback.
2 Significant developments in psychosomatic research.
3 Epidemiological factors identifying risks to disease (eg coronary heart disease, cancer).
4 An increase in chronic disease; and reduction in acute infectious disease.
5 Higher costs of health care and an increasing interest in illness prevention.
6 A public interest in self-control methods and health behaviour.

The growth of such approaches has been matched with a variety of definitions and titles in an attempt to give such efforts some identity and cohesion. The American Psychiatric Association has conceptualised psychosomatic medicine as the relationship between physical symptoms and psychological factors which precipitate, prolong or maintain the organic process. Among other definitions for behavioural medicine the Academy of Behavioural Medicine Research, as quoted by Schwartz and Weiss (1978) has defined it as:

> The interdisciplinary field concerned with the development and integration of behavioural and biomedical science, knowledge and techniques relevant to the understanding of health and illness and the application of this knowledge and these techniques to prevention, diagnosis and rehabilitation.

Leventhal and Hirschman (1982) agree that there was an increasing awareness of the importance of psychosocial factors in the delivery of health care, but there was also a need to give an interdisciplinary label to integrate behavioural research and prevention within the medical arena, so the term 'behavioural medicine' was coined.

A number of factors have caused the medical profession to seriously consider psychosocial influences. OPCS (Office of Population Censuses and Surveys) figures for 1981 show the three top causes of death as circulatory disorders; neoplasms; respiratory disease; and an increasing incidence of 'limiting longstanding illness' and 'longstanding illness' in comparison to 'acute sickness'. Public concern for health, costs of health care, and developments in psychological practice and clinical research, changing health patterns and clearer indications of the *relationship between risk behaviours and chronic disease*, have also influenced opinion.

Pomerleau (1982) in a recent paper on the subject summarises four major complementary lines of development in behavioural medicine which have produced a wealth of research reports and clinical application demonstrating the relevance to current health problems:

1 Interventions to modify behaviour or physiological response.
2 Interventions to modify behaviour of health care providers
3 Interventions to modify risk factors.
4 Interventions to modify compliance behaviours.

Without dwelling on these major areas it is perhaps enough to note here the clinical and research context surrounding the developments that have taken place both in health incidence and in behavioural medicine.

THE BIOMEDICAL MODEL

It is clear from population studies that the health needs of industrialised populations such as Britain have changed, but the model of health care has not. Indeed, John Powells (1974) suggests that even with increasing enthusiasm and spending on medicine this appears to be related to decreasing returns in health. Battling with disease has now given way to dealing with chronic conditions and problems arising from modes of living. Mortality and morbidity patterns are changing and health costs are rising. However, the system we work in is essentially based on a biomedical model which is a traditional model of symptom identification, treatment and cure, and the prevalent model of medical education.

Figure 1 demonstrates this system, which depends on a simple relationship between an agent, which disrupts a healthy process, produces a symptom and causes a seeking of health care. This is expected to result in a diagnosis, treatment and cure.

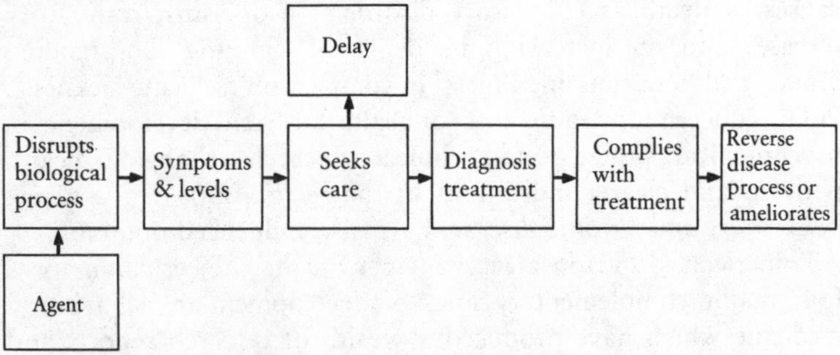

Figure 1 The Biomedical Model
based on Leventhal and Hirschman (1982)

It must be obvious immediately that there are intrinsic incompatibilities between biomedical and psychosocial approaches. The following points are derived largely from similar points made by Leventhal and Hirschman (1982).

AREAS OF CONFLICT BETWEEN BIOMEDICAL AND PSYCHOSOCIAL APPROACHES

CAUSATION AND TREATMENT

Significant and important disease processes often do not have a one-to-one relationship with causative agents. Indeed, most risk behaviours have multiple effects (see Eysenck, 1984). However, the traditional biomedical approach is based on an identification of direct causative agents which produce a disease process. Behavioural scientists have developed techniques of analysis to deal with these multi-factorial relationships (Cleary, 1983); and these are gaining increasing recognition.

THE CONCEPT OF DISABILITY

The medical perception of disability is physically based. However, psychosocial analyses recognise the complex inter-relationships between personal and social coping mechanisms, the environmental and behavioural contingencies which contribute (together with the extent of physical handicap) to the level of performance. Many physicians perceive disability mainly in physical terms, but behavioural scientists perceive overall functioning as a product of more complex inter-related variables.

MEASURES OF SUCCESS

The biomedical model measures 'cure' in terms of reduction of morbidity or mortality. Amelioration or coping is only a half-way measure, and does not feature as a 'success' in biomedical outcome research. Psychologists would see the adjustment to disability and improved functioning in spite of the handicap as an honourable goal, in improving quality of life and psychological well-being.

To take one example, much outcome research from treatment for chronic pain shows pain report varies little, although the effects on activity level and drug taking are often much improved (Fordyce, 1976). Psychologists would see this as an important goal in itself if the patient was coping better, but medical approaches will aim to cure the pain.

ATTITUDES TO HEALTH

Health is perceived as an absence of disease in medical approaches, rather than a positive goal in itself. This is not compatible with psychosocial approaches where health is seen as measurable on the dimension of 'healthiness'.

COMPLIANCE

An individual's failure to take advantage of medical investigations and treatment is often seen in the medical literature as a non-compliant personality trait, rather than a reflection upon the skills of negotiation in matching the needs of the client with those of the doctor. Indeed, it is quite clear that patients' experiences, beliefs, knowledge and self-perception of healthiness will all affect care-seeking behaviour and the acceptability of medical approaches. 'Compliance' is a service-based, not patient-based concept.

COMPLEXITY OF THE WHOLE PERSON APPROACH – PSYCHOLOGICAL TREATMENTS VERSUS MEDICAL TREATMENTS

Behavioural scientists see the process of treatment intervention as multi-faceted. These interventions are generally more complex than typical medical interventions.

For instance, if we compare the process of immunisation against disease with a programme for the management of chronic pain we notice the difference in the explanation of causation, and in the complexity of the therapeutic programme and the measures of success, when compared with biomedically-based explanation and intervention.

EXPERT-PATIENT COMMUNICATION VERSUS PATIENT PARTNERSHIP

These six topics briefly outlined must suggest some very basic conflicts when applying psychology in medicine, and now it must be perfectly clear that patient-based models of health care and health behaviour must be incompatible with the traditional expert/client role relationship we see in medical practice (Robin, 1984).

Because the prevailing philosophy is so different, Leventhal and Hirschman (1982) suggest some caution is needed when psychologists simply respond to demands for work from the power base in medical practice. If we only respond to the needs and preoccupations of these powerful members of the health service to improve existing medical practice we may be missing much more patient-relevant possibilities. Indeed they suggest that a wide range of promising applications have been limited by taking such a focus, and unless sufficient in-depth effort is put into investigating the explanatory mechanisms of health behaviour, we shall not have any clear understanding of illness processes or develop relevant intervention and prevention strategies.

> If behavioural medicine develops as a collection of technologies which are to be applied to specific practice problems and ignore underlying explanatory mechanisms, it will fail as a science and as a problem-solving technology. (Leventhal and Hirschman, 1982)

So the applications of psychology in medicine have very basic difficulties. These are the problems of incompatibility with the models used by the power holders, the commitment to examining explanatory mechanisms and the difficulties of taking a client-based view, which is antagonistic to the common 'expert role' adopted by health personnel.

In looking more closely at the patient-expert relationship, we can usefully examine the current problems patients experience in communicating with health professionals. Ley and Morris (1984) suggest in a review of the existing literature on the subject that the present clinician-patient oral communication:

1 Often fails to cover important topics.
2 Leaves patients dissatisfied.
3 Is often not understood by patients.

4 Is often forgotten by patients.
5 Often fails to produce the desired effect.

Patients are therefore often not being given the opportunity to know what is going on during their care and not being given the opportunity for informed decision-making about their own health. Indeed, these conclusions show us that health professionals guard information and do not allow the patient to actively participate in his/her treatment: a situation having serious ethical implications.

Caroline Faulder in her book *Whose Body is It?* (1985) suggests that shortcomings in communication cannot be placed simply at the door of the patient who may be seen by the clinician as of limited intellect, motivation or to have irresponsible personal characteristics. She suggests that the shortcomings in communication can originate from either or both sides. She suggests that doctors who are incapable of explaining plans of management should be questioning their own fitness to practice. She feels that an equal partnership is essential in medical management (and particularly in gaining informed consent) so both sides can meet as equals and both have a responsibility to communicate and to plan care.

She suggests that the balance is switching from the autocratic or 'expert' role, and due to medical progress and the changes in society's attitude, so doctors' authority is becoming eroded as they are being increasingly asked to participate more equally in decision making with patients. She suggests that the whole issue of doctor-patient communication is based on a much more fundamental issue of co-equal partnership, and challenges the necessity to monitor the expert role of care.

In an effort to clarify the difficulties of applying psychology in medicine in a service generally not accepting this patient partnership, and operating within different models of practice, the topic of health promotion will be discussed as a subject basically antagonistic to a sickness-based service, and yet with some current useful psychosocial models which could be the basis of fruitful research and intervention.

Due to the previously mentioned changing patterns of chronic disease, the escalating cost of health care (particularly in maintaining those with chronic illness), and the increasing public awareness and interest in health behaviour, the subject of health promotion is one of major concern and of prime interest to a clinical psychologist.

One must begin from a person-based perspective when examining the attitudes and behaviours that can increase health-related behaviour. But this makes essential challenges to the biomedical model, the foremost challenge being to the doctor's expert role. If we take the view that patient experience, motivation, and health beliefs are important factors and valuable assets to bring into the health care system, then the patient can be seen as the expert on his health and should be given equal responsibility in the decisions made relating to his own health. This, in turn, suggests that patients need much fuller information to make informed choices; and an opportunity to effect their care.

This has implications for the notion of informed consent to treatment:

> from an ethical point of view, the presumption by physicians that patients are incapable of adhering to therapies of self-management is inconsistent with the principle of informed consent, which requires presenting to a patient all the therapeutic options that any reasonable person would wish to weigh (Guttmacher *et al.*, 1981).

These authors, in studying borderline hypertension, argue that doctors often reduce the options available to people because they fear non-compliance, but they argue that anticipating non-compliance is not a valid reason for withholding any option to an individual. The authors suggest that the pay-offs for health care professionals (particularly physicians) are greater if the patient can become dependent on prescribed drugs and medical attendances. By encouraging dependency, little attention is paid to the prime causes of risk behaviours and risk conditions, thereby maintaining the predominant sickness-oriented medical service and the dependency of patients on that service.

In reflecting on this study and the ethical issues it highlights, one notices a sharp distinction between the American system where physicians are dependent on fee-for-service, and therefore have an interest in their patients' continued attendance. But the British salaried system has no such direct financial gain of that nature, within the NHS.

However, although the systems are different, the analysis does suggest to us that physicians will take decisions about people's competence to evaluate information and make choices, and this 'reduces the solicitation of informed consent to a hollow gesture'

(Guttmacher *et al.*, 1981). There is every reason to believe that the same attitudes prevail within the British system, although the contingencies are clearly different in a different market context.

PSYCHOLOGICAL EXPLANATION AND HEALTH BEHAVIOUR

Research on health behaviour would indicate to us that people are actively concerned with their own health. As people experience a new physical symptom so they generally attempt to problem-solve. Williamson and Danaher (1978) show that 63 per cent of cases will self-care, 12 per cent will self-care and visit their GP and 8 per cent will use the doctor's visit alone. Sixteen per cent will do nothing. This study demonstrates that most people will take an active problem-solving approach to their own symptoms when at the early stages in symptom experience, and will only seek health care in a minority of cases. So people are taking active coping steps already, long before they reach the medical services. They will derive their strategies from within their own health belief systems and previous experiences, and it is such factors that will affect their perceived need to refer and their availability to treatment once they enter the health care system. It is these processes that are fundamental to health behaviour, and that seem, to the psychologist, essential to understand.

In developing work in the area and using such theoretical analyses as the Self-Regulation Model (Leventhal and Hirschman, 1982), Health Belief Model (Becker 1974), or Locus of Control (Wallston and Wallston, 1981) or self-efficacy (O'Leary, 1985) psychologists have attempted to focus on explanations for health-related behaviours.

Such authors suggest that there is a major role for psychologists in identifying or explaining the processes involved in choices for healthy living, as well as concentrating on studying the appropriateness of uptake of health services and the variables effecting reinforcement contingencies that exist for health professionals. Unless these processes can be better understood and relevant interventions are matched, we can expect no greater efficiency without interventions.

SELF-REGULATION

Bearing in mind that people arrive within the health care system with their own active beliefs and problem-solving experiences, health promotion efforts must be concerned with the patient's perspectives: and not merely with information-giving.

Hollis *et al.* (1982) state:

> Knowledge of itself rarely leads to lasting behaviour change
> So:
> Before bombarding people with facts their interests, goals, health belief systems and current level of understanding should be taken into account.

It is too simplistic to suggest that giving information will produce acceptance, which will lead to behaviour change.

The self-regulation model, as outlined by Leventhal and Hirschman (1982), suggests a feedback system where health action is motivated by cultural standards of health, assimilated into personal health goals, and the actions themselves will lead to certain experiences (affective, behavioural and physiological). These experiences can either be positive or negative. It is these changes that will lead to further goal setting and further health action in a feedback loop. (See Figure 2.)

This model described only briefly here allows the actor to become an active problem-solver and to modify his behaviour according to the information he is aware of, in terms of his own health belief system and satisfaction with the changed experience.

HEALTH BELIEFS AND LOCUS OF CONTROL

The Health Belief Model (Becker, 1974) has also addressed relevant aspects of this decision-making process regarding health behaviours, and the Health Locus of Control literature suggests that insufficient attention has been paid to the notion of tailoring treatment programmes to individual's Health Locus of Control, so matching individuals to programmes. The theoretical analysis suggests that people tend to make internally or externally-based health choices, although their style will vary according to the value of the situation demands. However, Janis and Rodin (1979) suggest that:

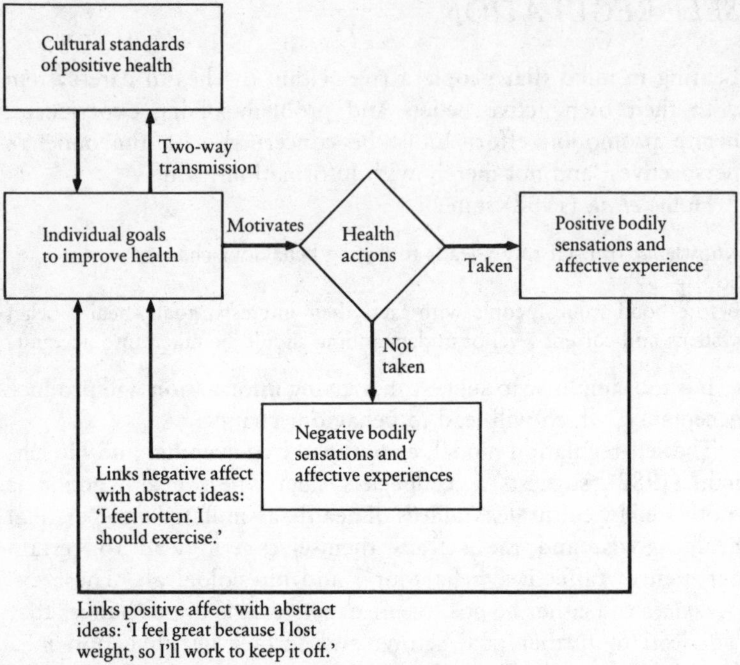

Figure 2 Self regulation of health promotion based on Leventhal and Hirschman (1982)

For any treatment, medical regime or daily health practice that requires voluntary action by the patient without constant surveillance by the therapist, internalisation is essential.

One might conclude that individuals with an internal Locus of Control were better targets for health programmes requiring 'internalisation', but Wallston and Wallston (1978) quote studies which demonstrate that with chronic conditions, such as diabetes, long-term diabetics who were internally controlled tended to ignore diets and to miss appointments. They suggest that the uncontrollable nature of the problem led the internals to assert control. The failure is not in the patient, but in the effectiveness of instruction given on that person's perceived healthiness. Internally controlled people certainly seem to seek more information, and it seems likely that increasing internality can help people to hold more internal beliefs and can affect their own health behaviour.

It must be emphasised that because people can be described as internally or externally controlled in certain situations, it does not mean we have the easy answer to health promotion programmes, matching different programmes to the person's Locus of Control. Internalisation can be shaped by efficient and relevant programmes, but the relationship between internality and effectiveness of intervention is still not clear by any means; nor are the associations between different contingencies and motivations and how this effects the Locus of Control.

The costs and benefits of particular situations can alter with different information, etc., so it is essential to look more closely at the situation demands rather than seeing internality or externality as a basic personality characteristic.

SELF-EFFICACY

With increasing recognition of the significance of behavioural patterns in chronic disease and the identification of risk factors in lifestyle, behavioural approaches in helping control certain habits are many and varied, although some theories have attempted to describe a macro-concept (summarised by O'Leary, 1985) derived from Bandura's work on social learning theory. As a construct, self-efficacy theory provides a common mechanism that encapsulates the issue of motivation and health behaviours. It appears that people who feel able to cope (both cognitively and behaviourally) will indeed cope better (as shown in measures like lowered blood pressure and heart rate when in stressful situations). So health information needs to take into account also beliefs in the person's abilities to affect their own health.

HEALTH CAREER AND CHANGING PATIENT-EXPERT RELATIONSHIP

In examining patient motivation for health behaviour it has become increasingly recognised that active and passive patient behaviour is elicited at different stages of health care, so the doctor-patient interaction changes considerably over time allowing more and less participation at different times.

Kotarba (1982) in his interesting book reverses our usual service-based view. In discussing the social dimensions of pain and taking a patient-based view he highlights the fact that some people approach the health care system more actively and that different people, at different times in their career are more and less capable of getting the health care system to work for them. He suggests that the active patient can get the health care system to perform better. In my own clinical experience, patients perceive themselves as more and less in control of the health care system at certain times in their health career, and this depends very much on the amount of active participation the health carers will allow.

At the first point of contact, as has already been suggested, the patient arrives with active ideas of his own health and treatment, but the doctor's expert role appears to strengthen as the patient's career develops through the system, and as the patient becomes more dependent. As he understands less of the investigations he is undergoing, he feels more vulnerable and passive. As technology takes over he depends more and more on expert opinion. Although many people are clearly helped by biomedical practice, a large number of people with chronic conditions inexorably progress to the chronic or rehabilitative phase. Here the doctors suggest a lot of the progress is 'up to him'. It appears that the doctor has done everything that he can in a curative sense and the patient is told to make the best of it, he is again put in an active role. He is again responsible for his care.

In summary, as the patient enters into the health care system he brings with him beliefs, expectancies about his health, and a history of previous experiences of the health care system which he has either found positive or negative. During his progress through his health career he is more or less available for active/passive approaches and only at certain times able to use his own problem-solving skills. As these dynamics change and as the person's career proceeds, different types of opportunities open up for patient-based and active programmes. At different stages in his career he will find the opportunity to participate equally will vary.

PATIENT PARTNERSHIP

It seems necessary from the above evidence that psychologists begin to develop clearer models of explanation to clarify the decision making people undergo when making health choices. Also, further investigation is needed on the changes in the balance of power in the patient's health career, which encourage active or passive participation at different stages. In order to promote healthier behaviours and to mobilise patient participation in different ways at different stages in the patient's career in sickness-based services, it is essential to have a firm theoretical foundation for these observations.

This focus on equal patient participation seems essential if health behaviours are to be promoted. Health promoters would suggest that a real challenge is needed to those health carers who firmly defend their expert role.

Indeed, the research on compliance rates would suggest that we have a severe problem and a waste of resources in helping patients follow instructions given by experts. For instance, Becker *et al.* (1972) report that only 51 per cent of mothers followed recommended medical schedules for the administration of antibiotics for their children with middle ear infection. They also report on the 'half rule', which reflects the rates of compliance for the treatment of hypertension. Thus, only half the clients measured as hypertensive came back for a necessary second measurement, and, of those who returned, and had measurable hypertension, only half were controlled adequately with the medication given. This means that only 12.5 per cent of the total group were adequately controlled for hypertension. Later studies have shown fairly similar low rates of compliance, although these tend to be closer to 30 per cent uncontrolled (Ward, 1977). There is an obvious need to improve our understanding of patient motivation and to match patient need with relevant interventions. Thus the concept of compliance with expert advice needs reconceptualising so patient partnership is increased. Perhaps the notion of equal sharing and partnership in care can lead to goal-setting and negotiation methods to achieving these goals. The client, by taking action he understands and wants himself, has every reason to 'comply'.

So psychologists, who are clearly experts in examining attitudes, beliefs and behaviours, have a clear role in explaining the patient's perspective in such interactions with the health care system, even though health carers may wish to guard their expert knowledge and position.

SUMMARY

This chapter has focused on the problems of increasing patient partnership and active involvement in health behaviours particularly in relation to the expert medical practitioner. It is suggested that the current biomedical model, which has such power in current health service delivery, is in some ways incompatible with current health needs and reduces patient responsibility and ability to take control and make choices. Some suggestions have been made as to why the health care system may not be sympathetic to psychosocial approaches. The issue of health promotion and the development of health behaviour has been the major focus of concern, emphasising current theoretical models that are useful but possibly incompatible with prevailing biomedical models. Psychologists need to develop more patient-based interventions from these theoretical bases and encourage the lessening of the expert role and the strengthening of patient partnership. In this way research topics may change, and the application of psychology in medicine will be more relevant to the consumer and match the service provided more closely to patient need; thereby improving effectiveness and more informed participation.

REFERENCES

Agras, W.S. (1982), 'Behavioural medicine in the 1980s: Non-random connections', *Journal of Consulting and Clinical Psychology*, 50, 6, pp.797–803.

Becker, M.H. (1974), 'The health belief model and personal health behaviour', *Health Education Monographs*, 2, pp.324–508.

Becker, M.H., Drachman, R.H. and Kirscht, J.P. (1972), 'Predicting mothers' compliance with paediatric medical regimens', *The Journal of Pediatrics, 81*, pp.843–54.

Becker, M.H. and Rosenstock, I.M. (1984), 'Compliance with medical advice', in A. Steptoe, *Health Care and Human Behaviour*, London, Academic Press.

Cleary, P.D. (1983), 'Multivariate analysis: Basic approaches to health data', in D. Mechanic, *Handbook of Health, Health Care and the Health Professions*, New York, Free Press.

Eysenck, H.J. (1984), 'Personality, stress and lung cancer', in J. Rachman, *Contributions to Medical Psychology,* Vol. 3, Oxford, Pergamon Press.

Faulder, C., (1985), '*Whose Body is It? The Troubling Issue of Informed Consent!*, London, Virago.

Fordyce, W.E. (1976), *Behavioural Methods for Chronic Pain and Illness*', St Louis, Morby.

Guttmacher, S., Teitelman, G., Chapin, G., Garbowski, G. and Schnall, P. (1981), 'Ethics and preventive medicine: The case for borderline hypertension', *Hastings Centre Report*, pp.12–20.

Hollis, J.P., Conners, W.E. and Mattarazzo, J.D. (1982), 'Lifestyle, behavioural health and heart disease', in R.J. Gatchel, H. Baum and J.E. Singer, *Handbook of Psychology and Health*, London, Lawrence Erlbaum Associates, pp.465–502.

Janis, I.L. and Rodin, J. (1979), 'Attribution, control and decision making; social psychology and health care', in G.C. Stone, F. Cohen and N.E. Alder (eds), *Health Psychology*, San Francisco, Jossey Bass, pp.487–521.

Kotarba, J.A. (1982), *Chronic Pain: Its Social Dimensions*, London, Sage Publications.

Leventhal, H. and Hirschman, R.S. (1982), 'Social psychology and prevention', in G. Sanders and J. Suls (eds), *Social Psychology of Health and Illness*, Lawrence Erlbaum Associates, pp.183–226.

Ley, P. and Morris, C. (1984), 'Psychological aspects of written information for patients', in S. Rachman (ed.), *Contributions to Medical Psychology,* Vol. 3, Oxford, Pergamon Press.

Office of Population Censuses and Surveys 1981, *Mortality Statistics, England and Wales*, London, HMSO.

O'Leary, A. (1985), 'Self-efficacy and health', *Behaviour Research and Therapy*, 23, 4, pp.437–51.

Pomerleau, O.F. (1982), 'A discourse on behavioural medicine: Current status and future trends', *Journal of Consulting and Clinical Psychology*, 50, 6, pp.1030–39.

Powells, J. (1974), 'On the limitations of modern medicine', in D. Mechanic,(ed.) *Readings: Medical Psychology*, London, Free Press.

Robin, E.D. (1984), *Matters of Life and Death. Risks and Benefits of Medical Care*, San Francisco, Freeman Press.

Schwartz, G.E. and Weiss, S.M. (1978), 'Yale Conference on Behavioral Medicine: A Proposed Definition and Statement of Goals', *Journal of Behavioural Medicine*, vol.1, pp.3–12.

Wallston, B.S. and Wallston, K.A. (1978), 'Locus of Control and Health: A review of the literature', *Health Education Monographs*, pp.107–15.

Wallston, K.A. and Wallston, B.S. (1981), 'Health Locus of Control Scales', *Research with the Locus of Control Construct,* Vol. 1, Assessment Methods, London, Academic Press, pp.189–243.

Ward, G. (1977), 'Keynote Address' at National Conference on High BP Control, Washington DC.

Weiss, S.M. (1981), 'Behavioural medicine in the United States: Research, clinical, and training opportunities', *International Journal of Mental Health, 9*, pp.182–96.

Williamson, J.D. and Danaher, K. (1978), *Self-Care in Health*, New York, Neale Watson, Academic Publications.

'To Do or Not to Do?': Ethical Problems for Behavioural Medicine

Rob Sanson-Fisher and Deborah Turnbull

The aim of this chapter is to determine some of the ethical problems confronting those attempting to change the lifestyles of the community. In recent years, community based interventions have become popular as a means of modifying health behaviour. Thus the ethical problems involved in such approaches must be delineated as an immediate step in providing ethical guidelines for intervention. This chapter also briefly examines some of the ethical issues involved in training medical students in communication skills. Communication is an important component of the doctor-patient relationship. While the dynamics of this relationship are quite different to those which exist in broad based community interventions (where the patient population can number hundreds of individuals), similar themes exist. These include power of the manager of the intervention, the degree of coercion exercised, and autonomy of the patient.

ETHICAL ISSUES INVOLVED IN COMMUNITY INTERVENTIONS

Community interventions into health risk behaviour have been widespread in recent years. Interventions can be categorised using a number of different criteria, for example, the environment of the intervention, including schools (Evans, Rozelle, Mittelmark,

Hansen, Bane and Havis, 1978) or the workplace (Rose, Tunstall-Pedoe and Heller, 1983). Similarly, they can be categorised according to the mode of intervention – health education, legislation, taxes and fines, or behaviourally orientated community intervention.

Interventions can also be arranged along a continuum of coercion. At one end of the continuum are educational approaches which attempt to provide information and restore choice. Behaviourally orientated interventions can be argued to be more coercive than educational strategies since the former attempt to modify actual behaviour by modifying the environment external to the individual. Paternalistic interventions such as legislation, taxes and fines can be placed at the most coercive end of the continuum since they effectively restrict freedom of choice. Those working in the area of health behaviour change are confronted by the ethics of each of these interventions either directly (for example when implementing preventive strategies) or indirectly (for example when confronted with aspects of the law). The following section will discuss the ethical issues involved in each of these interventions in turn.

TYPES OF INTERVENTIONS

Health Education

Health education is a relatively mild coercive strategy since it attempts to provide information. This generally increases the individual's power to make an informed choice. Consequently, health education requires less ethical justification (Wikler, 1978). It can be argued that withholding information may be coercive because knowledge is needed for informed decision making. If this is accepted then recent findings which indicate that 20 per cent of the American public do not know that smoking causes cancer must be a cause for concern (Federal Trade Commission, 1981). Such data suggests that large numbers of people are not acting on the basis of accurate knowledge about health risks and are therefore apparently deprived of informed choice.

Health education can also be viewed as counterbalancing information which promotes health risk behaviour. Cigarettes for example, are the most heavily advertised commodity in the United States (Federal Trade Commission, 1981). Similarly in Australia, tobacco advertising is currently estimated as worth A$60 million annually (Chapman and Carroll, 1984).

Another justification of education programmes is provided by the NIH/American College of Preventive Medicine Task Force. This group maintains that the justification for health education depends 'on the conviction that good health demands individual knowledge, individual responsibility and individual participation . . .' (Cohen and Cohen, 1978

The above arguments assume that the education strategies are aimed at providing information which enables a rational person to engage in free choice. This is distinct from the subtle use of media to manipulate choices covertly even for positive purposes (Pellegrino, 1981). It is very difficult to distinguish between covert manipulation and informational approaches designed to enhance free choice. Theoretically the latter would provide valid fact statements which would optimise self-determination. Decision making ability would be enhanced by providing alternative behaviour. In comparison, coercive presentations would be based on contentious information and disregard personal responsibility for health status (Pellegrino, 1981). Wikler (1978) maintains that educational approaches may become coercive when they attempt not only to provide information, but also manipulate attitudes and motivations.

While optimal health education programmes may provide free choice, and hence be seen to be ethical, they have not generally been effective in altering behaviour (Cohen and Cohen, 1978). The reasons for ineffectiveness can be related to the widespread discrepancy between health knowledge, and attitudes and behaviour (Telch, Killen, McAlister, Perry and Maccoby, 1982; Cohen and Cohen, 1978). This data has implications for the concept of autonomy. Beauchamp and Childress (1979) define a concept of autonomy which maintains that true autonomy involves not only knowledge and decision making but the capability to act upon such decisions. Thus according to such a definition, education programmes which provide information about the dangers of certain behaviours, but do not provide information and skills to actually change behaviour, do not ensure true autonomy.

Behaviourally orientated community interventions

In response to the low success rate of educational procedures, the use of 'psychological' or behaviourally oriented approaches has been proposed (Haggerty, 1977; Ubell, 1972). Pomerlau, Bass and Crown (1975) cite the Canadian Government Working Document which discusses the desirability of using behaviour modification for health problems on a national scale. An intervention applying social-psychological techniques is provided by Evans, Rozelle, Maxwell, Raines, Dill, Guthrie, Henderson and Hill (1981). This intervention used a deterrence strategy within a social learning and persuasive communication framework to deter junior high school students from smoking. Other smoking prevention studies have used relevant peer role models and active individual role playing as intervention agents (Hurd, Johnson, Pechacek, Bast, Jacobs and Leupker, 1980).

Using the Beauchamp and Childress (1979) definition of autonomy which incorporates decision making and the capability to act, behavioural approaches may be viewed as ensuring autonomy because they provide the techniques to alter behaviour. It must be noted, however, that behaviour change must be based on the individual's deliberation because both features (choice and ability to act) are salient in this concept of autonomy.

On the other hand, behaviourally orientated approaches can be argued to be more coercive than educative approaches. Educative approaches aim to restore a choice via information. Behaviourally orientated approaches go one step further than this. Behaviour modification aims at altering the external environment of the patient via methods such as contingency management or stimulus control. These methods directly modify the behaviour of the individual (Pomerlau *et al.*, 1975). Thus the ability of the individual to maintain behaviour is diminished because of forces outside his/her control. The individual's behaviour (after consent for treatment is given) is subject to external manipulation of the environment by the programme manager rather than internal decision making (as aimed at in educative approaches). Thus he or she becomes passively acted upon by actions of others.

Self-control methods are slightly different to behaviour modification methods, in self-control procedures the person modifies aspects of the environment that in turn modify the problem behaviour.

Hence the passive role of the patient is transformed into the role of active participant (Pomerlau *et al.* 1975). In this sense, self-control methods might be regarded as less coercive than traditional behaviour modification techniques. On the continuum of coercion, these methods might be placed somewhere between education and traditional behaviour modification. While they give more direct guidelines for behaviour change than do purely educative approaches, they involve the participant more actively than orthodox behaviour modification.

One large scale study to use self-control methods is the Stanford Heart Disease Prevention Programme (Maccoby, Farquhar, Wood and Alexander, 1977). Two communities involved in this programme were subjected to a mass media campaign (in one of these an intensive instruction programme was also used with high risk subjects). The mass media campaign was designed not only to inform and motivate the adult population about risk factors for cardiovascular disease but also to illustrate methods for self-assessment of risk related habits. These methods were designed to provide a basis for self-directed behaviour modification.

In justifying the use of behaviourally orientated techniques, Pomerlau *et al.* stress their effectiveness compared with other treatment methods. They cite a study by Meyer and Henderson (1974) which compares the effectiveness of such techniques with other treatment methods in reducing the risk of cardiovascular disease in an industrial population. Thirty six employees identified as being at risk of cariovascular disease were randomly assigned to one of the following treatment groups: 12 group-based behaviour modification sessions using self-control techniques; nine 15 minute individual counselling sessions with a health educator or one 20 minute counselling session with a physician. Results indicated that although all three procedures resulted in improvements in physiologic measurements of risk, the behavioural techniques produced greater changes in health habits than the other methods and that the improvements were more lasting.

Behaviourally oriented community interventions have been widely criticised on ethical grounds. Weingarten (1975) maintained that the ethics of such interventions are related to considerations besides efficacy. Firstly, the effect of modifying disease patterns on environmental resources, population dynamics, social organisations and human behaviour should be considered. Gori and Richter

(1978), for example, have examined the long term effects of successful prevention of what are now the major causes of mortality and morbidity. These include an increase in new competing causes of mortality and morbidity and a major restructuring of old age pensions and social security as the population becomes older. That is, while one disease may be eliminated, other health risk factors may appear or increase, although at later ages. Also, eventually, the growing increase in the retired population could result in economic difficulties as more pension funds and social security payments are required.

Secondly, Weingarten points to the ancient dilemma of individual rights and social responsibility and how it is often difficult to reconcile the two. An example of this is the smoker who many would see as having the social responsibility not to pollute others, but at the same time, the individual right to smoke.

Paternalistic interventions – legislation, taxes and fines

At the extreme end of the coercion continuum are those interventions which are imposed upon individuals. This can be achieved via legislation, taxes and fines. Social values when reinforced by the law become mechanisms of social control (Weingarten, 1978), since laws affect all people including those who do not or cannot give consent. Hence paternalistic strategies demand considerable debate (Wikler, 1978). Paternalism assumes that those who make laws or influence the process, such as health educators, know more about the morality, costs and benefits of health behaviour than those exhibiting health risk behaviours. Thus legislative intervention can be justified since it protects individuals against their own apparently ill advised risk behaviour. There is little doubt that paternalistic intervention can prevent individuals being harmed (Wikler, 1978). For example, seat belt legislation has been estimated to have saved approximately 2,000 lives over a seven year period in New South Wales (Herbert, 1980). At the same time, however, there are a number of practical and theoretical problems associated with these interventions. These are discussed in the following section.

Practical problems with paternalistic approaches

There are a number of practical problems associated with paternalistic interventions. First, interventions such as taxation may have serious side-effects. For example, raising the price of cigarettes may decrease the number of cigarettes smoked but lead smokers to smoke each cigarette longer and farther down leading to the same risk (Childress, 1982). There is data to suggest that smokers of middle-tar cigarettes may adjust their smoking habits to obtain a greater than expected nicotine intake from 'weaker' cigarettes (Ashton, Stepney and Thompson, 1979).

Second, paternalistic policies are only feasible for a limited number of health risks such as cigarette smoking, but not for risks that hold no market transactions such as lack of exercise (Childress, 1982). Third, such interventions may disproportionately affect the poor as they generally experience higher levels of health risk behaviour such as smoking (Todd, 1976) and drinking (Hetzel, 1974). Pellegrino (1981) for this reason favours inducements rather than disincentives.

Theoretical problems with paternalistic approaches

One reason for questioning the ethical justifiability of paternalistic interventions is the notion of harm (Wikler, 1978). What may be seen as harmful by one person may be viewed as beneficial by another. For example, a smoker may regard the 'beneficial' aspects of smoking such as stress reduction as compensating for the harmful or negative effects such as shortness of breath and increased risk of cancer and cardiovascular disease. Wikler notes that it is difficult to defer to authority in notions of harm and good because each individual often feels that his/her personal preferences are based on the values of reasonable people.

Paternalism also presupposes that intervention should only occur when the individual's autonomy is in jeopardy – that is when the potentially self-destructive activity is involuntary. However, it is difficult to determine when a person's actions are voluntary or coming from externally imposed values. These include those stressed by advertising or reinforced by ignorance. Thus, it is impossible to determine an individual's 'true' values (Wikler, 1978). John Stuart Mill maintained that interventions in voluntary individual behaviour are not justified even though the behaviour may be harmful. However, conduct that adversely effects others may be modified under certain conditions. Interventions in behaviours that are involuntary due to decreased decision making ability may be justified (Childress, 1982). Mill cited instances of limited or weak paternalism which maintained respect for the individual. Thus he argued for the labelling of dangerous drugs rather than their prohibition (Childress, 1982).

Many critics of Mill maintain that few lifestyles only affect the individual. Examples of this would include passive smoking and the effect of alcoholism on the family and society. Luce and Schweitzer (1978) estimate that the direct health-care cost alone that is attributable to, or associated with, smoking and alcohol abuse to be US$20.2 billion in 1976. This represents nearly 20 per cent of the total estimated cost of direct medical care in the United States. Mill also did not deny that harm to others can occur, but argued that it must be related to relevant considerations. These include whether the harm outweighs the loss of liberty and consent of the victim (Childress, 1982).

Thus, the previous section discusses a number of different types of lifestyle interventions. These have been categorised along a continuum of coercion. At one end of the continuum is health education and, at the other end, paternalistic interventions including taxes and fines. Each type of intervention has been demonstrated to involve ethical advantages and disadvantages. For example, while education programmes may provide information to enhance decision making ability, they may not be effective in altering actual behaviour and hence may not provide the individual with true autonomy. Alternatively, legislation may have greater efficacy in altering behaviour, but may ignore issues such as individual rights. Thus both positive and negative ethical aspects need to be considered when designing and implementing intervention programmes.

GENERAL ETHICAL PROBLEMS OF COMMUNITY INTERVENTIONS

As noted by Rust (1979) the question isn't whether or not we should modify behaviour, because each of us modifies others' behaviour every day simply through interaction. Rather, the issue is what ethical guidelines should be assumed. A number of general problems confronting workers who attempt to change the lifestyle of the community are discussed in the following section.

Possible negative effects of preventive strategies

In examining the ethical basis for preventive strategies, the possibility of side-effects must be considered. First, negative effects may be produced in individuals participating in the intervention. This has been indicated in a recent study of screening and referral for hypertension (Haynes, Sackett, Taylor, Gibson and Johnson, 1978). Results indicated that after screening and referral, absenteeism rose by 80 per cent compared with a 9 per cent rise in the general employee population during the period. The application of attempts to promote compliance with therapy did not influence absenteeism. One explanation offered to explain these findings is that the labelling of a person as hypertensive is deleterious because it causes many patients with newly labelled hypertension to adopt the 'sick role' and treat themselves as more fragile. The possible adverse effects of health education practices designed to scare or worry people into seeking medical attention has also been indicated by Schneider (1975). He cites the work of Hackett, Cassem and Baker (1973) who reported that people who worried more about cancer tended to delay more in going for medical help when symptoms of cancer became manifest.

Second, Holtzman (1979) also notes that campaigns for lifestyle change are most likely to succeed in those with the lightest burden of illness (usually those of higher socioeconomic class). Thus preventive strategies are more likely to increase the disparity in health between rich and poor and detract from more effective eclectic approaches. These utilise not only preventive strategies but also late intervention medical care and legal regulation. A number of studies have indicated the positive relationship between socioeconomic class and the utilisation of preventive care. In general, it has been indicated that socially disadvantaged families have higher consultation rates for morbidity and tend to under-utilise preventive health services (Fergusson, Horwood, Beautrais and Shannon, 1981).

Third, emphasis on prevention through individual responsibility may detract from other sources of illness such as unsafe working conditions and environmental health hazards (Wikler, 1978).

Recent research in Sweden, for example, indicates that more than one third of occupational accidents (114 non-fatal and 201 fatal cases) occurred because of insufficient safety measures for which employers were responsible (Grondstrom, Jarl and Thorson, 1980). Another study by Saari and Lahtela (1979) indicates that factories with a higher than average annual accident frequency had a greater prevalence of dangers such as unguarded machine parts. Moreover, undue stress upon the individual's role in the cause of illness could lead to a 'blame the victim' mentality. This could be used as an excuse for not making curative services available (Wikler, 1978).

Whose values?

In intervening in the lifestyle of individuals, it must be asked (Oliver and Rogers, 1985), why we are trying to change behaviour, for whose benefit and whose values are we espousing? In attempting to prevent individuals engaging in health risk behaviours, are we simply replacing one set of values with another? This is especially the case when we consider that the majority of those who engage in health risk behaviour are of lower socioeconomic class and the managers of intervention generally are of the middle class. It can be asked, then, are middle-class values simply being superimposed on those of the working class? Oliver and Rogers (1985) maintain that because we are social animals it is impossible for the manager of intervention to practise 'amorally' even though he or she may pretend to. That is, the manager cannot intervene without referring to his/her own value system and social experiences of what constitutes acceptable behaviour.

'Overism'

The ethical issue of overism arises from 'doing too much, too soon, too energetically, without assessing the impact of one's community intervention' (Perlman, 1977, p.53). When the community worker rigidly adheres to a particular theory or model without review by peers there is a distinct danger that he/she will come to see him/herself as a 'public protector of the community's mental health' (p.53). Perlman identifies possible dangers as when too much concern can become meddling. Secondly he notes that the line between prevention and protection of citizens against themselves is at times difficult to distinguish. Thirdly, early intervention when applied inappropriately can be an invasion of privacy.

An example of overism is given by Weisburger (1977) who indicates the haphazard and premature nature of many of the claims for cancer hazards. He notes in particular the repeated unsubstantiated claims in the American press of the relationship between specific chemicals and food additives and their relationship to cancer. Also presumed carcinogenic hazards have been presented before government agencies and the Congress without a full documentation of the facts. This has only alarmed the public.

Unique nature of community interventions

The very nature of community based interventions preclude the application of guidelines which are often used in individual clinical interventions. A campaign such as the 1972 Stanford Heart Disease Prevention Programme (Maccoby *et al.*, 1977) cannot ensure guidelines such as informed consent by every individual exposed to the multi-media campaign. Nor can there exist a therapist-client joint determination of the goals of therapy (or intervention).

POSSIBLE GUIDELINES OF PREVENTION

The question remains, at what point do we interfere in individual lifestyles to establish the 'common good'? Since the early critical review of periodic health screening by Frame and Carlson (1975), a number of documents outlining guidelines of prevention have appeared (Battista, Beaulieu, Feightner, Mann and Owen, 1984). Two models are offered by Pellegrino (1981) and the Canadian Task Force on the Periodic Health Examination (1979).

Pellegrino

Pellegrino (1981) maintains that, because voluntary measures promise to be ineffective for the good of all, measures to enforce personal compliance are justified; however, two things are required as a minimum. First, whatever measures are selected for universal application must be demonstrably effective. Three categories of effectiveness are suggested – certainty, suggestive or speculative. When the evidence is very strong or certain that the behaviour causes the disease (eg cigarette smoking and lung cancer), then coercive measures are justified. When the evidence linking the behaviour to specific illness is only suggestive (such as the relationship between high fat diets and cancer of the colon), involuntary measures would be less justified and education programmes are recommended so that the individual can decide. When the evidence is merely speculative, only information emphasising the uncertainties would be justified.

Second, Pellegrino suggests that a set of explicit moral principles must be met. These include proportionality and self-determination. Proportionality assumes that coercive measures are to be considered only when their effectiveness is unequivocal for large numbers of people and when effecting control extends over a limited sector of life. Examples include immunisation and sanitation. Second, a measure must meet as closely as possible the democratic principle of self-determination. Accordingly, voluntary measures must be seen as inadequate at the outset or must have failed before coercive measures are contemplated. When justified, coercion should be of the mildest form compatible with achieving the desired change in behaviour. To forestall the imposition of involuntary measures, valid information to enhance decision making must be provided. Coercive measures should be severely limited in matters that are personal and private including sex and family. Restrictions should be placed on those who engage in health risk behaviour and not on the victims of such behaviour (eg passive smokers). Regulations should always be in favour of those who cannot consent (eg children).

Canadian Task Force on the Periodic Health Examination

One important set of guidelines have been developed by the Canadian Task Force on the Periodic Health Examination. The thrust of the report is aimed at examining guidelines for the use of the periodic health examination as compared with the annual examination. Other preventive strategies however, could be examined with reference to the objectives of the report.

The report suggests guidelines for prevention based on their efficacy, effectiveness, efficiency and safety (Battista *et al.*, 1984). Firstly, the task force and its consultants attempted to identify potentially preventable conditions. In deciding whether the conditions should be included in a periodic health examination three aspects were studied (a) the current burden of mortality, morbidity and suffering caused by the condition (both on the individual and society); (b) the validity and acceptability of the manoeuvre (the risks and benefits; sensitivity; specificity and predictive value; safety; simplicity; cost and acceptability to the patient); (c) the effectiveness of the intervention. This was graded according to the quality of evidence. At the top end of the grade was evidence obtained from at least one properly randomised controlled trial. At the bottom end of the scale was evidence supported by opinions of respected authorities, based on clinical experience, descriptive studies, or reports of expert committees. (Canadian Task Force on the Periodic Health Examination, 1979).

Cost-benefit analysis

As maintained in the Canadian Task Force Report, an important aspect of prevention is validity and acceptability of the manoeuvre. One component of this involves cost of the intervention. Cost-benefit aspects of interventions are highly problematic and pose further problems for those working in the area of health behaviour change. One reason for this is the haphazard manner in which prevention and cost-benefit analyses have been approached in the past. This is evident in a recent study by Rogers, Eaton and Bruhn (1981). In this study, a literature review surveyed applications in promotion of a healthy lifestyle. The scope of the review covers the literature published from 1969 through 1979 in English language journals. The review indicated confusion regarding definitions of such concepts as health education, disease detection and health protection. The review also revealed several approaches to cost analysis in the short and long term evaluation of programmes. Results indicated few evaluations included appropriate cost analysis techniques or long range follow-up of the effects of the programme. It is concluded then that the overall cost effectiveness of services to promote health cannot be determined.

Rob Sanson-Fisher and Deborah Turnbull

ETHICAL ISSUES INVOLVED IN TRAINING MEDICAL STUDENTS TO BE EFFECTIVE COMMUNICATORS

This chapter also attempts to examine some of the issues involved in training medical students to become more effective communicators. As stated in the introduction, communication is an important component of the doctor-patient relationship. While the dynamics of this relationship are quite different to those which exist in community intervention, similar themes exist. These include power and coercion exercised by the intervention manager and autonomy of the client. Before discussing the issues involved in communication between doctor and patient, a general introduction to autonomy and power in this relationship is required.

AUTONOMY AND POWER IN THE DOCTOR-PATIENT RELATIONSHIP

These themes were recently discussed by Komrad (1983). Komrad views the patient as being in a state of diminished autonomy simply because of the fact that he/she is ill. Thus illness requires some degree of paternalistic intervention. The question, however, is what degree of paternalism is justified? Komrad views paternalism as a response to incapacity rather than a negation of rights. A continuous update of the patient's autonomy is required to modulate the doctor's paternalism. As the patient recovers there is a decrease in paternalism – the paternalism nurtures the patient's autonomy.

The imbalance of power in the therapist-patient relationship is also noted by Stolz, Wienckowski and Brown (1975). They view this imbalance as being essentially structural in cause. Typically, the therapist is from the more powerful classes or has a higher status within an institution. The client, on the other hand, is usually from a less powerful class and has a lower status in the institution.

COMMUNICATION IN THE DOCTOR-PATIENT RELATIONSHIP

Specific communication skills include interviewing, basic counselling skills, methods of giving information to patients, and the use of interpersonal styles which have been demonstrated to enhance satisfaction and compliance (Sanson-Fisher and Maguire, 1980).

In recent years, there has been an increasing interest in doctors' communication skills. Much of the research has been aimed at criticising the current lack of teaching of these skills. A recent study reported on the responses of 16,500 medical practitioners in Australia (Maguire, 1983). Some 80 per cent of the sample considered the medical education system to be deficient in teaching counselling skills (though some were referring to their undergraduate days and could not comment on today's teaching).

In response to reports such as these, a number of researchers have examined different techniques of teaching skills to medical students. For example, a recent study examined the value of feedback in teaching interviewing skills (Maguire, Roe, Goldberg, Jones, Hyde and O'Dowd, 1978).

The rationale for improving skills is that they effect most aspects of the patient-doctor interaction. These include adequacy of clinical interviews, patient's satisfaction, recall of offered advice, compliance and the impact of potentially distressing medical and surgical procedures (Sanson-Fisher and Maguire, 1980). Moreover, improving communication skills may also improve detection of psychiatric morbidity. This is essential considering the suspected high rates of non-detection (Goldberg and Blackwell, 1970) and the implications psychiatric morbidity has for quality of life.

Improper use of communication skills, however, could be argued to increase the power of the doctor over his/her patient. For example, the doctor might circumvent the patient's poorly formulated but personally valid objections to a particular intervention. Similarly, increasing compliance may be seen as reducing the patient's autonomy in cases where the patient has reasons for non-compliance which he/she views as justified.

Whether improving communication skills is used for increasing the doctor's power is largely dependent on the definition of communication and how the skills are taught. If they are taught in a manner which facilitates the doctor's 'salesmanship' techniques they will indeed increase the power of the doctor to 'talk over' a patient's objections to a particular intervention. In this sense, they might be seen as increasing the doctor's skills of coercion. Rather, teaching must ensure skills which enhance two-way communication. Here the doctor does not simply improve skills in persuasion but is taught to listen to the patient's fears and insecurities. Moreover, the doctor is taught to facilitate and encourage the patient's expression of feelings. Positive communication then must provide the patient with both beneficial and negative aspects of intervention. It also involves active involvement by the patient in the planning of acceptable treatment. Thus the doctor-patient interaction must ensure autonomy of the patient and enhance his/her decision making ability.

The approach being proposed here is similar to the 'mutual participation' model of doctor-patient interaction proposed by Szasz and Hollender (1956). This model is based on a mature doctor-patient relationship involving mutual participation and respect. This is in contrast to the unequal parent-child relationship which some researchers believe physicians seem to prefer (Hyatt, 1980). The model is not suitable for all types of therapeutic interactions. For example, those between doctor and child or the comatose patient.

This model has advantages and disadvantages for both doctors and patient. On the one hand, more responsibility is placed with the patient, and therefore pressure on the doctor to produce a 'cure' for a lifestyle which the patient may not wish to alter is decreased. Alternatively the doctor may lose the power which he/she values in the therapeutic relationship.

This type of relationship stresses an informal role structure and participation by both doctor and patient. This may produce stress and ambivalence. This may occur, for example, when the doctor must decide when the patient's decision making ability is intact or being compromised by outside pressures from family and friends. Secondly, the doctor is placed in a dilemma in instances when the patient, after being presented with all alternatives, decides on a course of action with which the doctor disagrees. Here the doctor is faced with two courses of action – simply becoming an agent of the patient and performing the intervention anyway, or refusing to perform the intervention, and referring the patient to a willing colleague.

Similar issues relate to the patient. While increased autonomy may be valued by many patients, some may prefer and feel more comfortable in the paternalistic interaction where the doctor behaves like a parent and the patient assumes the role of the child. Anxiety may be produced in highly defensive patients who prefer to be told what to do.

A number of studies have indicated that issues of autonomy and negotiation are a major source of conflict between the patient and doctor (Hyatt, 1980; Warner, 1977). Hyatt for example found significant disagreement about the power relationship between patients and doctors including issues such as placing pressure on the patient to accept the physician's advice, and doctor and patient perceptions of whether the patient prefers to be told what to do. In both cases the patient preferred a more autonomous role than the doctor perceived. Similarly Ley (1977) presents research which indicates a conflict of views about the amount of information which should be given to a dying patient. Research indicates that most patients with a potentially terminal disease wish to be fully informed (Reynolds, Sanson-Fisher, Poole, Harker and Byrne, 1981), while the traditional view among doctors is that such people should not be informed (Cartwright, Hockey and Anderson, 1973). Recent research in Newcastle, Australia, also indicates that while both doctors and patients express the desire for a mutually reciprocative relationship, this does not appear to be occurring in the general practice consultation (Cockburn, Reid and Sanson-Fisher (submitted for publication).

Hence it also appears that patients and increasing numbers of doctors are coming to prefer the more autonomous and equally based therapeutic interaction being recommended here.

CONCLUSIONS

Thus the purpose of this chapter has been twofold. First, to examine the problems of those working in the area of community based lifestyle interventions; second, to briefly outline the problems involved in teaching communication skills to medical students. Similar themes pervade including those of autonomy and power. In outlining the problems in intervening in the lifestyle of the community, this chapter has aimed at emphasising the need for a more formal ethics of prevention. This has also been noted by Pellegrino (1981) and Simonds (1978). Although guidelines have been developed (for example those of the Canadian Task Force on the Periodic Health Examination), more work is required. This is especially the case considering the fact that prevention is considered an essential strategy in altering current trends in mortality and morbidity.

The purpose of both community and individual clinical interventions is not to turn individuals into automated unthinking beings, but rather to improve certain skills and, hopefully, to enhance decision-making options (Stolz, Wienckowski and Brown, 1975). Although no absolute consensus will be achieved in a democratic society (Pellegrino, 1981), because prevention is now both possible and necessary, some degree of ethics should prevail.

REFERENCES

Ashton, H., Stepney R. and Thompson J.W. (1979), 'Self-titration by cigarette smokers', *British Medical Journal, 2*, pp.357–60.

Battista, R.N., Beaulieu, M.D., Feightner J.W., Mann, K.V., and Owen, G. (1984), 'The periodic health examination: 3 An evolving concept', *Canadian Medical Association Journal, 130*, pp.1288–92.

Beauchamp, T. and Childress, J. (1979), *Principles of Biomedical Ethics*, New York, Oxford University Press.

Canadian Task Force on the Periodic Health Examination (1979), 'The periodic health examination', *Canadian Medical Association Journal, 121*, pp.1193–254.

Cartwright, T.A., Hockey, L. and Anderson J.L. (1973), *Life Before Death*, London, Routledge & Kegan Paul.

Chapman, S. and Carroll, T. (eds) (1984), *Quit for Life. Community Information and Resource Manual*, (2nd edn), NSW, Department of Health.

Childress, J.F. (1982), *Who Should Decide? Paternalism in Health Care*, New York, Oxford University Press.

Cockburn, J., Reid, A. and Sanson-Fisher, R. submitted for publication.

Cohen, C.I. and Cohen E.J. (1978), 'Sounding Board. Health education: panacea, pernicious or pointless?', *New England Journal of Medicine, 299(13)*, pp.718–20.

Evans, R.I., Rozelle, R.M., Maxwell, S.E., Raines, B.E., Dill, C.A., Guthrie, T.J., Henderson, A.H. and Hill, P.C. (1981), 'Social modelling films to deter smoking in adolescents: results of a three-year field investigation', *Journal of Applied Psychology, 66(4)*, pp.399–414.

Evans, R.I., Rozelle, R.M., Mittelmark, M.B., Hansen, W.B., Bane, A.L. and Havis, J. (1978), 'Deterring the onset of smoking in children: knowledge of immediate physiological effects and coping with peer pressure, media pressure, and parent modeling', *Journal of Applied Social Psychology, 8(2)*, pp.126–35.

Federal Trade Commission (May 1981), *Staff Report on the Cigarette Advertising Investigation*, Washington DC, FTC.

Fergusson, D.M., Horwood, L.J., Beautrais, A.L. and Shannon, F.T. (1981), 'Health Care utilization in a New Zealand birth cohort', *Community Health Studies, 5(1)*, pp.53–60.

Frame, P.S. and Carlson, S.J. (1975), 'A critical review of periodic health screening using specific screening criteria, Part 1, Selected diseases of respiratory, cardiovascular and central nervous systems', *Journal of Family Practice*, vol.2, pp.29–36.

Goldberg, D.P. and Blackwell, B. (1970), 'Psychiatric illness in general practice. A detailed study using a new method of case identification', *British Medical Journal, 2*, pp.439–43.

Gori, G.B. and Richter, B.J. (1978), 'Macroeconomics of disease prevention in the United States', *Science, 200*, pp.1124–30.

Grondstrom, R., Jarl, T., and Thorson, J. (1980), 'Serious occupational accidents – an investigation of causes', *Journal of Occupational Accidents, 2*, pp.283–9.

Hackett, T.P., Cassen, N.H. and Baker, J.W. (1973), 'Patient Delay in Cancer', *New England Journal of Medicine*, vol.289, no.1, pp.14–20.

Haggerty, R.J. (1977), 'Changing lifestyles to improve health', *Preventive Medicine, 6(2)*, pp.276–89.

Haynes, R.B., Sackett, D.L., Taylor, W., Gibson, E.S. and Johnson, A.L. (1978), 'Increased absenteeism from work after detection and labelling of hypertensive patients', *New England Journal of Medicine, 299(14)*, pp.741–4.

Herbert, D.C. (1980), *Road Safety in the Seventies: Lessons for the Eighties. TARU Research Report No. 4180*, NSW, Department of Motor Transport.

Hetzel, B.S. (1974), *Health and Australian Society*, Victoria, Penguin.

Holtzman, N.A. (1979), 'Prevention: Rhetoric and Reality', *International Journal of Health Services, 9(1)*, pp.25–39.

Hurd, P.D., Johnson, C.A., Pechacek, T., Bast, L.P., Jacobs, D.R. and Leupker, R.V. (1980), 'Prevention of cigarette smoking in seventh grade students', *Journal of Behavioural Medicine, 3(1)*, pp.15–28.

Hyatt, J.D. (1980), 'Perceptions of the family physician by patients and family physicians', *Journal of Family Practice, 10(2)*, pp.295–300.

Komrad, M.S. (1983), 'A defence of medical paternalism: maximising patients' autonomy', *Journal of Medical Ethics, 9(1)*, pp.38–44.

Ley, P. (1977), 'Psychological studies of doctor-patient communication', in S. Rachman (ed.), *Contributions to Medical Psychology*, vol.1, Oxford, Pergamon Press, pp.9–42.

Luce, B.R. and Schweitzer, S.O. (1978), 'Smoking and alcohol abuse: a comparison of their economic consequences', *New England Journal Medicine, 298(10)*, pp.569–71.

Maccoby, N., Farquhar, J.W., Wood, P.D. and Alexander, J. (1977), 'Reducing the risk of cardivascular disease: Effects of a community-based campaign on knowledge and behaviour', *Journal of Community Health, 3(2)*, pp.100–14.

Maguire, P., Roe, P., Goldberg, D., Jones, S., Hyde, C. and O'Dowd, T. (1978), 'The value of feedback in teaching interviewing skills to medical students', *Psychological Medicine, 8*, pp.695–704.

Maguire, P. (1983), 'Many say counselling skills are inadequate', Special Report, *Medical Practice*, pp.23–4.

Meyer, A.J. and Henderson, J.B. (1974), 'Multiple risk factor reduction in the prevention of cardiovascular disease', *Preventive Medicine*, vol.3, pp.225–36.

Oliver, P., and Rogers, S.J. (1985), *Should Psychologists (and other Social scientists) Continue to Pretend to Practise Amorally*.

Pellegrino, E.D. (1981), 'Health promotion as public policy: The need for moral groundings', *Preventive Medicine, 10*, pp.371–8.

Perlman, B. (1977), 'Ethical concerns in community mental health', *Amercian Journal of Community Psychology, 5(1)*, pp.45–57.

Pomerleau, O., Bass, F. and Crown, V. (1975), 'Role of behaviour modification in preventive medicine', *New England Journal of Medicine, 292(24)*, pp.1277–82.

Reynolds, P.M., Sanson-Fisher, R.W., Poole, A.D., Harker, J. and Byrne, M.J. (1981), 'Cancer and communication: information-giving in an oncology clinic', *British Medical Journal, 282*, pp.1449–51.

Rogers, P.J., Eaton, E.K. and Bruhn, J.G. (1981), 'Is health promotion cost effective?', *Preventive Medicine, 10*, pp.324–39.

Rose, G., Tunstall-Pedoe, H.D. and Heller, R.F. (1983), UK Heart Disease Prevention Project, 'Incidence and mortality results', *Lancet, i*, pp.1062–5.

Rust, M.D. (1979), 'Issues in behaviour control: An exchange of views', I, *Man and Medicine, 4(1)*, pp.22–5.

Saari, J.T. and Lahtela, J. (1979), 'Characteristics of jobs in high and low accident frequency companies in the light metal working industry', *Accident Analysis and Prevention, 11(1)*, pp.51–60.

Sanson-Fisher, R. and Maguire, P. (1980), 'Should skills in communicating with patients be taught in medical schools?' *Lancet, ii*, pp.523–6.
Schneider, H.L. (1975), 'Letter to the editor', *New England Journal of Medicine, 293(10)*, p.510.
Simonds, S.K. (1978), 'Health education: facing issues of policy, ethics and social justice', *Health Education Monographs, 6*, Supplement 1, pp.18–27.
Stolz, S.B., Wienckowski, L.A. and Brown, B.S. (1975), 'Behaviour modification. A perspective on critical issues', *American Psychologist, 30(11)*, pp.1027–48.
Szasz, T.S. and Hollender, M.H. (1956), 'A contribution to the philosophy of medicine. The basic models of the doctor-patient relationship', *Archives of Internal Medicine, 97*, pp.585–92.
Telch, M.J., Killen, J.D., McAlister, A.L., Perry, C.L. and Maccoby, N. (1982), 'Long-term follow-up of a pilot project on smoking prevention with adolescents', *Journal of Behavioural Medicine, 5(1)*, pp.1–8.
Todd, G.F. (1976), *Social Class Variations in Cigarette Smoking and in Mortality from Associated Diseases. Occasional Paper* 2, London, Tobacco Research Council.
Ubell, E. (1972), 'Health behaviour change: A political model', *Preventive Medicine, 1(2)*, pp.209–21.
Warner, M.M. (1977), 'Consumers, family physicians, allied health workers, and sociomedical problems', *Journal of the Royal College of General Practitioners, 27(180)*, pp.431–5.
Weingarten, R. (1975), 'Behaviour modification', Letter to the editor, *New England Journal of Medicine, 293*, pp.509–10.
Weisburger, J.H. (1977), 'Social and ethical implications of claims for cancer hazards', *Medical and Pediatric Oncology, 3*, pp.137–40.
Wikler, D.I. (1978), 'Persuasion and coercion for health. Ethical issues in government efforts to change life-styles', *Milbank Memorial Fund Quarterly/Health and Society, 56(3)*, pp.303—38.

Psychotherapy as Essential Care

Richard Lindley

In their classic study of mental health care provision, Hollingshead and Redlich (1958) found that in New Haven, Connecticut there were striking inequalities in the treatment provided for people from different social classes. Unskilled and semi-skilled workers of poor education were much more likely than those from higher-ranked social classes to receive physiological treatments, such as electro-convulsive therapy, drugs and brain surgery. They rarely received psychotherapy, and, where they did, it was usually of a perfunctory nature. In contrast, psychotherapy *was* widely available for those from the top two social classes – the executive-professionals and the managerial-professionals.

Since then there has been an increasing trend to combine psychotherapy with other treatments, such as drug therapies, as is evidenced by Redlich and Kellert (1978). Nevertheless, it remains true that the distribution of psychotherapeutic services is much more unevenly distributed (according to social class, sex and geographical location) than other forms of health care – certainly within the United Kingdom and the United States. For example, in a recent study, Holmes (1985) found that working-class patients and women were seriously under-represented among those referred for psychotherapy by their general practitioner.

It is also true that the distribution of swimming pools and world cruises is very unequal. The fact that some people own swimming pools and spend vast amounts on world cruises, is a scandal in a world where millions die of hunger, thirst and avoidable disease every year. However, the fact that ability to pay determines who has swimming pools and expensive holidays is not in itself a ground for serious complaint.

Perhaps the most fundamental principle of the British National Health Service, established in 1948, has been that everyone who needed medical care or treatment should be able to receive it irrespective of ability to pay. During the 1960s and 1970s a similar principle was accepted in the government-funded Medicaid and Medicare in the United States.

The central question of this paper is whether psychotherapy should be regarded like private swimming pools and world cruises, as basically a luxury available to those able and willing to pay for it; or whether it should be treated as a part of essential care, to which everyone should be entitled – equally – irrespective of ability to pay. But first, I shall say a little about why, in a society without absolute scarcity of essential resources, basic *health* care should be available to all who need it.

BASIC HEALTH CARE

A case for distribution of health care facilities according to need, irrespective of ability to pay was confidently expressed by Bernard Williams (1962) in the following:

> Leaving aside preventive medicine, the proper ground of distribution of medical care is ill health: this is a necessary truth. Now in very many societies, while ill health may work as a necessary condition of receiving treatment, it does not work as a sufficient condition, since such treatment costs money and not all who are ill have the money; hence the possession of sufficient money becomes in fact an additional necessary condition of actually receiving treatment. . . . When we have the situation in which . . . wealth is a further necessary condition of the receipt of medical treatment, we can . . . apply the notions of equality and inequality: not . . . in connection with the inequality between the well and the ill, but in connection with the inequality between the rich ill and the poor ill, since we have straightforwardly the situation of those whose needs are the same not receiving the same treatment, though the needs are the grounds of the treatment. This is an irrational state of affairs . . . it is a situation in which reasons are insufficiently operative; it is a situation insufficiently controlled by reasons – and hence by reason itself (Williams, 1962, pp.121–2).

In an incisive criticism Robert Nozick (1974, pp.233–4) has

shown that Williams's argument is uncompelling as it stands. The claim that health care should be distributed according to user need rests on the supposition that where a service has an 'internal goal', it is a necessary truth that the proper basis for distributing that service is to serve the goal; and the 'internal goal' of medical treatment is the eradication of ill health or the cure of disease. If the principle behind this claim were accepted, then barbering services, gardening services, and any other service with an internal goal should be allocated strictly according to need, irrespective of ability or preparedness to pay. Nozick suggests that barbers and gardeners have the right to use their talents, and to allocate their services, as they wish. The implication is that, because this is true of gardeners and barbers, it should be true of other providers of services – including medical practitioners.

To defend the claim that health care should be available to all, according to their needs, we require an argument for why, amongst services with internal goals, health care is special. If this could be shown, Nozick's concern for the liberty of practitioners would, admittedly, still have to be considered. We would have a conflict between two plausible principles: that health care should be available to all, and that people should have the liberty to work for whom they choose. How such a conflict should be resolved would take us beyond the scope of this paper. The point is that, unless health care *is* special, the extreme libertarian about practitioners' rights might not even have a case to answer.

Norman Daniels (1985) has argued that health care is special, on the grounds that ill-health restricts a person's ability to pursue the 'normal opportunity range' for the society in which he or she lives. The normal opportunity range for a particular society is 'the array of life plans reasonable persons in it are likely to construct for themselves'. This range will vary from society to society – according to the level of material and social development. However, it is likely that in any society, diseases, which Daniels defines as: 'deviations from the natural functional organization of a typical member of a species', will reduce the opportunities of those suffering from them to below the norm for their society. Health care should be available to all – in the name of social justice – on the grounds that ill-health denies people the basic equality of opportunity to pursue their own plans of life, in accordance with their own conceptions of a worthwhile life:

Life plans for which we are otherwise suited and which we have a reasonable expectation of finding satisfying or happiness-producing are rendered unreasonable by impairments of normal functioning. Consequently, if persons have a fundamental interest in preserving the opportunity to revise their conceptions of the good through time, then they will have a pressing interest in maintaining normal species functioning . . . by establishing institutions, such as health-care systems, which do just that (Daniels, 1985, p.28).

The general rationale for belief in fair equality of opportunity is that respect for people requires that nobody is denied access to essential goods through arbitary decisions, its main application is in the field of employment. Jobs and careers should be allocated according to ability and inclination to do them – not according to skin colour, sex, or social background. Because people's opportunities are so fundamentally restricted by ill health, fair equality of opportunity requires that health care be available to everyone.

Of course this argument does not appeal to those who reject the principle of fair equality of opportunity, since it rests on an application of that principle. However, the equal opportunity principle is widely accepted – at least officially; so the argument is certainly relevant. However, I think it leaves important questions unanswered – apart from those which challenge the fair equality of opportunity principle itself.

Champions of the principle of fair equality of opportunity do not intend the principle to extend to all parts of life. They do not, for instance, believe that everyone should have the same opportunity to go on expensive world cruises – irrespective of ability and desire to pay. And yet lack of money certainly reduces many people's chances of pursuing such an apparently happiness-producing project. There is a need to identify those parts of life over which the equality of opportunity principle should apply and, within that area, a set of priorities needs to be worked out. Where is equality of opportunity most important?

To solve these problems it is necessary to devise a theory of primary goods and posit the existence of a hierarchy of needs. A need is a necessary condition for something. Thus to say that X needs Y is in itself incomplete. What is required in addition is a specification of what good lack-of-Y denies X. Artefacts, such as car engines, have needs – for instance for an effective cooling system, fuel, and finely-adjusted tappets. The first two are more basic needs than the last, since the engine will not work at all without them, whereas if its tappets are slightly out of adjustment it will function, but not as efficiently as it might. Needs of artefacts are necessary conditions for the artefacts to function as intended. The needs of living things, on the other hand, are the necessary conditions for them to flourish. As with artefacts, some needs are more basic than others. For a human being the need for oxygen is more basic than the need for a well-balanced diet. However, there is, and will continue to be, controversy over how to determine the relative importance of needs once one moves away from the necessary conditions for maintaining any existence at all.

This is especially important if one believes that a key role of society should be to ensure that people's basic needs are met. To try to resolve this controversy John Rawls (1973) makes considerable use of the concept of what he calls 'primary goods', which he characterises as follows:

> . . . things that every rational man is presumed to want. These goods normally have a use whatever a person's rational plan of life . . . the chief primary goods at the disposition of society are rights and liberties, powers and opportunities, income and wealth . . . These are the primary social goods. Other primary goods such as health and vigor, intelligence and imagination are natural goods; although their possession is influenced by the basic structure, they are not so directly under its control (Rawls, 1973, p.62).

Although health is not so directly the product of the basic structure of society as are basic liberties, it certainly is very heavily influenced by society's structure. The structure of a society certainly affects who has access to health care, and what sort of health care is regarded as essential. The Rawlsian claim is that if a society is to show a basic respect for its citizens, then, so far as it is within its power, it will ensure that primary goods are fairly distributed. Therefore, in so far as health is a primary good, and health care provision is within the control of a society, the society should have a structure which distributes health care fairly between people. This means, amongst other things, that nobody will be denied health care for arbitrary reasons, including inability to afford such care.

Whereas health is a primary good, having professionally-trimmed hair and lawns certainly are not. People are able to flourish without the services of barbers and gardeners, even if these people do improve the quality of life of some. On the other hand, ill-health is itself an impediment to flourishing – for anybody.

I think that a theory of primary goods is useful in defining the legitimate area of concern of a society. However, we still require an independent theory which recognises a hierarchy of needs or interests, and enables us to rank priorities – even amongst primary goods themselves. For example, although we may suppose that civil liberties are primary goods, in an imperfect world, we have to ask how important particular liberties are compared with others, and compared with other primary goods. Although health is a primary good, it does not follow that the proper responsibility of society should be to ensure that everybody is as healthy as possible. For there are other primary goods which may compete with health, and it may be that there is a level of health beyond which further improvements in health are of little moral significance, compared with that of attaining this level.

There is widespread agreement across the political spectrum that a certain level of health is so important to anyone, that a society which respects its individual citizens should, where possible, ensure that at least this level is attained by all. Where it is not possible (as in the case of those who suffer from certain diseases), this should not be due to lack of proper resource provision from society, and is a proper subject for compensation (as in the case of mobility allowances for the physically handicapped).

Controversy abounds, and will continue to do so, over just what level of health is to be taken as a norm for societal responsibility. This is in part because it cannot be settled by the technical application of biomedical science. Recall Daniels's characterisation of diseases as 'deviations from the natural functional organization of a typical member of a species'. It is implausible to claim that all such deviations are equally important. Furthermore, given that we are able to control so much of the 'natural' environment, why should policy-makers be fixated on what is *merely* natural for a typical member of the species? Nature is morally blind.

Having said this, there is little serious dispute in regard to many diseases, both over whether they are serious enough to be society's responsibility, and over what sort of treatment should be available for them. However, to provide a general answer to the question about what sort of health care should be guaranteed by a relatively affluent society for its members, one needs a positive account of human flourishing. Such accounts are not amenable to formal proof, and have been the subject of fierce argument, certainly since the time of Socrates. For an interesting account of the role of conceptions of human flourishing in ethics see Harman (1983).

THE CASE OF PSYCHOTHERAPY

Nowhere is the need for an account of human flourishing more pressing than in the controversy over whether psychotherapy should be regarded as essential care. Some people claim that psychotherapy should not be so regarded on the grounds that, even by reference to its own goals, it is inefficacious. Research findings on this subject are controversial, and difficult to assess. However, I refer the reader to Luborsky *et al.* (1985) and Aveline (1984) for two recent studies which describe circumstances in which psychotherapy is likely to be efficacious. Others, whilst not denying that psychotherapy may succeed in achieving its goals, question these goals – either on the grounds that they are not genuinely matters of health, or that they are not essential, or both. As psychotherapy may be more expensive (certainly in therapist-time) than drug treatments and pure behaviour modification programmes, so the argument goes, it is a luxury which society has no responsibility to provide, since a person's essential health care can be adequately provided by these other means.

Although psychotherapy has been attempted on severely psychotic patients, and in such cases is clearly offering (however successfully) a form of essential health care, much psychotherapy is practised on people who are more or less in touch with reality, and more or less able to cope with life. This has generated an extreme aversion to the possible extension of psychotherapeutic services to wider sections of the community, typified in this extract from a letter to the *British Journal of Psychiatry*:

> The present controversy about psychotherapy seems to me a great deal of talk about new methods of treating sprain whilst ignoring the fractures. As long as there is insufficient manpower and resources to deal adequately with the diseased and the disabled, it would seem that the distressed and dissatisfied warrant a lower priority, rather than the reverse which seems to apply at present . . . (Hunt, 1985, p.670).

Are the distinctive concerns of psychotherapy really matters of health? The World Health Organisation defines health as '. . . a state of complete physical, mental, and social well-being, and not merely the absence of disease and infirmity'. On *this* definition it is clear that psychotherapy is directly concerned to promote the health of its clients. However, there are several grounds on which the WHO definition can be challenged. Perhaps the most telling is that it revises existing linguistic conventions in a way which obscures distinctions which have hitherto been useful. Health has traditionally been regarded as a necessary, but not sufficient condition for overall well-being. If a person is not doing well this may be because he is unhealthy, or due to external constraints. Nelson Mandela may have been in surprisingly good *health* throughout most of his long prison sentence; however, his imprisonment and harsh treatment have horribly reduced his overall well-being. It is useful to be able to distinguish internal disorders from external obstacles to well-being. Adoption of the WHO definition might obscure this distinction. Nevertheless, the WHO revisionary definition draws our attention to an important truth, easily overlooked, which is especially relevant to arguments about psychotherapy: The central substantive aim of health care is to promote the well-being of its beneficiaries, rather than just to promote health (narrowly defined) for its own sake. Whether or not psychotherapy for the non-psychotic should be regarded as a genuine form of *health* care is not the key issue. The key issue is whether the care offered by psychotherapists is essential for the reasonable well-being of its clients.

Psychotherapy is a form of care practised by a variety of types of carer – including social workers, marriage guidance counsellors, lay analysts and psychiatrists. Rather than argue over whether the aim of psychotherapy is strictly-speaking the *health* of its clients, we need to focus on whether what it seeks to give them is an essential part of human well-being or flourishing (I use the expressions interchangeably). This is because the arguments for a minimum level of *health* care to be guaranteed for all are really part of a larger argument about a minimum level of well-being which society should, so far as it is in its power, provide for all.

Although there is something in Hunt's claim that the diseased and disabled have a stronger claim to scarce resources for care than do the (merely) distressed and dissatisfied, it would be a mistake to conclude (as Hunt, 1985, seems to) that public-funded psychotherapy should be held in abeyance until 'the last psychotic patient is reasonably free of distressing and troublesome symptomatology . . .'. There are several reasons for this; here are two. First, it is by no means clear that a reduction in psychotherapy for the non-psychotic would significantly improve the lot of the psychotic, whereas it might make prospective beneficiaries of psychotherapy significantly worse off. Second, even though the needs of psychotics are, perhaps, even more pressing than those of non-psychotics seeking psychotherapy, the needs of the latter might give them a stronger claim on public resources than *other* possible beneficiaries. If the resources devoted to psychological care as a whole are woefully inadequate, rather than arguing that the claims of one group are stronger than those of the other, it would be legitimate, and more constructive, to argue that adequate resources should be provided for the service as a whole. Imagine an argument that nobody should have a hip replacement until the last cancer patient is cured!

In what follows I shall discuss two accounts of human well-being, one of which is decidedly more favourable to the view that psychotherapy aims at something vitally important for human flourishing. The grandest aspiration of a defender of psychotherapy would be to prove that psychotherapy should be available to everyone – as a part of essential care. My aim in this paper is far more modest. I seek to show that, on the more plausible view of human flourishing, which makes best sense of principles of liberal democracy, the aims of psychotherapy include the promotion of essential interests of its clients. If this is accepted, then, amongst liberal democrats, the argument about whether psychotherapy should be available to everyone as part of essential care will be restricted to internal questions about the efficacy of therapeutic practice – in its own terms.

HUMAN FLOURISHING

For a plant or animal to flourish is for it to be a good specimen of its kind. A flourishing oak tree will have a healthy foliage and root system, and a sturdy trunk. A flourishing lion will have a healthy diet, be relatively free of diseases and parasites, and have his own pride. But what about human beings? What is a flourishing human being? A flourishing human being is, similarly, a good specimen of a human being. The more complex the behaviour of an organism, the more scope there is for disagreement about what are essential goods for that organism. Anything which is good for an organism is either *intrinsically* good, that is, something which in itself is good for the organism, independently of any further effects it might have, or it is only *instrumentally*, good, that is, its worth consists in having effects which are beneficial for the organism. Thus, in the case of a plant, we may say that having a beautiful scent is an instrumental good, since this will help the plant to attract pollinating insects, which will enable it to reproduce successfully, which is good in itself for the plant. What are the intrinsic goods for human beings? One reason this question is hard to answer is that human beings have such a diversity of interests. So what may be good for a lover of loud music might be terrible for a lover of peaceful solitude. Nevertheless, there are some goods which are instrumentally valuable to people, no matter what their specific interests (health is one), and it may be that there are certain states of affairs which constitute *intrinsic* goods for everyone, no matter what their specific interests. For one attempt to describe an intrinsic good for people, consider the following passage by David Hume.

> Ask a man why he uses exercise; he will answer, because he desires to keep his health. If you then enquire, why he desires his health, he will readily reply, because sickness is painful. If you push your enquiries further, and desire a reason why he hates pain, it is impossible that he can give any. This is an ultimate end, and is never referred to any other object. (Hume, 1751, p.293.)

According to classical utilitarianism as systematically developed by Jeremy Bentham, pleasure and the avoidance of pain are the *only* intrinsic goods for people. Pleasure and pain are mental states which are to be compared according to their duration and intensity. The good for any individual is entirely determined by what gives him/her pleasure and causes him/her pain.

This account certainly makes a lot of sense of many moral prohibitions and prescriptions. Hunger and disease are both evils – for anybody – because they cause their victims pain, and deprive them of pleasure. Deception, robbery and violence are all condemned on Benthamite principles, because their practice reduces net pleasure in the world. The Benthamite account is also appealing to those who would question traditional values. Of any moral principle, one may ask 'What is its contribution to the net balance of pleasure over pain?' If its pursuit fails to make one, the principle should be dropped. For example, principles proscribing pre-marital sex should be abandoned unless it could be shown that following them increases the net balance of pleasure over pain in the world.

What, in the most general terms, would be the effects of applying this model of the good for people to the problems of priorities of care? It is clear that the model does not offer a substitute for the hard work of planning social policy. However, it provides a coherent principle, by ultimate appeal to which, theoretically, disputes could be settled.

On this model of the good for human beings, the ultimate aim of society in general, and the caring professions in particular, should be to maximise pleasure (in other words those psychological states which are pleasant) and to minimise pain. The prime responsibility of doctors is to relieve their patients of the pain associated with their illnesses. The aim of any system of priorities for resource allocation should be quite simply to make the biggest impact on pain and pleasure. Leaving aside duration and intensity, any pain or pleasure should count for as much as any other – no matter who is the victim or beneficiary.

What would be the consequences of applying this model to the care of those with psychological problems? The sole ultimate rationale for intervention would be, as with all things, reducing pain and promoting pleasure. In principle, psychological welfare is just as important as physical welfare, since, for example, the pain of depression may be at least as awful as that of migraine. Furthermore, a psychological condition, such as chronic anxiety, might deny its victim the chance to enjoy him/herself, to just the same extent as might chronic asthma.

In both mental and physical care, the prime aim is the relief of pain (as opposed to the positive promotion of pleasure). This is for a variety of reasons, one of them being that the elimination or reduction of pain is a relatively well-defined, frequently attainable goal, whereas its positive counterpart is perhaps more ill-defined, and less attainable.

Acceptance of the above model of human well-being would make it most unlikely that psychotherapy would receive special status in the fight for scarce resources – as a part of essential care. For there already is a wide range of drugs, which are arguably more efficient and effective *at pain relief* than is psychotherapy. This, I suppose, is not surprising, and should not dismay supporters of psychotherapy; for psychotherapy has other aims. A defender of psychotherapy could argue 'Simply as means for the alleviation of pain, psychotherapy may be ineffective; but the relief of pain is only one of the fundamental aims of care.' The claim that pain is the only intrinsic ill that can befall a person, and that pleasant mental states constitute the only intrinsic good, is a false and dangerous oversimplification. The true value of psychotherapy can be appreciated only when this is understood.

The classical utilitarian assumption that pleasure and the avoidance of pain are the only intrinsic goods, is not without appeal, particularly as an aid to resisting outmoded superstitious restrictions on people doing what they want. However, few people accept it; it seems to leave something out.

Perhaps the closest approximation to an ideal classical utilitarian society is that described in Aldous Huxley's *Brave New World*. A policy of positive eugenics combined with intensive behaviour modification and subliminal learning throughout childhood ensures that the majority of the population are well-suited to whatever social role they are allotted. There is material abundance and it is possible for people to enjoy a range of thrilling experiences. For those who begin to feel anxious, angry or depressed, help is immediately available in the form of *soma*, a psychotropic drug, which induces a general sense of well-being in its taker, frequently based on the harmless indulgence of fantasy. By any plausible calculus of pleasure and pain *Brave New World* is a very pleasant, pain-free place. Yet Huxley wrote his novel as a warning about what he feared might befall the Western world if we were not very careful. The world described by him is horrific – even though its citizens are more contented than most of us will ever be.

The fact that people in *Brave New World* live an immensely pleasant and pain-free life cannot in itself be a point against that society. So if the society really is awful it must be because it lacks something which is even more important than pleasure and the absence of pain. There are various ways of trying to express what is missing: The people are not in control of their own lives; their pleasure is based on illusion; they are manipulated; their relationships are shallow; their lives lack authenticity; they are denied autonomy.

The strongest objections raised in liberal democratic societies to totalitarian regimes is not that life within them is inevitably painful. It is rather that the centralised control over people's lives is excessive. The state interferes with almost all aspects of people's lives and they are not able to pursue their own projects according to their own conceptions of a good life. If human beings were to become contented automata, this would not be a great triumph of civilisation, but a catastrophe for humanity. I don't think it could be *proved* that such a change would be catastrophic; but amongst supporters of liberal democracy the belief is widespread. What follows is addressed to those who share this belief about totalitarianism.

The most fundamental moral objection to totalitarianism is that it prevents its subjects from developing and exercising their capacity for autonomy. Choices of lifestyle, political organisation, religious practice, abode and movement, may all be controlled – and this is thought to be inimical to a respect for people.

Underlying this objection is a belief that human beings have a vital interest in their own autonomy. In many circumstances autonomy (self-rule or self-determination) helps people effectively to avoid pain and pursue pleasure. For autonomous people are less likely to make bad decisions, and more likely to be able to devise and follow successful long-term strategies. However, people's interests in autonomy and pleasant mental states may sometimes conflict. In these cases Benthamite principles would recommend that priority be given to the latter; for autonomy is, on that account, only of instrumental value.

Bentham's most illustrious pupil John Stuart Mill remained a utilitarian throughout his life, maintaining that the ultimate aim of society should be 'the general happiness' or 'the general good'. However, he developed an account of happiness or 'the good for human beings' which included an acceptance of the fundamental value of autonomy. Mill believed not only that autonomy is an intrinsic good for people, but that it might be more important to be autonomous than simply contented. He maintained that those who had developed their autonomy would prefer to retain it, even if this cost them some pain. Of this preference for autonomy over mere contentment he wrote:

Whoever supposes that this preference takes place at a sacrifice of happiness . . . confounds the two very different ideas, of happiness, and content. It is indisputable that the being whose capacities of enjoyment are low, has the greatest chance of having them fully satisfied; and a highly endowed being will always feel that any happiness which he can look for, as the world is constituted, is imperfect. But he can learn to bear its imperfections, if they are at all bearable; and they will not make him envy the being who is indeed unconscious of the imperfections, but only because he feels not at all the good which those imperfections qualify. It is better to be a human being dissatisfied than a pig satisfied; better to be Socrates disastisfied than a fool satisfied. (Mill, 1861, p.9.)

How does a happy person's life differ from that of someone who is merely contented? To be happy is to be doing well as a human being – to flourish. For Mill, our capacity for rational choice is perhaps the most morally important fact about human beings. Having the capacity to deliberate, and to choose to act in accordance with our own conceptions of what is good or worthwhile, creates the possibility of our enjoying different qualities of pleasure. The ultimate criterion of what constitutes human well-being is whatever would be preferred by people whose choices are not constrained by ignorance and/or irrationality. Mill believed that the vast majority of people, who understand what it is to be autonomous, would not be prepared to abandon their autonomy for even huge gains in pleasure, and:

Of two pleasures, if there be one to which all or almost all who have experience of both give a decided preference, irrespective of any feeling of moral obligation to prefer it, that is the more desirable pleasure. If one of the two is, by those who are competently acquainted with both, placed so far above the other that they prefer it, even though knowing it to be attended with a greater amount of discontent, and would not resign it for any quantity of the other pleasure . . . we are justified in ascribing to the preferred enjoyment a superiority in quality, so far outweighing quantity as to render it, in comparison, of small account (ibid., p.8).

A further objection to the World Health Organisation's definition of 'health' is that, according to it, the goal of health for all is obviously unattainable, and it provides no clue for the allocation of relatively scarce resources. Mill's aim of 'the general happiness' is, in contrast, a goal which he thought was attainable. Once again there is a clear difference from Bentham. For Bentham there is no such thing as achieving a state of happiness – or well-being – for degree of happiness is measured simply by duration and intensity of pleasant (and unpleasant) psychological states. And no matter how pleasant a person's experiences may be, they could always be even pleasanter. Mill, however, defined happiness as:

> . . .not a life of rapture; but moments of such, in an existence made up of few and transitory pains, many and various pleasures, with a decided predominance of the active over the passive, and having as the foundation of the whole not to expect more from life than it is capable of bestowing. A life thus composed, to those who have been fortunate enough to obtain it, has always appeared worthy of the name of happiness. And such an existence is even now the lot of many, during some considerable portion of their lives. The present wretched education, and wretched social arrangements, are the only real hindrance to its being attainable by almost all (ibid., p.12).

The Millian version of utilitarianism has a built-in respect for the individual and a substantial egalitarianism. The ultimate aim of society is 'the general happiness'. Although Mill sometimes talks as if this is meant in Bentham's quantitative sense, I think the most plausible way of interpreting it is as 'a state where happiness is general', that is, a state where as many people as possible have attained the state described above. There is a level of well-being which is such that, beyond it, further gains are morally insignificant compared with the moral importance of attaining it.

Happiness, so interpreted, requires a balance of pleasure over pain; but also an active, relatively autonomous existence – neither based on illusion nor ignorant conformity. I do not think that Mill's view of happiness can be proved to be the only rationally compelling conception, since its foundation lies in the 'choice criterion' (what is best for people is what they would choose were they rational and fully informed), which itself is questionable (see Lindley, 1986). However, this conception is widely held, and something like it is needed for a moral justification of liberal democracy (where there is universal suffrage and a large sphere of private life is protected from governmental scrutiny and concern).

PSYCHOTHERAPY, AUTONOMY AND HUMAN FLOURISHING

There are so many practices which go under the name 'psychotherapy' that it is hard to say anything interesting about the aims of psychotherapy as a whole. One exception, I think, is that psychotherapy is especially concerned to enable its clients to free themselves from obstacles to autonomy. There is a widespread belief in the value of self-determination. Although psychotherapists aim to alleviate the pain of their clients, and one way of doing this is by helping them to become more autonomous, most psychotherapies (if not all) are predicated on the assumption that taking control of one's own life is *in itself* an essential part of human flourishing. Thus Freud spoke of replacing 'hysterical misery' with 'ordinary unhappiness', the former being worse, though not simply because it is more *painful*.

If a Millian conception of human flourishing were correct, it would follow that there is a level of autonomy, which is such that anyone who has failed to attain it is, *ipso facto*, not flourishing. Psychotherapy would undoubtedly be an essential form of care if it were able to make the difference for its clients between being below this level and attaining it. It would also be of great benefit if it could substantially increase the autonomy of those below the level, even it it were not sufficient to bring them up to it. Only in so far as psychotherapy is practised on those above the level, in order to take them yet further above it, could it be regarded as a luxury.

Of course none of the above should be taken as a general indictment of the use of drugs or behaviour modification programmes in the treatment of mental disorder. It is undoubtedly true that a judicious use of these treatments sometimes is the best way both of relieving pain and alleviating the symptoms of the grosser forms of heteronomy (as in, say, endogenous depression or agoraphobia). It would be a mistake to regard psychotherapy and these other therapies as mutually exclusive and opposed alternatives. The main problem, from the point of view of those who take autonomy seriously, is not that drug therapy and behaviour modification therapy are widely used, but rather that psychotherapy is not more widely available, and is so unevenly distributed.

What implications does this paper have for the practice of individual therapists, as opposed to public policy? The strongest reason for believing that psychotherapy should be taken seriously is that autonomy is a vital interest which cannot be adequately promoted by other therapies alone. However, the relation between psychotherapy and autonomy is by no means simple and straightforward. Joel Feinberg (1973) usefully characterised autonomy in the following way: 'I am autonomous if I rule me, and no-one else rules I', that is, the 'I' which rules 'me' is not in turn ruled by anyone else. In so far as psychotherapists are to help clients regain their autonomy or develop it for the first time, it is necessary to identify different types of heteronomy (limitations on people's autonomy).

In line with Feinberg's characterisation we may divide the obstacles to autonomy into external and internal. External obstacles such as poverty, a soul-destroying work environment, and other material deprivations cannot be obviously overcome by psychotherapy; and 'solutions' which simply consist in changing people's expectations so they do not mind such objectively demeaning existences could not appeal to those who take autonomy seriously. 'Internal autonomy' requires of a person an active rationality. This includes the ability to respond appropriately and in new ways to new situations, an ability and desire to face reality: 'I'd rather know the truth, even if it's painful'. This in turn requires the self-esteem which can only come about through being taken seriously oneself.

The problem of the uneven distribution of psychotherapy is in part due to the lack of public funding available. But it is also due to lack of demand amongst deprived groups who are arguably most in need of therapy. This situation is analogous to higher education, which is enjoyed by a disproportionately small number of people from working class backgrounds; indeed there are many analogies between education and psychotherapy (see Holmes, 1985). According to Holmes, to overcome the problem of lack of demand among the needy for psychotherapy:

> Psychotherapists must deliver psychotherapy where, and in a way that makes sense to ordinary people. For the most part this will mean in general practice. This in turn means counsellors, family therapists, group workers, marriage guidance counsellors and analytic therapists working and training in primary care.

Finally, because in a sense the whole rationale of psychotherapy depends on a recognition of the value of autonomy, therapists have a special responsibility to respect the autonomy of their patients – in particular to avoid deception and manipulation, and to ensure, where possible, that their patients' consent to therapy is based on an accurate understanding of the nature and likely efficacy of the therapy (see Lindley, 1986a).

CONCLUSION

If, as I have suggested, psychotherapy is an essential form of care, then not only should there be far greater provision, but psychotherapists themselves should change in order to make their services more appealing and accessible to those who need it most and benefit from it least.

It would be wildly implausible to suppose that scarcity will be abolished in the foreseeable future – even in the more affluent countries. By this I mean that it is inevitable that, no matter what policies are adopted by governments, some essential needs will not be met. In order to make any claim for public provision of psychotherapeutic services it is necessary to argue that the needs which psychotherapy seeks to meet are *at least* essential. I think a good case can be made for such a conclusion, based on acceptance of a Millian view of human flourishing. Although it is not possible to prove that a Millian view is correct, I do believe that it is widely held, and that something like it is essential to a moral defence of liberal democracy. I realise that this paper leaves many (perhaps most) of the important questions about psychotherapy and public policy unanswered. However, I do hope I have said enough to convince the reader that there is a pressing need to answer them; for psychotherapy, unlike world cruises and private swimming pools, is, whatever it is, not just a luxurious self-indulgence.[1]

1 I would like to thank Gregory DesJardins, Gavin and Susan Fairbairn for helpful comments on an earlier draft.

REFERENCES

Aveline, M. (1984), 'What Price Psychotherapy?', *Lancet*, 13 October.

Daniels, N. (1985), *Just Health Care*, Cambridge, Cambridge University Press.

Feinberg, J. (1973), *Social Philosophy*, Englewood Cliffs, Prentice Hall.

Harman, G. (1983), 'Human Flourishing, Ethics and Liberty', *Philosophy and Public Affairs*, vol.12, no.3.

Hollingshead, A.B. and Redlich, F.C. (1958), *Class and Mental Illness*, New York, Wiley.

Holmes, J. (1985), 'Psychotherapy Broking in General Practice: An analysis of 50 cases sent for assessment', paper presented to conference on Psychiatry and General Practice, November 1985 – to be published.

Hume, D. (1751), *Enquiry Concerning the Principles of Morals*, (page reference is to the reprint of the Selby-Bigge edition of Hume's *Enquiries*, 1972, Oxford, Oxford University Press).

Hunt, M. (1985), 'Psychotherapy and Psychiatric Need', *British Journal of Psychiatry*, vol.146.

Lindley, R. (1986), *Autonomy*, London, Macmillan.

Lindley, R. (1986a), 'Family therapy and Respect for People' in S. Walrond-Skinner and D. Watson (eds), *Ethical Issues in Family Therapy*, London, Routledge & Kegan Paul.

Luborsky, L., McLellan, A., Woody, G., O'Brien, C. and Auerbach, A. (1985), 'Therapist Success and its Determinants', *Archives of General Psychiatry*, vol.42, pp.602–11.

Mill, J.S. (1861), *Utilitarianism*, (page references are to *Utilitarianism, On Liberty, and Considerations on Representative Government*, 1972, London, Dent).

Nozick, R. (1974), *Anarchy, State and Utopia*, Oxford, Blackwell.

Rawls, J. (1973), *A Theory of Justice*, Oxford, Oxford University Press.

Redlich, F.C., and Kellert, S.R. (1978), 'Trends in American Mental Health', *American Journal of Psychiatry*, vol.135.

Williams, B. (1962), 'The Idea of Equality', in P. Laslett and W. Runciman (eds), *Philosophy, Politics and Society*, Oxford, Blackwell.

Avoiding the Big Issues and Attending to the Small

Dorothy Rowe

Psychologists are nice people. They care. They are reasonable, modest and co-operative. They don't brawl or back-stab or climb to the top over the bodies of their colleagues, not like certain members of other professions. They give serious attention to all the serious issues of the human condition. That is, all the serious issues of the human condition except one. The extinction of the human race.

Psychologists, on the whole, show very little interest in the fact that the human race is facing extinction. Nuclear and ecological issues rarely feature in conference programmes. James Thompson and his colleagues produced the thoughtful and carefully argued *Psychological Aspects of Nuclear War* but Psychologists for Peace is a small, exclusive organisation, composed, like most peace organisations, of the young and the old. The middle-aged are elsewhere, attending to matters more important than the continuation of life on earth.

There is, in the UK at least, no shortage of information about the fate of the earth. Anyone who reads the newspapers and watches television must be aware of the increasing nuclear arsenal, the ease with which this arsenal could come into use, either by intent or accident, and the consequent 'nuclear winter' which would damage irreparably the delicate ecological balance which maintains life on the planet. Similarly, anyone who reads newspapers and watches television must be aware of the destruction of the forests, the pollution of the atmosphere and the increasing numbers of people which together now are creating deserts, dead rivers and lakes, and starvation, and which, eventually, possibly in no more than 150 years, will render the planet uninhabitable. The best that the human race can look forward to is a degradation of the conditions of life, something far more unpleasant than the primitive life from whence we came, when nature was fresh and sweet. The worst that the human race can look forward to is its annihilation. No thinking, intelligent person in the UK could be unaware of this. Yet most people act as if they are. Most psychologists act as if they are unaware.

This unawareness contains a curious irony. Academic psychologists might, in the ivory tower tradition, ignore ordinary life, but clinical psychologists should be keenly aware of what is ordinary and real, for in their work, in one way or another, they have to assess how crazy each of their clients is. The test of madness is how unaware the person is of reality. Thus in the thinking of many clinical psychologists it is mad to deny your immediate surroundings and to claim that the Russians are using powerful rays to insert evil thoughts in your mind, but it is not mad to pay attention to your immediate surroundings and to deny that the Russians really do have nuclear weapons targeted on your home.

I spent a year asking every person I came across, many of them psychologists, 'How do you live with the threat of a nuclear war?' Some answered passionately, 'I think about it all the time', or 'I never make a major decision without considering it', or 'I try to ignore it but then I look at my small children and remember'. But many people looked surprised when I asked. Sometimes the surprise was at the raising of such an unimportant, boring subject. Sometimes the surprise was at the raising of such an indelicate subject. This reaction reminded me of how polite people, in the pre-pill, pre-feminist days, would react when sex was mentioned. How could you be so *crude*?

For some people the surprise was that I should be worried about such matters. Did I not know that the ending of life on earth is a trivial matter, just one unimportant facet of the 'Grand Design'? Hindu psychologists treated me with the gentle condescension one gives to a child. I did not understand that I was deluded into thinking that the world was a reality when in fact it was an illusion and, as such, it would change. 'The Lord giveth and the Lord taketh away.' For the true believer there was no cause for alarm. What alarmed me was that Mrs Gandhi was a true believer, and she had nuclear bombs at her disposal. Let us hope that now Rajiv Gandhi sees these bombs as sufficiently real as to provide a protection against Pakistan's development of a nuclear arsenal.

Hinduism conceives of rebirth as the passage of some essential essence, the *jiva*, from one life form to another with the purpose of merging eventually with the Great Oneness. The *jiva* is not a self-conscious individual identity, analogous to the Christian concept of the soul. Many erstwhile Christians believe in reincarnation where the individual self passes from body to body in successive generations. Faced with the possibility that there may be no future generations to inhabit, some believers in reincarnation posit a kind of limbo where they can wait the millions of years necessary for the earth to become habitable again. Everything will, eventually, turn out well.

Similarly confident are those people who see the essence of life as some form of spirituality where the self or soul continues on a higher plane of existence, irrespective of what happens to mere earthly things. Most confident of all are the various sects of the Fundamentalist Christians who await the inevitable and imminent Armageddon with confidence and satisfaction, knowing that they will be transferred to Heaven, safe from the effects of Armageddon, the destruction of life on earth. Such committed Fundamentalists include Ronald Reagan and Caspa Weinberger.

Of course, not all Christians are Fundamentalists. Many see their tasks as to preserve God's creation, and so they play an active part in the anti-nuclear and ecological movements and in charities to assist the poor and starving. They observe the Buddha's injunction to eschew metaphysical speculation and to concentrate their efforts on alleviating suffering. They do not protect themselves from painful reality by retreating into the magical thinking which religious belief makes available, any more than they retreat into the magical beliefs which patriotism makes available. (On my travels in the USA and the USSR I have found the strongly held magical belief that, come what may, the strength and purity of the USA/USSR will prevail.)

In therapy the therapist has again and again to uncover and confront the magical thinking of the client, the defence which has been built to protect against intolerable pain. It is a very difficult task to help the client to face the pain, to relinquish the security of the magical belief and to accept the insecurity of hope. (Hope is possible only when there is insecurity; complete security is complete hopelessness.) Only therapists concern themselves with trying to understand and to change magical thinking, and then only in selected individuals seeking help. Yet it is the magical thinking of religion and patriotism which is plunging us further into peril. Should not psychologists pay attention to this?

Many psychologists react with the helplessness that many people feel. What can we do against the might of government and armies? Yet, again, we know something about 'learned helplessness'. Is there some essential difference between asserting yourself before a shop assistant and asserting yourself before your government? But, take care. What would happen if everybody knew how to assert themselves, to stand up for their own rights? Doesn't the stability of society depend on the docility of most of its members? If psychologists started using their knowledge of learned helplessness to assist people generally to assert their rights to continuing life, would not psychologists then be seen as dangerous revolutionaries? We would become objects of hate in the media, our reputations would be slandered, our phones would be tapped, our passports taken away. We would receive hate mail, death threats, even bombs and bullets. Quite unthinkable. Psychologists are respectable people.

But we know that learned helplessness turns into self-hate and despair, and that self-hate and despair is what is called depression. We know that while a depressed person may appear to be still and quiet, inside is a boiling volcano of hate and envy, the source of powerful destructive urges. We know that the depressed person's desire to destroy includes not merely himself but the evil, imperfect world. We know too how prevalent depression is and that it is not confined to women, the poor and the inadequate. The retreat into the prison of depression is available not least to those who, having climbed the pinnacles of success and power, find nothing but a barren loneliness which, combined with a ravenous hunger for power and adulation, produces self-hate and murderous envy which are presented to the world as superior virtue. The Ayatollah Khomeini remembers how the Iraqis once refused him shelter, and sends thousands of men to their death. Since death in a *jihad*, a holy war, means, to the devout Muslim, immediate transfer to Paradise, such slaughter is not viewed with horror but with fervent patriotic joy. That such joy in death and destruction is not confined to devout Muslims could be seen in the Falklands War.

Should psychologists concern themselves with such matters? Or should they leave such matters to the politicians and militarist? There are some people who would argue that these matters are none of our business, that we cannot apply the knowledge that we have of ordinary people to people holding enormous power and influence, or even to large groups of people. I have been taken to task for applying the knowledge we have of child rearing practices and the production of cruelty to countries such as El Salvador where the extremes of cruelty are ubiquitous and are handed down from generation to generation like the family jewels. Somehow, to some people, politics and economics are matters divorced from individual behaviour, and thus there is nothing that a psychologist could say which has any relevance for politics and economics. Such a point of view denies that politics and economics are simply names for some of the theories and practices of human beings. Such a point of view is in itself a denial of personal responsibility, an attitude which we deplore in the people of the USSR who give to the State the responsibility for making those decisions which in a democracy are regarded as the responsibility of the individual. *We are all human beings in one world, and we are all responsible for what happens here.*

The concept of personal responsibility is central to therapy. We are not the helpless victims of our genes or of our history. We have the power to reflect upon our experience and to change how we respond to our experience. We can reassess and redefine our experience. We can change how we evaluate ourselves and how we relate to others. Self-reflection and understanding open an endless vista of creative possibilities.

Or do they? Are there limits to self-reflection and understanding? Why has the human brought itself to the verge of extinction? Is it simply through a lack of self-reflection and understanding? Or is it because human beings can live no other way? In short, is the peril we face a moral issue or a scientific inevitability?

When I began to give serious consideration to what might be called 'nuclear issues', I held the belief and hope of therapists that the profound and beneficial changes which can come from self-reflection and understanding could resolve the conflicts between nations which threaten all of us. I doubted if the various national leaders, the militarists and the armament manufacturers would be prepared to undertake the perilous, painful path to self-knowledge, but I still believed that the possibilities of such action and change were there. But then I started thinking and writing about these issues. I wanted to go beyond the wearisome unilateralist/multilateralist arguments about disarmament and look, in Personal Construct Psychology terms, at the constructs of envy, greed and power which maintained armies and put barriers to friendship and tolerance. As I worked, my belief in the limitless possibilities of change in how we construe ourselves was undermined.

Some time before, I had been forced through my studies in 'laddering' constructs to admit that Eysenck was right. There are extroverts and introverts, and they differ in how they construe their existence and their annihilation. (Annihilation is worse than bodily death. It is the wiping out of the sense of being. We can feel the pain of the threat of this whenever someone treats us as a thing of no value, or when we feel that we have made a huge, irreparable mistake, or when events show us that we are not in control of our lives.) At the top of the extroverts' ladder are constructs concerning existence as being part of a group and annihilation as expulsion from that group, while for introverts existence is construed as the continuing development of individual clarity and authenticity while annihilation is falling into chaos. These differences relate to how extroverts and introverts perceive inner and outer reality. For extroverts outer reality is more real and substantial than inner reality, and for introverts the opposite is the case. Since how we construe our existence and our annihilation underpins every decision, however trivial, which we make, this 'core construct' is of immense importance in human life.

I often have the opportunity to 'ladder' an extrovert and an introvert in the presence of one another, usually in the context of exploring why they, as a married couple, are having difficulties in getting along altogether. I find that usually neither member of the couple has perceived that the other holds such a profound and differing view of existence and annihilation. This is not necessarily because of a lack of perception and caring. Some couples know one another very well. It is because our way of construing our existence and annihilation is the primary stuff of living. It provides the dimensions of our world. It is hard for an extrovert to perceive, appreciate and understand the introvert's construction of existence and annihilation, just as it is hard for an introvert to make the same empathetic leap of imagination into the world of the extrovert. To change from one perception of existence and annihilation to another is impossible, just as it is impossible for us to change from seeing the world in three dimensions to seeing it in seven. Perhaps there is, as Eysenck argues, an underlying neural pattern which distinguishes introverts from extroverts and which we can no more choose to change than we can choose to change the colour of our eyes.

Extroverts get into difficulties and fall into madness when they perceive themselves as alone, and introverts get into difficulties and fall into madness when they perceive themselves as losing control and falling into chaos. The 'cure' for each has to be within the context of their own particular perception of existence and annihilation. If this is not possible, if the extrovert is irretrievably expelled from the group, if the introvert cannot create some order and control, then the fear and the defences against the fear (the symptoms of neurosis and psychosis) persist, no matter what brilliant psychotherapy or skilful drug manipulation be available. Our perception of our existence and our annihilation sets limits to our freedom of choice.

It seems that there are similar limits in the way in which we live in groups and define those groups. *It seems that a necessary condition of human life is to have enemies, and that this necessary condition of our life will mean our inevitable death.*

For human beings to survive they need air, food, water and shelter from the extremes of temperature. To satisfy these needs we have to be able to perceive the world around us, and *to perceive anything we must be aware of a contrast.* If we are presented with sameness we perceive nothing. To perceive and to know something, we need some kind of contrast or differential to be present. To know black we must know white; to know good we must know bad; to know life we must know death; to know friend we must know foe.

The process whereby we perceive and know is the process whereby we create structures. These structures become our self and our world. To make ourselves feel secure we try to forget that what we perceive, know and believe are structures, and we act as if these fictional structures are Absolute Reality. Whenever we are threatened with the possibility of the structural nature of our perceptions, knowledge and beliefs being revealed and disproved, be it when a door which we believed was unlocked refuses to open or when someone seeks to disprove our most cherished metaphysical beliefs, we react with anger and aggression.

We create ourselves and our world out of structures which, when threatened, we defend with aggression.

We begin forming these structures from the moment of birth, and these structures are called forth and become important in the context of our relationship with others. A newborn baby structures sights and sounds, and from those structures differentiates a mother's face and a mother's voice. If these relational structures are not available the baby does not thrive, and if these relational structures prove to be unpredictable then the baby is greatly distressed. For the baby to survive with some degree of sanity it has to be part of a group.

As we get older this does not change. We have to be part of a group. From the records of human torture and from the research on sensory deprivation we know that complete isolation for an indefinite period produces great suffering and the eventual breakdown of the structures of self and the world. Not even introverts involved in the most intense pursuit of personal aims can live outside a group. Extroverts need other people to reflect and confirm their existence, and introverts need other people to set standards, give approval and prevent the introvert from disappearing into the private world of inner reality. If other people are not available, we turn animals into pets and relate to them as we would to people. After all, dogs are more faithful and trustworthy than people and cats more cuddly. So,

To become and remain a person we must be a member of a group.

The only way we can perceive and so define our group is in terms of a contrast. There is inside the group and outside the group, like the members of my group/not like members of my group.

The difference which we perceive between inside and outside the group can be divided into *objective* and *subjective* differences.

Objective differences are those which everyone, whether part of the group or not can easily perceive. Males are different from females. This group lives in England; that group lives in Germany. Those people have a legal right; these do not. Objective differences can be discussed rationally, modified, and accepted as differences which are not dangerous. Concepts of masculinity and femininity can be analysed and discussed, and, sometimes, from this changes in the relationships between men and women emerge. Governments in England and Germany can abandon their respective claims to empire and merge much of their financial and trading interests. The legal profession flourishes on the concept of legal right. The observation, discussion and modification of objective differences can take place with a minimum of fear and anger.

Not so with subjective differences. These are differences which lie only in the eye of the beholder. To the outside observer there seems to be no reason why the Protestants and and Catholics in Northern Ireland should not sink their differences, or the Afikaaners not give the blacks the vote, or the Muslims, Druse and Christians in Lebanon not realise that they share one country. But to the members of these groups the reasons for hating their enemies and refusing all compromises are clear, absolute and unchangeable. They fear and hate their enemies. They seek to destroy their enemies, and they will defend themselves from their enemies to the death.

Subjective differences can be expressed in a variety of ways – they are the infidels / we are the faithful; they are subhuman / we are superhuman; they are lazy and untrustworthy / we are hard working and honest; they are seeking world domination / we want nothing but peace – but the underlying construct is always the same. They are bad : We are good.

The goodness of the group is something very precious to every member of the group. Each person has available the comforting thought that, 'Even though I may be weak, bad, inadequate, I belong to the best family / class / race / creed / nation in the world.' The more weak, bad and inadequate the person feels, the more loyal the person is to the group and defends it more fiercely. The greater the danger from the enemy (ie, the weaker the people in the group feel) the more closely the members of the group adhere together. Such closeness can be very pleasant, giving us the kind of sustenance which we enjoyed, and lost, as small children, and which, to some degree, we long for all the rest of our lives. The current nostalgia in England for the Second World War is a memory of the closeness which the dangers of that war created. (Such nostalgia blinds some people from the realisation that a Third World War would be very different from the Second World War.)

The process by which the awareness of subjective differences is created is well documented in the annals of child development and psychotherapy. When a baby comes into the world it is quite pleased with being itself. But the group it has joined soon starts making demands that it should conform to the standards of the group.

The group exercises its power as the definer of who and what the baby is. (Power is the right to make your definitions prevail over other people's definitions.) So the baby learns what sex it is, but not simply that it is a boy or a girl, but that it is 'a wonderful boy' or 'a bad boy', 'Daddy's little girl' or 'a disappointment she's a girl'. Along with these definitions come the rules and expectations which, though they may never be made explicit, become the unseen and omnipresent dimensions of the child's world – 'Men never cry', 'It is unfeminine to be aggressive, and unfeminine girls are never loved', 'If you do not do as you are told your parents will not love you', 'Don't upset Mother', 'Always try to please your father', 'Blood is thicker than water', 'People of other nationality, class and creed are dangerous'.

Many of the definitions and rules we are taught in childhood we discard as we get older, sometimes because they simply become irrelevant and sometimes because we acquire other rules and definitions because we want to establish our separateness from our parents. But other rules and definitions we continue to use because the sanctions if we drop the rules and definitions are too dangerous for us to contemplate. Many of us spend our entire lives trying to please our parents, or to earn their love, or to avoid their wrath, even though our parents may have died many years before. Many of us cling to the rules and definitions because to do otherwise would be to reawaken the greatest terror of our lives.

When we were small we knew that we were unable to care for ourselves. We knew that we were dependent on the adults around us, and to be secure we needed to know that those adults were good people who loved and cared for us. We needed parents who were infallible and just and whose love for us was without end. But, of course, what we had for parents were mere human beings who were far from infallible, often unjust, whose love could be blotted out by their anger or fear and who might suddenly and inexplicably disappear from us. Thus we might find ourselves in head-on collision with them over where we should defecate or what we should eat. We might find ourselves being punished unfairly, or shamed and humiliated, or being abandoned to the care of strangers. These events could produce in us the extremes of rage and hatred for our parents, a hatred which made us see our parents as bad. But such a perception could create a danger which threatened to annihilate us. Our parents were bad and we were alone.

Such a peril is usually too great for a small child to bear. One way to save oneself is to redefine who was good and who was bad. Instead of knowing that:

'I am being punished by my bad parents'
the situation is redefined as:
'I am bad and am being punished by my good parents.'

Now we are safe again in the care of good parents who know what is best for us.

But such safety is purchased at a high price. We are condemned to a lifetime of trying to be good, so as to overcome this sense of inherent badness. Now we have to earn our right to exist. Now we see some parts of our self as no longer acceptable. We have to label some parts of our self as bad. These might be our anger, aggression, or our weakness and vulnerability to pain. These might be our greed and envy, or our desire to play and to be irresponsible. Whatever aspects of our self we now regard as bad and unacceptable we have to keep unacknowledged. We must constantly be on guard against our self. We can never simply be ourselves again.

Very often the dangers from the evil within become too great to bear, and then we have to find some way of protecting ourselves. When our reality becomes intolerable we can always resort to denial that it is so. We can always say, 'It didn't happen', or 'I forget', or 'I'm not upset', or 'It's not me. It's them' – the defence mechanisms of denial, repression, isolation and projection. Each is effective up to a point, and each has its disadvantages. We each have our favourite, but the one most useful for groups is projection. 'They are evil : we are good.' The advantage of projecting all our unacceptable parts on to our enemies, and then reviling our enemies for being what we despise, is that it does have an element of truth. Our enemies, being human like us, do have all the human vices we despise. They are angry, aggressive, weak, vulnerable to pain, greedy, envious, childlike, and irresponsible, and everything else in the range of human possibilities in humanness. All we have to do is to concentrate on their vices and ignore their humanness.

But the trouble is that when we project the despised and dangerous elements of ourselves on to others, then we see those elements in others being directed towards us and punishing us. We give up our personal greed and desire for individual power to belong to a communist state, and we see ourselves threatened by the powerful and limitless greed of capitalism. We give up our childish irresponsibility and desire for play to belong to the righteous and hard-working, and we see ourselves threatened by the shiftless blacks and/or the work-shy scroungers. Such a perception increases our sense of danger and our need for our group to protect us. Thus the process whereby we gave up part of ourselves in order to become a member of a group increases our dependence on that group.

Along with the process whereby we learn the subjective differences between our group and our enemies can go another process of change. On many occasions when we discover that the people who should be protecting us are in fact persecuting us, the degree of cruelty we suffer forces us to protect ourselves by not merely defining our aggressor as good and ourselves as bad, but by deciding to share in some way the goodness of the aggressor. We resolve that we shall become like the aggressor. We shall punish others in the way that we were punished. In adulthood we say, 'I was beaten as a child and it never did me any harm.'

The defence of identifying with the aggressor is the process whereby the human race perpetuates its cruelty. This is the process whereby we destroy the empathetic imagination and allow ourselves to see other people, animals, and the world in which we live as mere objects to be used and destroyed as we please.

Subjective differences are very important. They give us a sense of belonging, of being with people who are like us. They make crisp, clear and permanent divisions in the seamless, changing universe. In reality other people are not very different from us. They are in the business of, at worst, surviving, and, at best, maximising their assets. They all love, hate, envy, get angry, feel frightened. They all have to face loss, loneliness, old age and death. But there are so many of them. How can *I*, one lone person have any significance? So, if I cannot achieve significance, then my group can, for it is the best and greatest group the universe has ever seen.

We all have claims to greatness. The Jews are the Chosen Ones, the Christians have been Saved, while the Japanese rest assuredly in the knowledge that their race alone, unsullied by foreign blood for over a thousand years, is the only human race. The rest, the *gaijin*, are not really human. I can laugh at all this nonsense because I was born a Presbyterian and know myself to be among the Infallible Elect. Moreover, if harassed by other nationals, especially the English, I can fall back on the natural superiority of the Australians.

The subjective differences between our group and all others not only maintains our self-esteem, it allows us to indulge in hatred and revenge. While these emotions are deplorable if exercised by one individual towards another, when exercised by one group against another they become virtues. Even more than virtues, they can become a way of life, a description of a total identity. If some gigantic miracle occurred in Northern Ireland or in Lebanon to stop the fighting and to bring peace and reconciliation, many of the people in those countries would lose both their sense of identity and their purpose in living. They would be even more lost than those poor Falashas transferred from their Ethiopian desert to an Israeli city. Perhaps this is one of the issues which psychologists should be examining. How can we repair the damage to the development of children caused by war, cruelty and starvation? But we cannot eradicate these inflictions unless we can change the fundamental way in which we form our groups.

Can we live without enemies? is the most important question which has ever faced the human race. With the knowledge and skills we have as psychologists we should be able to confront it and find whether the salvation of the human race can come, not from moral exhortations, but only from a profound alteration in what it is to be a human animal. No matter what the answer is to this question, it is our duty as scientists to face it. We should not go blind and heedless to our end.

REFERENCES

Miller, A. (1981), *For Your Own Good. The Hidden Roots of Violence*, London, Faber.

Rowe, D. (1985), *Living with the Bomb*, London, Routledge & Kegan Paul.

Thompson, J. (1985), *Psychological Aspects of Nuclear War*, Chichester, British Psychological Society and John Wiley and Sons.

Responsibility, Respect for Persons and Psychological Change

Gavin Fairbairn

This chapter is concerned with the philosophical notion of respect for persons and with some of the ways in which clinical psychologists and their clients may be said to be responsible. I will argue that if the changes brought about by psychologists[1] are to be evaluated positively in an ethical sense, then they will have to be underpinned by respect for the individuals who are changed, as persons. To behave ethically in relation to others is minimally to regard and act in relation to them in ways that take account of their being people. This seems fundamental to any ethics of persons.

Respecting others as people involves helping them to make responsible decisions about their lives, because taking responsibility for one's life is at least part of what it is to function fully as a person. Later in the chapter I will discuss some different senses of the term 'responsibility' and relate these to psychological practice in terms of both the responsibility of the psychologist and of the responsibility of the client.

RESPECT FOR PERSONS

Biestek and Gehrig (1978) write that the social work profession 'selects as its supreme value the innate dignity and value of the human person. It maintains that nothing in the world is more precious and noble than the person, and that every person is worthy of respect.'

Most practitioners of the caring professions would probably

embrace the sentiments that this statement attributes to social workers, though fewer may be able to be precise in telling what they understand by it or how they think it will influence their professional practice. In it Biestek and Gehrig seem to be outlining the ethical principle most often referred to as 'respect for persons' but which is also referred to in other ways, for example as 'respect for others' or 'respect for the individual'.

Downie and Telfer (1969) maintain that respect for persons is the central value in the caring professions. Certainly it is frequently referred to in discussions of ethics in the caring professions. For example, the BPS 'A Code of Conduct for Psychologists' (1985) mentions it, although it does not refer to respect for persons separately, but discusses people and evidence in the same breath, as it were, when it asserts that 'In all their work psychologists shall value integrity, impartiality and respect for persons and evidence . . .' ('A Code of Conduct for Psychologists', 1).

Timms (1983) writes that respect for persons is

> . . . more like a summary of a way of life or a morality than a single moral principle. It resembles the basis of rules or the reason for helping to achieve human purposes rather than a rule or purpose.

Its rather general character has led some people to criticise the place that this principle has been given in elaborations of the ethical stance of professional carers. For example, Simpkin (1979) asserts that it gives no guide for practice. It is true that the principle of respect for persons cannot guide practice in the sense of dictating actions in particular situations. It shares this with all general ethical principles. However, this does not mean that it does not represent a sound ethical foundation. As I have already said, respect for persons must underlie any ethics that has people as its primary focus, because to behave ethically towards others requires minimally that we should regard and act towards them in ways that take account of their being people.

Respect for persons is an expression of the high regard in which human beings hold their fellows. It is about cherishing folk for being folk and not things. It is about caring for them in ways that enable them to express their being as people in the best ways they can. Downie and Telfer (1969) write:

> to cherish a thing is to care about its essential features – those which, as we say, 'make it what it is' – and to consider important not only that it should

continue to exist but also that it should flourish. Hence, to respect a person as an end is to respect him for those features which make him what he is as a person and which, when developed, constitute his flourishing.

In his discussion of psychotherapy as essential care, Richard Lindley (chapter 12, this volume) argues that many psychotherapies, because they aim at increasing autonomy, are predicated on the assumption that '. . . taking control of one's own life is in itself an essential part of human flourishing'. If Lindley is correct then such therapies would seem to be based upon respect for persons, in Downie and Telfer's terms.

Campbell (1975) focuses on the need to respect the wishes and aspirations of others if we are to treat them with respect as persons. He writes:

> Respect . . . implies a relationship of involvement with others such that our choices and intentions are governed by their aims and aspirations as well as our own. To acknowledge another person is to acknowledge the possibility of other centres of choice and intention by which our personal aspirations may be modified.

Harris (1985) takes a wider view and asserts that respect for persons has two essential elements:

1 Concern for their welfare.
2 Respect for their wishes.

Although he further asserts that these two are essential '. . . just in the sense that no one could coherently claim to respect others if they failed to exhibit both dimensions', Harris seems to regard 'respect for wishes' as the more important element of respect for persons. He thus places himself with those who believe that part of what it is to flourish as a human being is to be autonomous. In a real sense, a person's ability to have wishes and to be responsible depends upon their physical state; one could not be a human person in the way that we are all human persons without a physical body with which to express our wishes, feelings, attitudes, intentions and so on. Nevertheless I am inclined to regard respect for wishes as more important than respect for welfare because the higher and more 'personal' aspects of personhood seem so closely bound up with the way in which people can make choices, form intentions and wishes, and embrace their living in a responsible way.

Harris seems to be construing welfare quite narrowly to include only physical welfare. But welfare may be construed as having as much to do with psychological, even spiritual well-being as it is to do with physical well-being, in which case there is an overlap between respecting wishes and caring for an individual's welfare. Cartainly, caring for a person's welfare will at least sometimes involve respecting his wishes even where these suggest courses of action that are contrary to what caring for physical welfare, in a simplistic kind of way, might suggest. I am thinking of situations where physical welfare seems less important than psychological or spiritual welfare. Some of the most clear cut cases are to be found in relation to moral problems about suicide and voluntary euthanasia where what is at stake is the question of whether it can ever be in a person's best interest to die rather than continue to live the life that he is living.

Discussing a patient with advanced cancer, the heart transplant surgeon, Christian Barnard (1986), illustrates how important it can be to respect an individual's wishes, even at the expense of our ideas of how his physical welfare might best be served, if we are to respect him as a person. The patient, Eli Khan, has told the doctors that they mustn't try to save his life. 'I am ready to die. The machine is worn out, and the mechanic must now give up.' The doctors have told Mr Khan that they do not work in a hospital where patients are simply allowed to die and he protests 'But doctor, what is wrong with death? I have lived a very happy life and a very proud life. My children have all been proud of their father, and I want them to remember me as a *Mensch*, a human being.' In this case the doctors are adopting a primitive notion of welfare. They want to protect Mr Khan's welfare, no doubt with the best of intentions, but they fail to see that his welfare does not consist in his physical life continuing for as long as possible; it also consists in his making a good death, of dying with the knowledge that at the end he was still regarded and treated with respect and care, as a person.

Respecting a person's wishes is essentially about respecting the person as autonomous, that is as a self-governing being. And this, I want to suggest, is the most important aspect of the attitude of respect for persons. However, it is as well to note some possible objections that can be raised against taking respect for wishes as more fundamental than respect for physical welfare. These are concerned with the possibility that a person's wishes might not be in her best interests because the attempt to fulfil them might greatly reduce her opportunities for autonomy in the future.[2,3] I am thinking, for example, of a person who wishes to end her life, and who attempts suicide but fails and as a result is severely disabled, such that her opportunities to direct her own life and arrange that wishes she holds will be fulfilled, are greatly reduced. The argument in favour of (or against refraining from) interfering in an individual's attempt to end her life, where that attempt at suicide seems unlikely to succeed, would then be that if the attempt is not stopped, her autonomy interests are likely to be injured. Of course this argument only works in circumstances where we are aware that the suicide attempt is more likely to fail with horrible results than it is to be successful. In the case of an individual whose suicide attempt seems very likely to succeed, the argument would not work, because in that case no adverse effects in terms of the individual's autonomy would ensue from our stopping the attempt at suicide, unless that is the attempt, say, at suicide by overdosing has already caused irreparable damage. The difficulty of course would be making an accurate prediction about the likely after-effects of a given suicide attempt.

Unsuccessful suicide attempts are significantly different from successful ones in that when suicide is successful it is not strictly true that the individual will have less autonomy in future; being dead is not a state that people experience and hence a person who commits suicide, is not, as it were, around to suffer any loss of autonomy. Something similar is true in the case of someone who refuses life saving medical treatment. The most common example is when a Jehovah's Witness, as a matter of religious principle, will not accept a blood transfusion. Such a person, if he persists in his demands to make decisions about his own, life and is successful in persuading others that he should be permitted to do so, will in all probability have no future wishes at all, although this is less certain than it is with successful suicide. A more difficult though perhaps less dramatic case might be when an individual, perhaps a senile person or someone suffering the aftermath of a serious overdose, who is quite incapable of caring for herself, asks to be discharged from hospital. Part of the difficulty in all of these cases, where an individual's wishes seem likely to result in their being harmed, is in determining whether their expressed wishes are truly indicative of their preferences rather than of a disturbed psychological state. The case of the person wishing to be discharged from hospital is more difficult because of the increased likelihood that the wishes of the individual involved are the result of a disturbed psychological state. Someone who is suffering from senile dementia may very well be unaware realistically of her abilities; this may also be the case for someone who is suffering from the physical and psychological trauma of a recent massive overdose.

It is difficult for the psychologist to decide what she should do when it seems that the welfare of clients will not be served by the actions that they wish to take. Of course it is not only in life threatening situations such as threatened suicide that she might find herself facing such a dilemma. I cannot enter into a detailed discussion of the many questions that surround the problems of how we can best respect others in such situations, for example the question of whether the psychologist is ever justified in acting paternalistically towards her clients. There are no simple answers to such questions. The answers we give will depend not only upon the assessment we make of the individual's mental state, of the extent to which expressed wishes truly represent what she would want in her most rational state of mind, but also upon the emphasis that we place upon caring for an individual's physical welfare as against her psychological or spiritual welfare. An interesting account of some of the problems that surround paternalism and caring for others, may be found in Lindley (1987) and a more general account of the nature of autonomy and paternalism may be found in Lindley (1986). One observation that I would like to make, however, is that much of what passes for paternalism seems to be more concerned with protecting its perpetrator than with caring for the welfare of the individual in question. I don't intend to sound moralistic here; protecting one's interests can in some circumstances be both understandable and I think morally acceptable. Although I think that respecting another as a person will most often involve respecting her wishes, there are circumstances in which I think one can override them without qualms. One such situation would be where an individual comes across another's suicide attempt and is hence faced with deciding what to do about it. An individual who attempts suicide in such a way that others may discover her before she dies cannot expect others who do not share her views of the rightness and wrongness or rationality of suicide, for example, to stand by and allow her to die. In a sense, attempting suicide in circumstances that mean she may be discovered is an offence against those who discover her, it fails to respect them as people. When working as a psychiatric social worker I once prevented a suicide attempt on the part of a client more because I had a selfish interest in preserving her life than because I was convinced that to do so would serve a good purpose for her. As it happens, in this case the person concerned expressed afterwards that she was glad she had not died. However, even if she had been furious with me I think my actions would stand as having been morally sound. She, as far as I can tell, would in that case have had further opportunities for suicide in the future; indeed she would have had the added advantage that having once been prevented from dying, she would have been in a better position to arrange her successful demise. I, for my part, did not have my career ruined, as it surely would have been had I allowed her to die in the particular circumstances, and was therefore still in a position to help my other clients. Perhaps in honesty I should make it clear that I can envisage circumstances in which I think it would be morally right to allow a suicide attempt to succeed.

Both Harris and Campbell, in their accounts of the attitude – and by implication behaviour – required if we are to respect others as persons, begin to attend to the central importance of reciprocity in personal relationships, and of recognising the other as a person who, like ourselves, has aspirations and wishes. In relation to persons, the range of responses and attitudes that is appropriate is very different from that which is appropriate to non-persons. Some of the other chapters in this book draw attention to the difference between the ways in which it is appropriate to regard persons and objects. For example, in chapter 5 Peter Trower draws attention to the way in which scientific behaviour therapy seeks to persuade clients that they are '. . . deficient organisms rather than fallible agents' and in chapter 2 David Smail talks of '. . . the unquestioning confidence we have in technological solutions and our readiness to conceptualise ourselves as machines . . .'. It seems inappropriate to view therapy as a technical enterprise, that is, as an activity in which it is appropriate to apply techniques rather in the way motor mechanics might apply techniques to the putting right of other people's cars, because to do so is to degrade and dehumanise the subjects of one's caring attention by treating them as objects. One aspect of the attitude which is respect for persons, for psychologists, must be for them to take seriously the nature not only of the client but of themselves, as personal agents.

Perhaps the most straightforward statements of respect for persons is the Golden Rule that we should 'Do unto others as you would have them do unto you'. This injunction seems to make the reciprocity of respectful personal relationships even more explicit than either Harris or Campbell. We may assume that the individual attempting to afford respect to others wishes herself to be treated as a person. Obeying the Golden Rule would then imply that the psychologist should afford clients the opportunity to express their personhood as fully as may be. I have already suggested that being a person is at least partly about being and becoming responsible. If we are the kind of individuals who take responsibility for our lives, doing unto others what we would like them to do unto us would then involve giving others, for whom we have responsibility and over whom we can exert power or influence, opportunities to be, and encouragement in being, responsible for themselves. For some clients it would involve affording opportunities for exercising choice and directing the course of their own lives. This is perhaps especially true in the context of long stay psychiatric and mental handicap wards where rather than affording patients the opportunity to be responsible, opportunities for responsible choice and decision making may be systematically removed in the interests of safe, secure and easily maintained wards. However, attention to the importance of choice in developing responsibility in clients is also important in other contexts including individual psychotherapy, where rather than affording opportunities for choice, drawing attention to the choices that are available, will be important.

RESPONSIBILITY

The various senses in which we can be responsible have been elaborated in many different ways (see for example Fairbairn, 1985; Downie, 1971; Hart, 1965; Benn and Peters, 1959) and so I will not enter into a detailed discussion here. However, it is probably worth beginning by saying a little about the different ways in which the concept of responsibility may be used as a preliminary to the discussion of responsibility in psychological practice that follows.

SOME DIFFERENT SENSES OF RESPONSIBILITY

In a purely *causal* sense we are responsible for the things we do and for the things that happen as a result of what we do. Recently, for example, I was responsible for not attending sufficiently when pulling away from traffic lights in my car and also, unfortunately, for the damage to the car in front that occurred as a result. It is not possible to avoid causal responsibility. In the same way that Watzlawick *et al.* (1967) maintain that 'One cannot not communicate', one cannot not be responsible, in this causal sense. Clearly psychologists want to be causally responsible for good outcomes in terms of client welfare and any attempt to demonstrate the efficacy of a therapeutic approach depends upon the attempt to demonstrate that psychological interventions, and no other variables, have been responsible for benefits that may be seen to have occurred.

Causal responsibility for something which we have intentionally brought about may make us morally praiseworthy or blameworthy depending on whether we have been instrumental in bringing about desirable or undesirable states of affairs. Our causal responsibility for a state of affairs that we have not brought about intentionally may also make us morally blameworthy if this state of affairs came about as a result of our lack of attention, or negligence. If a car driver deliberately drives at a pedestrian she will be morally as well as causally responsible for the pedestrian's injuries because of her intention to hit him. In the case where she injures the pedestrian because he steps out without warning, the driver, though causally responsible, will remain morally blameless. However, if she hit him because she was driving without due care and attention, for example under the influence of alcohol, the driver will be morally responsible even though she did not intend to injure the pedestrian; here the driver's moral responsibility arises because of her negligent and irresponsible behaviour in drinking and driving. The morality of an event depends upon its coming about through the agency of a person and it is important to note that we can be agents in the world by refraining from acting, just as much as by acting; in the case of the negligent car driver, by refraining from attending to the seriousness of the pursuit of car driving. I will say more about moral responsibility for refrainings or 'acts of omission', later.

Another sense of responsibility is when it is used to mean much the same as *duty*. The BPS *Guidelines for the Professional Practice of Clinical Psychology* (1983) at times use the term 'duties' to refer to responsibilities that arise as a result of the psychologist's professional role. This sense of responsibility is closely related to that commonly referred to as *accountability*, because someone who has a duty to perform some task may be expected to account for the way in which she has done it or has attempted or failed to attempt to do it. Accountability usually attaches to a particular role and someone who is accountable may be expected to explain and justify what she has done or has not done. If we have a duty to carry out some task, and fail to do so, or fail in doing so, this might be morally important depending on what we have failed to do and upon the circumstances in which our failure has occurred. Consider, for example, a lifesaver whose duty it is to save or to attempt to save the lives of swimmers in difficulties. He will be morally blameless if he fails to save the life of a swimmer on his stretch of beach if he can account well for his attempt to do so. If, on the other hand, a swimmer dies because he was drunk instead of patrolling vigilantly looking for people in distress, then the fact that he cannot account plausibly for his failure to save the swimmer will leave him morally blameworthy.

The expression 'responsible' may also be used, essentially in a moral way, to refer to a person who we consider trustworthy and capable of making wise decisions; a '*responsible*' person is one we can trust to act sensibly, perhaps one we can trust to carry out duties to the best of her ability. Certain categories of person including mentally infirm people and young children are commonly thought incapable of responsibility of this kind. A result of this is that such individuals are often denied opportunities to grow in responsibility.

Being a responsible person in this sense depends on the ability to be aware of our actions, and the effects of our actions, and to accept that we were causally responsible for them. It also, as it happens, depends on its being true that we were at least to some extent free in our choice of actions, that our actions are not totally determined by sources outside ourselves, however much they may be influenced by them. The ability to be responsible in this sense is often thought to be one of the characteristics that distinguishes persons from non-persons. In a sense, then, to become more responsible is to become more of a person. There are implications here for the ways in which individuals who are thought to be incapable of responsibility are treated. If we treat someone as if they are incapable of responsibility, in a sense we deny their personhood; and if we do not give people the opportunity to take responsibility, to choose and make decisions about their lives, we deny them the opportunity to express their personhood, and to grow in personhood.

Let me say something finally about our responsibility for events and states of affairs that come about as a result of things that we fail to do. A number of philosophers have argued, very plausibly, that we are as responsible for harm that comes about as a result of our failure to act, that is for our refrainings, or acts of omission, as we are for harm that comes about because of our direct and intended action (see for example, Harris, 1980). Consider for example a man who sees a child drowning in the canal as he is out walking but decides that rather than saving the child he will hurry home for tea. Such a man is surely as responsible, both causally and morally for the child's death by drowning' as he would have been had he thrown her into the canal with the intention that she should drown.

Accepting the notion that our omissions are as morally significant as our direct and intended actions places very strenuous demands on conduct. The notion has been applied in many areas of practical concern. For example, James Rachels (1979) uses it in an elegant argument about the responsibility that those of us in the affluent countries might be said to have for the suffering of people in the Third World. The notion is also used in arguing that the distinction that is often made in medicine between 'killing' and 'letting die' is morally speaking a false one. For example, in relation to the debate about whether it can be permissible to allow severely handicapped infants to die, John Harris (1981) argues that 'non-treatment . . . is a death dealing device' and that hence when doctors do not help such babies to live but allow them to die, what they do is as significant, morally speaking, as killing them. In psychology the relevance of the notion may be seen by referring to situations where psychologists may refrain from acting in relation to situations where they disagree with others; this is perhaps most likely to happen where the psychologist is part of a multi-disciplinary team or committee. For example, they may refrain from speaking out against decisions either in relation to individual patients or in relation to matters of policy affecting large numbers of individuals, even where they disagree on theoretical, practical or ethical grounds. It should be clear from what I have said that in such a situation the individual psychologist certainly cannot take refuge in the knowledge that she did not agree with the decision in question; by refraining from speaking out she effectively condones it.

RESPONSIBILITY AND PSYCHOLOGICAL PRACTICE

Frequent references are made to 'responsibility' and other related concepts in discussions, not only of the ethics of the caring professions, but also in discussions of the nature of their caring. The BPS *Guidelines* (1983) contain frequent references to the responsibilities of clinical psychologists although these are often phrased in terms of other words such as 'obligations', 'duties' and so on. Other chapters in this book also make frequent references to responsibility, again often using such alternative words.

A consideration of responsibility in psychological practice may be focused in two ways. First, there are issues concerning the responsibility of the psychologist. Second, there are issues concerning the responsibility of the client. Let me consider these in turn.

The responsibility of the psychologist

Psychologists in clinical practice are normally considered responsible in the sense of being responsible people. They are accountable for their actions and for the results of those actions, to a number of different individuals and different groups; and they are accountable for occasions when they have failed to, or have refrained from, acting. For example, they must be able to account for their professional actions and decisions to the institutions in which they work, to the teams of which they are members and to other members of their profession. And, of course, psychologists are responsible to their clients for the service that they provide, for providing help in the best way that they are able, with integrity and commitment.

A client can reasonably expect that the psychologist who is offering him help, will endeavour to act in his best interests at all times and that she will be competent to offer the help that she does. The *Guidelines* state that 'Psychologists recognise the boundaries of their competence and the limitations of their techniques . . . and they provide only those services and use only those techniques for which their training and experience equip them' (*Guidelines*, 2.5). Of course, things are more complicated than this, as David Smail (chapter 2, this volume) points out in relation to psychotherapy. Being '. . . fully trained, paid up and approved . . .' in itself does not guaranteee that a psychologist is an effective therapist because this '. . . simply assumes the validity of the procedures in which therapists are trained'.

The psychologist is paid because she has developed skills in psychological problem solving and she must surely have some success in order to justify her salary. But neither the client nor anyone else can justifiably hold the psychologist wholly responsible for bringing about change but only for the part that she plays in the change process. All that the psychologist can reasonably be expected to do is to provide a therapeutic context in which she has good reason to believe that change can take place. Psychologists are not like heart transplant surgeons. Whereas the heart transplant patient can reasonably expect at the end of his operation that he will have a new heart (though at this stage in the development of such procedures he can expect very little else in addition, certainly not any specific amount of additional life), the client who comes to a psychologist cannot expect any particular product or benefit as a result of therapy.

For psychologists of different theoretical persuasions providing a context in which change can take place will mean different things. For example, for the behaviourist it will involve manipulating contingencies of reinforcement such that change is facilitated, whereas for the analytically oriented psychotherapist it will involve providing an environment in which the client is enabled to come to an understanding of the nature of his symptoms and the part they play in maintaining his psychological equilibrium. Psychologists of either of these persuasions may doubt the validity of the theoretical stance of the other and its resultant therapeutic approach. However, unless it can be shown unequivocally that the methods she uses are ineffective or damaging, it would seem wrong to hold the psychologist responsible if her clients fail to change or if changes of a negative kind occur during therapy, provided that she has engaged in sensible and well founded practice and has observed reasonable caution in doing so. If as a result of therapy a client's life does not change or changes in undesirable ways (and of course it is difficult to assess whether changes that do take place have taken place as a result of therapy and nothing else), the client must share responsibility with the psychologist. This must be the case if clients are to be treated with respect as persons. If it is to be based on respect for persons, the process of psychological change must be seen as a joint enterprise even in cases where the client has little ability to take responsibility. If it is not viewed in this way the client is likely to be treated more as an object to be manipulated than as an agent with whom to interact; and I have already suggested that therapeutic approaches which involve viewing clients in this way are disrespectful of them as people.

I have said that psychologists can reasonably be expected to provide a context in which they have good reason to believe that change can take place. It is worth considering what might constitute valid reasons for a psychologist to entertain such a belief. I do not intend to enter into a discussion of the extent to which psychology as a discipline is justifiably considered a science, or the extent to which different therapeutic approaches drawn from psychology are based on scientific knowledge, except to acknowledge that doubts about both are possible. However, if psychology is a science under whatever description of science, then it would be reasonable to expect that psychologists should undertake research of an appropriate kind to discover the efficacy of their methods. Ethical problems will arise whatever research methodology is adopted. Let me mention some that might arise with research into therapeutic practice that is based on traditional scientific methodology. In order to demonstrate that benefit which has occurred has been the result of a particular method of treatment, many people would consider it necessary to compare a group of individuals receiving that treatment with a control group. But adopting this methodology, what is a psychologist to do when she believes that the intervention under consideration is the best possible help available – is it not then unethical to refrain from offering it to everyone who could benefit? Issues of this kind have become relatively common in medicine, for example in relation to the question of whether mastectomy or lumpectomy is the most effective method of dealing with breast cancer and whether giving women folic acid during pregnancy can contribute to a decrease in the rate of children born with spina bifida. A further issue concerns the psychologist who becomes convinced that a particular intervention is effective in bringing about positive change and yet believes that for ideological or ethical reasons it is unacceptable, perhaps because it involves treating people in ways that she believes people should never be treated. What we have here is basically an argument about means and ends. For example, some psychologists may think that some means, perhaps aversion therapy for sex offenders or the use of paradoxical techniques in family therapy, are never justified, whatever the desired end and whatever their efficacy in achieving this end.

At times the different responsibilities of psychologists will conflict with one another. Responsibility to clients may at times bring moral conflicts both with employers and with members of other professions. For example, conflict may arise for a psychologist who is working as part of a multi-disciplinary team, when her view of a client's state, or about methods of working within a unit, say, differs from that of other team members. Such conflicts of course arise because as the BPS *Guidelines* state, when psychologists collaborate with members of other professions in providing health care, responsibility '. . . is shared between all the individuals concerned in that each has his or her own duty of care towards the patient' (*Guidelines*, 5.4). A particular difficulty may arise when assessments that a psychologist has made lead other colleagues towards courses of action that she does not believe are in the client's best interests. What responsibility does the psychologist have for the use to which the results of her assessment procedures are put by other people?

In circumstances where a psychologist holds views about the treatment or assessment of clients that conflict with those of colleagues, it seems that the interests of the client should be paramount, however difficult it may be to decide what those interests are. The *Guidelines* are explicit in stating that '. . . where conflict exists between the psychologist's obligations to the patient and his or her obligations to other health care professionals, in this respect . . . the psychologist's primary concern is that the patient receives the care that he or she is considered to require' (*Guidelines*, 5.5). This seems to suggest that in circumstances of conflict with other disciplines the psychologist's primary responsibility must be to the welfare of the patient, based on his/her assessment of what would be in that patient's best interests. But things are not quite this simple. The psychologist who is involved in a dispute with colleagues over a particular client is not concerned with that client alone. A balance has to be found between her responsibilities to do what she thinks is best for a particular client and maintaining reasonable working relationships with colleagues for the sake of other clients. Obstinate refusal to agree with a consultant or team decision may result in bad feeling which could be detrimental to working relationships and hence to the welfare of other clients in the future. And of course a balance needs to be found between 'sticking to one's guns' because one's ideological and theoretical views lead one to believe one has it right, and leaving room for some doubt that in a given instance one may be mistaken. It is important for psychologists, as it is for everyone, to remain aware of the possibility that they may be mistaken; to do otherwise would surely in itself be morally dubious.

The responsibility of the client

The extent to which clients are considered responsible depends upon a number of factors including their mental health or emotional state as assessed by members of the mental health team. Some clients are more likely than others to be thought capable of responsibility and this will probably have an effect on the kind of treatment they receive. If being responsible for one's life is part of what it is to be a person, then treatments that do not aim at maximising a client's ability to take responsibility are disrespectful of him as a person.

Psychotherapy, because of its emphasis on the development of autonomy, is perhaps the most obvious example of a treatment where encouraging responsibility is a primary aim. However, it is worth noting the emphasis that is placed upon client responsibility from a radical behaviourist standpoint by Glynn Owens (chapter 6, in this volume). In the case of individuals whose capacity to act responsibly is severely diminished by mental distress, infirmity or handicap, it may be appropriate to remove responsibility for some areas of life, for example those in which there might be a risk of injury, at least for a time. Compulsory treatment under the Mental Health legislation is largely about removing responsibility from individuals who are thought, at least for a time, to be incapable of responsible action such that they constitute a risk to themselves or others. The difficulty is in deciding just how much responsibility it is appropriate to remove or to give back. And even in such cases, it is disrespectful of an individual as a person to act such that responsibility of which they are capable is denied. Respect for clients as people demands that they be given the maximum amount of responsibility consistent with their welfare and with the welfare of those with whom they come in contact.

The widespread public debate about the issue of informed consent in medicine (see, for example, Faulder, 1985) is essentially concerned with the question of whether patients should be treated as responsible individuals able to take responsible decisions about their own welfare. The idea that ordinary people are capable of accepting at least some responsibility for their own health behaviour (in the sense of being responsible people; they cannot avoid being causally responsible for it to a certain extent), and for decisions regarding their medical care, is nowadays relatively commonly asserted. Perhaps two of the main manifestations of the movement towards this view are the campaign for more choice in the matter of pregnancy and childbirth and the growth of the 'Well Women' clinics. The move towards a more contractual form of doctor-patient relationship with more responsibility being expected of and afforded to patients may perhaps be reinforced by investigations of, for example, the effects, in terms of compliance with treatment, of giving patients information about their condition and its treatment. Of course this depends upon compliance being seen as responsible; it could be argued that it is only responsible if it makes sense to do 'what the doctor orders'. Psychologists working in medicine can help in developing client responsibility by contributing to the development of medical interviewing practice in ways that allow for negotiation of the complaint and for the education of patients. The process of negotiation, set out by Tuckett *et al.* (1985), places the patient in the position of becoming a responsible partner in his own treatment. Within such a doctor-patient relationship, the notion of compliance becomes more clearly about responsibility on the part of the patient, because by being 'compliant' the patient is then acting in accordance with the treatment he has negotiated with the doctor rather than in accordance with the doctor's orders.

Glynn Owens (chapter 6, this volume) argues for a process of negotiating with the client about the nature of the problem and the best way to handle it; he maintains that the role of the behavioural therapist is to give the client knowledge such that so far as is possible he becomes able to deal with the problem himself. This is essentially the same as what we would hope for in informed consent. Obtaining properly informed consent must inevitably involve consideration not only of the outcome desired from treatment but also of the means by which this is brought about. Therapists seeking to obtain informed consent will therefore negotiate with clients not only about the outcome they desire from treatment, but also about the way in which that outcome is to be reached. Negotiation of some kind is of course common in many approaches to psychotherapy. However, some therapeutic approaches depend significantly upon non-negotiation at some level. It is interesting to consider what it might mean to have informed consent to the use of certain psychological interventions. For example, what would it mean to have informed consent to involvement in a token economy? Could it make sense to have informed consent to the use of therapeutic paradox in individual or family therapy? Approaches where paradoxical messages are used in bringing about change, while they may involve negotiation at some level, depend upon some of the more important issues remaining non-negotiated. In a sense they are non-negotiable because to negotiate about their use would sabotage that use. Asking for consent would involve 'blowing the gaff' on the approach; whatever exponents of paradox say about the honesty of this technique, being straightforwardly honest about what is involved would make the therapeutic use of paradox impossible. And even where open negotiations about the tasks of therapy are carried out, the use of certain approaches may involve keeping important information from clients. For example, in strategic approaches to family therapy, information about hypotheses are witheld from the client (the family) as a matter of method; nevertheless the family therapist may maintain that the end goal of therapy is to help the members of the family to take responsibility for sorting out their own troubles.

Increasing client responsibility

I have suggested that respecting clients as people involves assisting them to express their personhood as well as may be, that being a person is at least partly about becoming and being responsible and therefore that respecting clients as people must involve assisting their growth as responsible people. One way of helping others to take responsiblity for their lives is by helping them to become realistically aware of the effects that they bring about in the world, for example, of their effects on other people. Helping their children to become aware of their responsibility for states of affairs that they bring about is arguably one of the most important tasks of parenthood. Helping her clients to become realistically aware of the responsibility they have and can take for their lives is arguably one of the chief ways a therapist can help them. One way of doing this is by helping them to become aware of the choices that they have and of those that they do not have.

An individual's choices are made public in his actions and also in his omissions to act. He is personally responsible for the choices that he makes even when these do not result in actions. For example, a man who decides to have his hair cut before going to an interview is responsible for the consequences of his decision to look smart; but he would also have been responsible for the consequences had he chosen to leave it long. At times we may allow things to happen to us, as objects, rather than choosing, as agents, to influence things to the extent that we are able. Such 'allowings' are choices of a kind because they represent the choice to allow things to happen; but rather than embracing responsibility when we choose to allow things to happen, we give up or deny responsibility. Another way in which we may deny responsibility is by denying that we have choices by which we can influence our lives. A person who has been diagnosed as mentally ill and who believes in his diagnosis may deny that he can do certain things or avoid doing others, claiming that his illness causes him to act in certain ways and prevents him from acting in others. Let me give a couple of examples. David, who had been diagnosed as suffering from a compulsive obsessional neurosis, thought that his habit of checking and rechecking what people said was caused by his illness and refused to acknowledge that whatever the effects of his 'illness' he also had a habit of not listening to what people said. And Liza, who had been hospitalised as a 'chronic schizophrenic' for years, denied her responsibility for managing some of the everyday affairs of her life such as paying the rent, keeping her house in some kind of order etc. by 'passing the buck' onto the illness. She would say that it was her 'schizophrenia' that prevented her from doing things. However, things she cared about, such as having an adequate supply of cigarettes in the house, or collecting her son from the train when he came to stay, she managed to do despite her condition.

Another way in which we can deny responsibility is by utilising language that displaces responsibility onto others, or onto the cosmos, as it were. The denial of responsibility may be embodied in statements such as 'It's always like this', 'Things are getting worse', 'Something's got to happen' and 'Somebody will have to do something'. Accepting such statements as straightforward accounts of the situation, passively allowing a client to totally locate responsibility outside himself, is rather like giving permission for him to deny his potential to act upon his problems. Allowing the client to deny his ability to make decisions about his life, however bad the alternatives might be, is to encourage him to give up responsibility for himself. This is not to treat him with respect as a person. A man may claim that he cannot do something when really he means that he will not do it because for some reason he has decided not to do so. For example, he may claim that he can't leave his wife when what he really means is that despite the inconvenience and distress it causes him, he would rather stay with her than suffer the alternative; in other words the benefits of staying in the system outweigh those of leaving. Or he may claim that he cannot do without tobacco and beer in order to allow enough money to pay the rent when really he means that he does not want to do this. Rudestam (1978) suggests that inviting clients to change their linguistic habits can be effective in encouraging them to take responsibility for themselves. For example, a person, who habitually says that he 'can't' do something when in fact he means that he 'won't' do it because he prefers not to do so, might be helped to regain his agency by insisting that he use the term 'won't' rather than 'can't' when describing the problems he is having in achieving goals he has set for himself.

CONSTRUING ACCOUNTABILITY AS BLAME

I have discussed the philosophical notion of respect for persons and some of the difficulties that may arise in implementing this principle in practice. I have discussed some different senses of responsibility and related these to the responsibility of the psychologist and the responsibility of the client. I want now to discuss the tendency to construe the accountability of practitioners mainly in terms of the possibility of being blamed when things go wrong. I will argue that when this happens, and it happens, I fear, alarmingly frequently, practice is likely to become more conservative, with emphasis being placed more on avoiding the possibility of accusations of lack of care than on enhancing client welfare. I will suggest that the adoption of a defensive stance is likely to lead to an attitude to clients in which they are less respected as people because they are less likely to be treated as responsible agents. Much of what I want to say is perhaps most relevant to those working with clients who might be considered incapable of acting responsibly (or at any rate as suffering from deficiencies such that they have very much reduced potential for responsible action), such as children, mentally handicapped, psychogeriatric and severely mentally ill clients, perhaps especially 'chronic' clients who have been in hospital for a very long time.

Attending to the possibility of being blamed when bad states of affairs occur is a common and understandable response on the part of the caring professions to the kind of media coverage that is often given to cases where services to clients may be construed as having failed in some way. For example, a child, known to have been abused by its parents in the past, might be severely injured after being returned to its parents following a period in care. Public outrage is likely to follow in such circumstances even where it is the case that the social workers and others involved acted in good faith, having taken all reasonable steps to establish that the child's best interests would be served by a return to the parents. And it is not only the public that can be outraged by such unfortunate incidents; agencies and institutions can also be thus outraged, or at any rate can act as if they are. Let me give an example. Mr Smith, who was about to be discharged from hospital after a period as an in-patient for a depressive illness, slipped getting out of a bath and broke his leg. The nurse in charge of the ward had decided that it was inappropriate for him to have his bathing supervised because the only staff available at the time were women and because Mr Smith was about to be discharged. It may seem in this instance that the nurse was respecting the man's wish for privacy rather than showing concern for his welfare. In fact, of course, given the man's good physical and mental health, concern for his physical welfare would not have dictated supervising his bath, though respect for the accepted procedures of the hospital might have, as might a predisposition on the part of the nurse to take precautionary steps to guard her reputation at the cost of the patient's dignity. The responsible nurse was disciplined as a result of this incident, presumably because her employers wished to avoid methods of work developing in which the physical welfare of patients was given second place relative to their psychological welfare. In some ways this seems paradoxical in a context in which people are treated primarily because of psychological problems.

Any allocation of blame depends upon decisions about the causes of an occurrence. If it can be shown that an agent or agency was causally responsible in bringing about an event or state of affairs, or could reasonably have been expected to have prevented it, then it can make sense to ask whether they should be held accountable for its occurrence. But causality is rarely a simple thing and it is difficult to assess the extent to which a psychologist is causally responsible for states of affairs and events that occur during her professional practice. For example, if a client in therapy commits suicide, except in very exceptional circumstances it would be wrong to say that the psychologist is causally (and, hence, morally) responsible. Whatever may have happened or not happened in the therapeutic sessions, many other factors in the client's life may have been involved in the decision to commit suicide. And, as the example of the man who broke his leg shows, even where an accident could perhaps have been prevented, it is not necessarily the case that it would amount to negligence to have refrained from action that might have prevented it. Indeed in that case, it could be argued that to have had Mr Smith's bathing supervised would have been an infringement on his privacy that was incompatible with caring for his psychological state and hence that to have placed a nurse 'on guard' over his ablutions would have constituted negligence and certainly lack of respect for him as a person.

The prevalence of this adversarial approach to bad occurrences in the health and welfare services is likely to have the result that caring professionals respond by becoming less willing to make 'high risk' decisions because they fear that if a bad result follows they will be attacked and accused of irresponsible action even where this results in poorer standards of care and even harm to clients. I have discussed this at length elsewhere (Fairbairn, 1985). The standardised procedures that social workers are required to carry out in relation to cases of suspected, or even possible, child abuse, the procedures nurses have for distributing drugs and many of the restrictive practices that are customary on wards dealing with individuals who are thought to be lacking in responsibility, for whatever reason, are all examples of responses of this kind. Such standardised procedures are arguably designed more to protect the credibility and reputation of agencies and institutions, than to help any individual client. But it is not just that standard procedures may arise as a result of construing accountability negatively. Individual practitioners are also likely to become more conservative in their decision making. Let me consider an example.

Alice was clinically depressed when she was admitted to hospital. After two years, the consultant psychiatrist and her psychologist had begun to think that she should return home to her husband and family. With this in mind the psychologist and a co-therapist had been visiting her home with Alice, to conduct family therapy sessions. Although there was continuing difficulty in the marital relationship, one Wednesday Alice came to see the psychologist and said that she now believed she should go home because she had responsibilities to fulfil in relation to her family. After consultation between Alice, the psychologist and the consultant, she was discharged and an arrangement made that she should telephone the psychologist on Friday morning to give an account of how she was managing at home. Friday morning came and Alice did not phone. However, later in the day, she arrived at the psychologist's office asking to be readmitted. The psychologist, who believed that her step in asking to be discharged had been Alice's first real step towards embracing responsibility for herself, explained that she thought that to come back into hospital would constitute a backwards move and urged Alice to reconsider. Alice went directly to the consultant and demanded to be taken back, adding that if she was not, she would kill herself. After much discussion, the consultant decided, in conjunction with the psychologist, that Alice should be readmitted. In this case the psychologist felt that she and her consultant colleague made a decision which allowed Alice to deny her responsible self, because they were afraid of the consequences of doing otherwise. A complicating factor was their awareness that no community nursing cover could be made available to check on Alice's condition over the weekend; and significantly over the past twelve months the hospital in question had had rather a large number of suicides and had received bad press coverage as a result.

In caring for mentally handicapped, severely mentally distressed or geriatric patients in hospitals or other residential institutions, decisions may be taken which reduce the possibility for the exercise of personal responsibility. David Clark (1974) writes that '. . . doctors and nurses are highly skilled at removing an individual's responsibility.' Of course it is not just doctors and nurses that remove responsibility from patients. Psychologists who recognise the truth of Clark's sentiment, perhaps particularly those concerned with the 'back wards' of large psychiatric hospitals or with mental handicap hospitals, might find themselves being concerned with finding ways of giving responsibility to clients. Clark writes that we

> . . . should always question any limitation of a person's responsibility . . . .In general people are more ready for responsibility than doctors and nurses will credit . . . many doctors and nurses . . . only too easily decide it will be done better and quicker if I do it myself . . . but it may be far more helpful to him to exercise his own responsibility, make his own mistakes, surmount his crisis and grow a little (Clark, 1974).

People have different capacities for responsibility. One thing that usually distinguishes mentally handicapped or distressed people is that they are less able to take responsibility for themselves than other people. However, it should not be the case that a person's having been assessed as mentally handicapped or diagnosed as suffering from a mental illness is taken to mean that he is incapable of any rational decision or choice. Although an individual may not be able to take much responsibility, respect for him as a person demands that he be enabled and encouraged to take whatever responsibility he can. For example, a mentally handicapped person may not be able to make complex decisions about his life on his own, but he may be capable of contributing to them. The idea that being given responsibility can help clients to grow and change clearly has implications for the ways in which all patients are treated. Of course it is not just, as implied by Clark, that it is convenient to deny patients the opportunity to exercise responsibility. They are likely to have things done for them, to be denied the possibility to do simple things for themselves such as making cups of tea, bathing unaided and so on, even where they could in all probability manage such things, because of the possibility of accidents and the resultant allocation of blame. Several years ago I was involved in an experiment in the use of a simple method of groupwork designed to bring about communication in very long stay patients in a large psychiatric hospital. The method of 'rotating dyads' (Landfield, 1977) in which group members engaged in discussion of different topics in a series of different pairs with other clients seemed to be quite successful in producing much free discussion among previously very inward and silent old ladies and gentlemen, mostly diagnosed as chronic schizophrenic. However, the most significant element in the method we employed was perhaps that at the end of each session the group members made tea for us all (under supervision) in the ward kitchen. It was noticeable that many colleagues, of all disciplines, who joined in the group sessions found it very hard to tolerate the risk that a patient might be injured during the tea making.

CONCLUSION

I am conscious that I have paid little attention to possible arguments that may be raised against what I have said. For example, I have not fully considered the difficulties that may arise with the idea that the psychologist best respects clients as people by encouraging them to be responsible; for example in circumstances when it seems to her that a client does not wish to be responsible. Many clients will come to a psychologist because they wish to get rid of uncomfortable feelings they have and yet they may be unprepared to make changes in their personal lives, or to see any changes in the family or other social systems of which they are a part of in order to achieve this end. Can't it sometimes be respectful of a client as a person, the argument would go, to simply accept his desire not to change? Wouldn't it be disrespectful of the client if the psychologist tried to force him into responsible decision making and action? The question of whether a psychologist should try to bring about change in a client when the client seems unwilling to change is related to the question of whether and when paternalistic interference in another's life is justified. To answer such questions in a detailed way would entail considering carefully what kind of relationship it is appropriate for clients and psychologists to make together. This would involve considering in detail the nature and stringency of the responsibilities the psychologist accepts when she enters into a therapeutic relationship and asking, for example, whether she can expect her clients to treat her with respect as a person. To answer such questions is beyond the scope of this chapter although I hope that some of what I have said may give an indication of how I might begin to answer them. However, if the objections that arise as a response to what I have said result in thought being given to such questions I will be well pleased.

NOTES

I would like to thank Sandra Canter, Miss MacMinn, Hazel Seidel and especially Susan Fairbairn for their help with this chapter.

1 Several people have sounded alarm bells at the idea that psychologists change people, as if psychologists are not in the business of psychological change. One analytically oriented psychotherapist said, for example, that all she is concerned to do is to help clients to come to an awareness of the nature of their symptoms. But surely helping clients to become aware of the significance of their symptoms is to change them psychologically? It seems to me that anyone working in therapy has got to be motivated to bring about some change in clients otherwise they are being paid for nothing. What is at issue, of course, is the question of whether the psychologist should be deciding upon what change should occur or should be endeavouring to bring about any particular change.

2 I am grateful to Richard Lindley for pointing out the difference, in terms of one's future autonomy, between killing oneself and making a rather poor attempt at killing oneself.

3 It might be argued that an individual who attempts 'suicide' and fails may actually have had the aim of injuring herself such that her autonomy would be reduced. In that case a lessening of her

autonomy would seem to be in accordance with the individual's wishes, if not in her interests (given that autonomy is in general considered to be a good thing). For example, it might have been thought that Sally who jumped from a first story window and ended up paraplegic, and whose husband Frank left the armed forces to stay at home and look after her, had intended to trade off her autonomy to gain the constant attention of her spouse, and had hence had her wish fulfilled by her paralysis. However, this would depend upon whether it was considered possible that a person could rationally entertain the intention to reduce her overall autonomy in this way. I am inclined to think that except in very exceptional circumstances a person could not wish to decrease their autonomy to such an extent whatever the trade-off.

REFERENCES

Barnard, C., 'The Need for Euthanasia', in A.B. Downing and B. Smoker (eds) (1986), *Voluntary Euthanasia; Experts Debate the Right to Die*, London, Peter Owen.

Benn, S.I. and Peters, R.S. (1959), *Social Principles and the Democratic State*, London, Allen and Unwin.

Biestek, F. and Gehrig, C. (1978), *Client Self Determination: A Fifty Year History*, Chicago Ill., Loyola University Press.

British Psychological Society (1983), *Guidelines for the Professional Practice of Clinical Psychology*, Leicester, BPS.

British Psychological Society (1985), 'A Code of Conduct for Psychologists', *Bulletin of the BPS*, vol.38.

Campbell, A. (1975), *Moral Dilemmas in Medicine*, second edition, Edinburgh, Churchill Livingstone.

Clark, D. (1974), *Social Therapy in Psychiatry*, Harmondsworth, Penguin.

Downie, R.S. (1971), *Roles and Values*, London, Methuen.

Downie, R.S. and Telfer, E. (1969), *Respect for Persons*, London, Allen & Unwin.

Fairbairn, G. (1985), 'Responsibility in Social Work', in D. Watson (ed.), (1985), *A Code of Ethics for Social Work: The Second Step*, London, Routledge & Kegan Paul.

Faulder, C. (1985), *Whose Body Is It? The Troubling Issue of Informed Consent*, London, Virago.

Harris, J. (1980), *Violence and Responsibility*, London, Routledge & Kegan Paul.

Harris, J. (1981), 'Ethical problems in the management of some severely

handicapped children', *Journal of Medical Ethics, 7*, pp.117–24.
Harris, J. (1985), *The Value of Life*, London, Routledge & Kegan Paul.
Hart, H.L.A. (1965), *Punishment and Responsibility*, Oxford, Oxford University Press.
Landfield, A. (1977), Personal communication during a workshop on 'rotating dyads' at the Conference on Personal Construct Theory, Christchurch College, University of Oxford.
Lindley, R. (1986), *Autonomy*, London, Macmillan.
Lindley, R. 'Paternalism and Caring' in G. Fairbairn and S. Fairbairn (eds) (1987), *Ethical Issues in Caring*, Aldershot, Gower.
Rachels, J. (1979), 'Killing and Starving to Death', *Philosophy*, vol.54.
Rudestam, K.E. (1978), 'Semantics and psychotherapy', *Psychotherapy, Theory, Research and Practice*, vol.15, no.2.
Simpkin, M. (1979), *Trapped Within Welfare*, London, Macmillan.
Timms, N. (1983), *Social Work Values: An Enquiry*, London, Routledge & Kegan Paul.
Tuckett, D. *et al.* (1985), *Meetings between experts, an approach to sharing ideas in medical consultation*, London and New York, Tavistock.
Watzlawick, P., Beavin, J.H., and Jackson, D.D. (1967), *Pragmatics of Human Communication*, New York, Norton.

Index